QUEENS

OF THE

KINGDOM

QUEENS

OF THE

KINGDOM

THE WOMEN OF
SAUDI ARABIA SPEAK

NICOLA SUTCLIFF

**SIMON &
SCHUSTER**

London · New York · Sydney · Toronto · New Delhi

A CBS COMPANY

First published in Great Britain by Simon & Schuster UK Ltd, 2019
A CBS COMPANY

Copyright © Nicola Sutcliff, 2019
Illustrations © Merieme Mesfioui, 2019

1 3 5 7 9 10 8 6 4 2

Simon & Schuster UK Ltd
1st Floor
222 Gray's Inn Road
London WC1X 8HB

www.simonandschuster.co.uk

Simon & Schuster Australia, Sydney
Simon & Schuster India, New Delhi

The author and publishers have made all reasonable efforts
to contact copyright-holders for permission, and apologise
for any omissions or errors in the form of credits given.
Corrections may be made to future printings.

A CIP catalogue record for this book
is available from the British Library

Trade Paperback ISBN: 978-1-4711-7967-9
eBook ISBN: 978-1-4711-7968-6

Typeset in Perpetua by M Rules
Printed and bound by CPI Group (UK) Ltd, Croydon, CR0 4YY

MIX
Paper from
responsible sources
FSC® C020471

Simon & Schuster UK Ltd are committed to sourcing paper
that is made from wood grown in sustainable forests and supports the Forest
Stewardship Council, the leading international forest certification organisation.
Our books displaying the FSC logo are printed on FSC certified paper.

CONTENTS

GLOSSARY

abaya	Women's long, loose-fitting cloak worn in public or in the company of non-related males; usually black
alhamduLillah	*Thanks/Praise be to God*
baba	*Dad*
Bedouin	*desert dwellers;* nomadic, Arabic peoples primarily inhabiting North Africa and the Arabian Peninsula
hadith	Recorded sayings and deeds of the Prophet Mohammed
hai'a	*committee;* colloquial name given to representatives of the Committee for the Promotion of Virtue and Prevention of Vice, externally referred to as the religious police
haram	*forbidden*, according to *Sharia*; opposite of *halal*
hijab	Modest code of dress that applies to both men and women; often used colloquially to refer to a woman's headscarf

imam	Islamic leader in worship and community life
insha'Allah	*God willing*
khalas	Exclamation equivalent to 'that's it!' / 'enough!'
khula	Divorce initiated by a woman, dependent on the surrender of her bridal dower
mahram	Any man a woman is prohibited from marrying due to kinship, e.g. her father, brothers, uncles, nephews
Majlis al Shura	The highest consultative assembly in Saudi Arabia's theocratic monarchy, charged with proposing legislation to the King; also known as the Shura Council
masha'Allah	*God has willed it;* frequently used in a context of gratitude, celebration or praise
muttawah	*volunteer;* deeply religious and pious individual(s) who practices *Sharia* according to its most literal interpretation and encourages others to do the same; colloquially used to refer to members of the Unit for the Promotion of Virtue and Prevention of Vice, externally referred to as the religious police
niqab	Women's face veil, revealing only the eyes; usually black.
Qabili	Families that claim to be able to trace their lineage back to one of two original tribes on the peninsula

Qur'an	The holy book of Islam, believed to be the original, unaltered words of Allah, as revealed to his prophet, Mohammed
Ramadan	The ninth month of the Islamic calendar, during which all Muslims of sound health participate in sunrise to sunset fasting from both food and water
riyal	Saudi currency
Salafism	Movement within Islam which advocates a return to the traditions and practices of the *salaf*: the first three generations of Muslims, including that of the Prophet Mohammed
Sharia	Islamic system of life and law based on the *Qur'an* and *Hadith*. *Sharia* may never be altered, but is open to interpretation
Shura Council	See *Majlis al Shura*
shisha	Water pipes used for smoking flavoured tobacco
Sunnah	Collected religious practices established by the Prophet Mohammed
tarha	Women's headscarf; in Saudi Arabia usually worn together with the *abaya*
thobe	Men's traditional long white tunic
Vision 2030	National development strategy which aims to diversify the economy away from oil-dependency and advance public, cultural and social sectors

w'Allah	*I swear it by God*
Wahhabism	Highly conservative branch of Islam based on literal interpretation of the *Qur'an* and *Hadith;* aims to purify the faith of modern distortions
wasta	Social and professional influence accrued through name, connections and the lending of favours
yanee	*it means;* a common filler in conversation, i.e. 'you know?'

AN INTRODUCTION

One day in my mid-twenties, my father sat me down for 'a talk' about my future. By this time I had worked as a teacher, a translator, a logistics coordinator and a research assistant and had lived in several countries. Nonetheless, my father was concerned for my professional and financial stability – it was time, he said, to settle on more gainful, long-term employment.

I took his words to heart. Three months later, on my next visit, I proudly informed him that I had been offered a permanent contract with a healthy salary and the opportunity to contribute to two of the fields that most inspired me: women's empowerment and transformative education. I had accepted a role at the first university for women – in Saudi Arabia. And with those two little words, his delighted smile froze.

My parents' concerns were understandable. We can only make judgements based on the information available to us, and Saudi Arabia had become the pantomime villain of the international media, rivalled only perhaps by North Korea.

It was a negative narrative cemented by its repetition. Every news article I read on the country seemed to follow the same copy-and-paste formula. The first paragraph outlined the headline issue, the second – regardless of the article's topic – offered commentary on the female driving ban, and the third helpfully informed the reader of any executions ordered by the state during the preceding months.

Sensationalist coverage of the region has been legitimised by the difficulties encountered by reporters in entering Saudi Arabia, combined with the lack of media output released by the country itself. Ironically, perhaps, it is the Kingdom's attempt to 'lay low', reinforced by the deep value attributed to privacy in Saudi society, which has made the country such an object of fascination; an interest that revolves primarily around the lives of its female citizens.

But, despite being the focus of so many column inches, the women around whom such articles centred were invariably reduced to two-dimensional stock images of black-veiled figures. The only female voices regularly emerging seemed to be those of state-sanctioned spokeswomen or frustrated activists and those who had escaped especially abusive circumstances.

My own interest was piqued, not by what we were told of the lives of women in Saudi Arabia, but by what we weren't. I have always believed that life is formed far more by shades of grey than the utopian or dystopian narratives that may be comfortably contained by the black-and-white print of the news column.

I also felt that, while I claimed to be a feminist and an 'ally' of women in their struggles worldwide, my own experience of womanhood had, until this point, been very narrow and very sheltered. Who was I to judge another woman's way of life when I had never walked a mile in her shoes, or indeed, her veil?

So I packed a single case, purchased a black *abaya* and *niqab*, the body-concealing cloak and face veil habitually worn by Saudi women in public, on eBay (both of my choices I was later to learn were shamefully unfashionable) and collected my ticket to Riyadh.

During my early days in the capital, certain things did unsettle me. Being locked in the back of a blacked-out car while the company driver collected my food from restaurants without 'family' sections. The absence of women on the streets, on billboards, on television; in my white privileged world I had never truly grasped, until this point, the importance of equal representation in media. It seemed that half of life was elsewhere.

But truthfully, what surprised me most was how little culture shock I actually suffered. Beyond these idiosyncrasies, daily life continued as usual. I did my groceries at Safeway, I bought my shoes from Marks & Spencer, I watched movies on Amazon Prime – and my Saudi counterparts did just the same.

In short, I was reassured in my conviction that, beyond culture and creed, we all have far more in common than we do apart; that despite what those attention-grabbing headlines would have us believe, Saudi women's primary concerns are not of *jihad*[1] or patriarchal oppression or the dimensions of the cloth that covers them, but rather of the standard of education enjoyed by their children, the challenges of balancing work and childcare, and, of course, when the next series of *The Walking Dead* is due to be released.

The first few months I lived in Riyadh, I adopted local customs as far as my limited knowledge would allow. I lived in the city centre, not a Western compound; I predominantly covered my face with the *niqab* – although it is not expected of foreign women; I shopped at *souqs*;[2] learned to cook with local ingredients; and subjected taxi drivers, shop assistants and students to my broken Egyptian Arabic, learnt through an app on my phone.

Despite my efforts, I found I was still at risk of disappearing into the expat bubble – a fate especially prevalent in the Kingdom, where family privacy is sacrosanct and Saudi and

---

1 *Struggle, effort*; can denote both an internal and external fight for the principles of Islam.
2 Marketplaces.

foreign workers each reside behind their own high walls. Aware of this, I consciously started talking with local women, asking them questions and listening to their stories.

At first, these personal histories were kept as keepsakes, shared only among family and friends; the basis, perhaps, of a rather unique scrapbook. But even here, I began to notice the humanising potential of storytelling. My parents stopped calling to ask if I was safe, and instead started asking after my Saudi friends and students. Was so-and-so feeling better? Would that student like some extra textbooks sent out? Or some help with her engineering application? I wished I could introduce more people, personally, to the women of the Kingdom.

I began to formalise my efforts. I made contact with influential Saudi women at embassy events in Riyadh and told them of my idea of compiling a book of interviews. To my enormous honour, and continuing gratitude, I was welcomed into the homes of senior princesses, members of national councils, and activists whose names I had only seen in newspapers.

Although it had only ever been my intention to speak with women with more 'everyday' occupations, given the language barrier and women's more frequent occupation of the domestic realm, this group actually proved far more difficult to access. But I was determined, and as my courage grew, I started to approach market vendors, shop assistants, supermarket cashiers, women waiting at airports or sitting next to me on trains. I called in favours and accepted invites to family gatherings.

I was also increasingly aware that I could not produce anything approaching a representative portrait of womanhood in such a large and diverse nation by expending my energies in the capital alone. And so I travelled, often alone, to the far eastern, western and northern reaches of the country, as well as into the desert in search of surviving Bedouin communities. Never once on these expeditions did I feel unsafe or unwelcome.

Nonetheless, each time I raised the question of an interview, I did so fully expecting to be rebuffed; an unfamiliar foreign woman with atrocious Arabic and full of probing questions. Instead, I was invited into family homes to share delicious local cuisine and stories of lives lived as in every part of the world, with their struggles and victories, joys and despairs.

In total, I conducted fifty recorded interviews along with dozens of informal discussions. The twenty-nine which I felt covered the most diverse range of backgrounds and viewpoints are published on the pages that follow. Despite my own misgivings, in the event, my requests for interviews, often from strangers, were politely refused only twice.

In many homes I was the first Westerner to cross the threshold; for some I was the first they had ever spoken to. In some cases language was a barrier and I was fortunate to count on the help of interpreters in the form of generous friends and curious relatives to bridge the void. Sometimes multiple interview sessions were necessary to cover all the areas on which I quizzed each of my interviewees – but gradually, I came to know the real women of the Kingdom.

Perhaps the greatest joy of all was finding that this learning process was a mutual one. At the end of my first semester teaching at a Saudi university, I was shyly approached by a quiet student from a deeply religious and conservative family who sheepishly announced, 'Miss Nicola, I used to hate Westerners, I thought you were all bad, but now I've met you and [name of colleague] . . . I love you!'

Because stereotypes, of course, run both ways. During the 1990s, when the isolationist Wahhabi-Salafi movement was at its peak and access to international media was severely constricted, a number of pamphlets decrying the plight of the Western woman were broadly circulated. According to one, 'When a Western woman ages, she goes through three stages:

first, she gets a dog to keep her company as she has no spouse and no child; secondly, she moves into a home for the elderly, as no one cares for her; and third, her money, if she has any, is taken for her upkeep, or she dies – like a dog – alone without anyone by her side.'

Still today, the women I spoke to, in their more honest moments, expressed their concerns that women in the West were routinely ejected from their parents' homes against their will on their eighteenth birthdays, that they 'spent every night sleeping in a different bed' and that prostitution was a mainstream career option. I made sure to allow time for them to interview me with their own questions at the end of each meeting.

While we largely succeeded in overcoming our cultural and linguistic differences, there were sometimes other, more subtle obstacles to our dialogues. Some women, especially from less privileged socio-economic backgrounds, lacked the language to give form to their dreams and their frustrations, never having been asked such questions before.

For women from such closed communities, it was not always easy to answer my more abstract questions, or, perhaps, for me to phrase them most helpfully. How can you objectively assess your role in society or your freedoms when you have never been exposed to an alternative? How easy would any of us find it to articulate our 'normal' comprehensively to someone raised in an entirely different way of life? It is perhaps unsurprising, then, that their thoughts on different topics occasionally appear to contradict one another.

It was as we navigated through these conversations that I began to notice the pervasive use of the term 'queen', which has been used to both empower and placate; from the ideal of a mother as the 'queen' of her family and household, to the oft-quoted local refrain that 'The queens don't drive.' It is a label that has been cherished by traditional women but often mocked by women's rights activists, dubbing their homeland, 'The Kingdom of one king and millions of queens'. Nonetheless, given the current atmosphere of reform, it is perhaps a title ripe to be reclaimed.

Regardless of their differing views on such matters, what united all of these women was their warm hospitality and their patriotism. These were not the oppressed victims in need of rescue or international intervention I had read about in the papers or online – I was looked at with utter bewilderment when I mentioned the efforts of international NGOs campaigning on their behalves. The barriers they have faced, and continue to face, in exercising their rights as full citizens of their country should not be underemphasised; but these were also women proud of their homeland, their families, and the changes they are witnessing – and instigating.

The interviews sampled in this book were conducted in the period 2014–2017. In retrospect, it was a remarkable period in Saudi and in global women's history. During this time, women in Saudi Arabia gained the right to vote, to work in retail, to accept employment without their male guardian's permission, and, indeed, to manage their own businesses. What I didn't realise at the time was that I was capturing a snapshot of a society on the cusp of far greater change.

The editing process has been considerably enlivened by the fall of the infamous female driving ban, the reopening of cinemas and various smaller amendments to guardianship, marriage and child custody regulations. The headlines of news providers have accordingly begun to shift from, 'x things that Saudi women still can't do,' to, 'Now Saudi women can . . . '

This impressive turnaround, while welcomed by international observers and many inside the country, has not been entirely pain-free. Internally, Saudi Arabia remains a deeply conservative country. Implementing such rapid social reform with the minimum of turmoil is a delicate procedure, and the country's rulers have made clear that these changes will be made only under their timetable and by their authority.

In May 2018, at least fourteen human rights activists, mostly women, some of whom I'd interviewed, were taken into custody in an entirely unanticipated sting operation. At the time of publishing, most remain incarcerated with little information released as to their whereabouts or the charges levelled against them. In the atmosphere of uncertainty following these sudden events, some of my interviewees requested anonymity.

As a consequence, not only of these developments but of the highly private nature of Saudi society in general, and regarding women in particular, the names and some personal details of some participants of this book have been changed, while preserving their personal stories and opinions.

I would like to apologise wholeheartedly for areas where the text in this tome already runs behind the rapid pace of current developments, for errors in my understanding of Islamic scripture and civil and *Sharia* legal principles, and for the necessity of forming certain generalisations in these limited pages. My Saudi friends and acquaintances have been extremely generous with their time in answering my questions and reviewing my words.

With the informal and often conversational nature of the dialogues recorded, it was also necessary to abridge and restructure the original reams of transcript amassed from each interview. In each case I have done my best to retain the women's original 'voices', making every effort not to distort the meaning of their words on the editing block.

This book was completed as a tribute to all those who opened their doors, poured endless cardamom coffee along with their stories and tears, and shared their intimate personal journeys with a stranger, without expectation of anything at all in return. It was written for the Queens of the Kingdom.

Author disclaimer: All contributors whose surnames are not printed in these pages have been anonymised. The views and opinions expressed in the chapters accompanying these interviews do not necessarily reflect those held by any individual interviewee.

I have endeavoured to be as accurate as possible, but do not claim to be a historian or religious expert. Any errors or missing details are unintentional. My apologies for any mistakes in these pages.

THE VILLAGER

Mama Muna

Great-grandmother, aged 100, Najd region

At 100 years of age, Mama Muna is older than the Kingdom itself. Born into a comparatively wealthy family in the barter economy of the time and raised in a mud house, she is one of the last remaining witnesses of a way of life that has now been extinguished as the country undergoes rapid modernisation. A mother of five surviving children, she has never moved, but has watched as her village has swelled into a bustling town around her. Mama Muna now lives in her granddaughter's large, modern home.

There were 130 houses in the village

I don't know how old I was when I lost my eye. I only remember I had three little ones by that time. I was out collecting firewood to cook the dinner and a stick swung up and jabbed me in the eye. I just remember the pain and the blood, blood, blood. I don't know how they got it out and cleaned me up. *AlhamduLillah*[3] it didn't stop me reaching a hundred!

I grew up in a mud house. There were 130 houses in the village back then, and a long wall that went all the way round us. There was just one big door to go in and out, and they locked it every night at evening prayers. If you got home late, you just

---

3 'Thanks be to God'.

had to sleep out in the sand till dawn. It kept us safe; there were no policemen in those days.

Life was work, from morning till night. There wasn't much time for anything else. Perhaps every five or six days a group of us women would come together to gossip, sew, weave baskets and share some watermelon. That was all there was.

There were no shops, our dresses we made ourselves – we just had the one pattern and two types of fabric. Maybe once a year, around *Eid*,[4] a woman would come from Riyadh with a big bag full of perfume, underwear and ready-made dresses. She would open it up in the middle of my kitchen floor, just like a treasure chest, and all the neighbours would dive in. That was our shopping spree.

A woman should look after her husband, care for her children

I didn't go to school; we didn't have one for the girls. When I was small, I tried to join in the girls *kuttub*;[5] we learned the alphabet, memorised *Qur'an*, all that – but I was a slow learner and the teacher, Miss Haya, used to beat me for every mistake. I came home most days in tears.

One day my mother – God rest her soul – just took my slate and snapped it, right in two. She said it wasn't worth me being so miserable, just for the sake of reading; I didn't need to go out to work like the boys anyway. From then on, I stayed at home with her.

It's better for a woman to be at home; she should look after her husband, care for her children. My husband wouldn't know how to bond with a baby. How would he? He didn't bring it into the world.

That doesn't mean a woman works less than a man. In the

4 One of two major Islamic festivals.
5 Informal study group based on religious teachings.

old days, I was up every day before dawn, chopping firewood, collecting water, sewing clothes, grinding wheat. Every day I cooked for fifteen people: my husband, my children and the farm boys. I did it all on an open fire in the kitchen.

Women don't work like that any more. They get their food from the restaurant, and give their children to the maid. You see them going out to work every which where. If a woman has to work, fine, she can teach, she can work in a school. But she shouldn't work with men. Mixing them now like they do in the city, this will only bring trouble.

She held my hand when it was time to meet him

One day, I came home and found Mama wearing her *abaya*[6] in the house. I asked her why she was wearing it inside. She just said, 'A man is coming.' That's how I found out I was going to be married. I was thirteen.

We had the wedding that same day. There was a big party – the women on one side of the house, the men on the other; everyone singing and dancing. They slaughtered a camel and five goats. There were three women just to make the bread – it was a big feast: fifteen plates!

I didn't eat though. I was inside by myself, waiting for my husband. Only the *ar-rabeya* stayed with me – it's a kind of maid who used to help, just with weddings. She arranged my hair, my make-up, talked to me about how I should behave with my new husband.

She held my hand when it was time to meet him; I was too frightened to go into the room by myself. I was young; I didn't understand anything. I remember she said to him, 'Here is your wife, now give me my money!' Then, *khalas*,[7] she was gone.

---

6 Women's long, loose-fitting cloak worn in public or in the company of non-related males, usually black.
7 Exclamation equivalent to 'that's it!' or 'enough!'

We stayed at home with my parents for one week before I joined his family home, with his brothers and all the other wives; nowadays of course, a girl won't marry unless she gets her own house. They all want to live alone – like cats! There were no cars then either; I walked to my new home by myself with the bridal trousseau that Mama gave me.

She gave me perfume, misk, saffron, gold jewellery and five long dresses – she made them herself. She was very clever, Mama; she made them extendable with buttons, so I could lengthen the sleeves and the skirt as I grew.

My husband must have been in his twenties, I suppose. We got on well enough. In a way I didn't know him that well; we were both so busy all day, working, working, working, I only saw him at night.

Now it's different. The girls meet the man before they marry, they talk on the phone and everything. But for me, no, I don't think it's decent. Better he comes to your parents and asks for your hand.

But maybe better when she's a little older than I was. I still don't know why they threw me on him like that. I was just a child.

I was a good mother – but they still died

When I was around fifteen, I started to get this strange feeling down in my belly. It was like something was moving in there. I tried to talk to the other women about it, but they just told me this was something that all women felt and not to worry about it.

But time went on, and I was worried; the thing was moving all the time and I was so swollen. I thought I must be sick, that maybe I would die. Finally, one day I went to my husband and I told him that there was something very wrong and I was going to visit my mother for help. That's when she told me about the baby.

I had no idea where babies came from. As a child, when the women sat down to talk, we were always sent away to play. Nobody ever explained anything to me. We were told that babies were delivered at the walls of the town, that's it.

When the pain started, I went back to Mama's house again. She took me to the bedroom, but then visitors arrived downstairs and she had to see them. As the pain got worse, I gripped onto a wooden pole and I prayed. Mama said the moment she closed the door on her guests, she heard a baby crying upstairs. My first boy. I did it all by myself.

The second one caught me by surprise. I was down in the cow shed when she came. I cut the cord with a knife and was cleaned up before anyone even knew what had happened.

Each time I would go back to stay with Mama for forty days. That's your resting time, when you learn how to do it all: feed the baby, hold her, dress her. I really took to it, *yanee*.[8] I was a good mother – but still they died.

I had ten children: seven girls and three boys. I lost three girls and one of the boys. Mostly it was – how do you call it? – measles. They got very hot, whatever I did I couldn't cool them down; then they came out in red spots all over and they stopped eating. I lost one one year, two the next, like that.

That's how it was in those days. We didn't have doctors, and the only water was from the well; it wasn't clean. When someone got sick, we waited for God to heal him – and if God chose death, then he died.

I myself was one of seven children. Only my brother and I survived. I remember two of my sisters died the same day; they went swimming in the lake, and when they came back they were coughing, coughing. They couldn't eat, and later they passed. Maybe it was malaria, I don't know. My youngest sister

---

8 Common filler in conversation; equivalent 'you know?'

was run down by a cow that got loose out in the street. The others died from measles, or something like it.

It's still difficult to talk about them now, my children and my siblings, even after all these years. I still carry them with me. That was a part of life you never got used to.

I covered, even my fingers

I cover because I'm afraid of God, I'm afraid of hellfire. If I don't cover I don't know where I'll go when I die.

We didn't have this niqab[9] when I was young. I just pulled a black veil over my face when I left the house. I still do. And the abayas weren't light little things like they are now. No, they were made of wool. They were hot. They were heavy.

Even when I carried the water jar on my head, I would pull the cloth right up over my hands so you couldn't see a finger. It's haram,[10] it's shameful for a woman to walk around showing herself in front of the men. Who would marry a girl like that?

We weren't afraid to talk to men though, not like they are now. We would greet each other on the street. We could even have male visitors to the house while the men were at work. We just didn't show them our faces.

We still kept ourselves pretty underneath for our husbands, mind. We made our own make-up. Kohl you make with the wood of the harmal tree; you burn it, then grind up the ashes with a little ithmid[11] stone. Then there's another tree, the diram we call it. Those sticks you chew until your lips turn pink. I still use it. And the henna on your hands; partly because it's beautiful, but also because it's a kind of medicine when you're working with your hands all day.

---

9 Women's face veil, revealing only the eyes.
10 Forbidden according to Sharia.
11 Antimony.

You don't need a guardian in a village

You only need a *mahram*[12] with you if you're making a long journey – *yanee*, to another city or so. It's in the religion, he has to accompany you. I never thought about it when I was younger; when I wanted to visit my mother, my sisters, my children, I just walked there. Everything was nearby. You don't need a guardian to walk across a village.

If I could have my wish, we'd just go back

I like the telephone; I can talk to my brother all the way in Riyadh. But the rest of it, you can keep it. Life was better before.

Before, I knew everyone in the village and everyone knew me. People helped one another. If the neighbours were cooking something good, they always dropped round with a plate or two to share. If you had a guest, all the women around came over to help you prepare. You were never lonely back then.

Before, during *Ramadan*, we would break our fast every night in a different house, even out in the street. Everyone brought a dish and we all sat together around the oil lamps, everyone laughing and talking. Nowadays everyone is in their houses with their high walls and they go to work far away in the city. I don't know who lives here any more.

If I could have my wish, we'd just go back, back to the way it was when there were 130 houses and a single gate in the wall.

---

12 Any man a woman is prohibited from marrying due to kinship. For example, her father, brothers, uncles, nephews.

THE BEDOUIN

Hafsa

Semi-nomadic Bedouin, mid-fifties, Tabuk area

Hafsa belongs to a Bedouin[13] tribe which has inhabited the north-west of the Arabian Peninsula since long before the creation of Saudi Arabia. A mother of eleven, she was raised according to a traditional nomadic way of life where tents and camels were the only shelter and transport available. Hafsa's family continues to spend part of the year roaming the deserts with her family; the rest they now spend settled on a small plot of land on the outskirts of Tabuk, where they have constructed more permanent shelters. Hafsa has no birth certificate but believes she is currently in her mid-fifties.

Fire was life

I gave birth to eleven children out there in the sands – five boys and six girls. There weren't any doctors; at least I'd never met one. *AlhamduLillah*, every one of them survived. And I did too.

We didn't have any of this technology. There was no electricity. Fire was life. When we're far out in the desert we still bury the meat in the sand to make it last longer. We take our milk from the goats and the camels, we shake it to make butter and curds. We grind the wheat to make flour for our bread. In

---

13 Nomadic desert peoples, primarily inhabiting North Africa and the Arabian Peninsula.

the old days that's all there was. Maybe we'd buy a little rice along the way. When I was younger, I had to do all of it with a baby on my back, too!

We're traveller Bedouins, *yanee*, we follow the rains; where there's rain, there's grass, and then you know your animals are safe. And when the plants go dry, that's it, you wrap up your life in the tent, tie it to the camels and move on. Before the Gulf War we used to roam right up into Jordan and stay there for a year at a time. It's all the same desert. But now, with all the new borders and such, we're stuck closer to home.[14] That's why we built the huts.

Now we spend maybe half the year travelling and half the year here, but even this – I consider it city life. You start to belong more to the village than to the dunes. Look, I have a phone now. We're drinking juice from a carton. You can't escape it. Half of me is happy for it, and half of me weeps.

There's no peace in the city

I get anxious when I come to visit my daughters in the city. There's no peace, inside your head or out of it. My sons keep trying to move me into an apartment but I won't do it. I'm not comfortable there. Sleeping in a bed hurts my back. I was born on this land, and I want to stay on it.

I don't think I'd be in such good shape if I lived in the city. Here you're always working, always moving. I believe Bedouins are stronger; we have more energy, we live longer too – I've never been to a hospital, not once in my life. If you put me in an apartment I think I'd seize up!

The city life is comfortable, but it's not good for you. Everyone gets sick more now; people are getting lazier – women

---

14 Following the 1990–1991 Gulf War, precipitated by the Iraqi invasion of Kuwait, many regional borders were formalized.

are getting lazier! I swear that's why young people get divorced these days – she doesn't know how to sew, how to clean, how to cook. You won't keep a man on instant noodles and eggs!

First of all is the man

First of all is the man, second is the mother of the man, and third are the wives. My husband is the leader of the family, *yanee*, he's the boss; I don't go anywhere out of this plot of land without his say-so.

The man has the freedom, but it's the women who bear the responsibilities. We're the ones who work. Everything you see around you, we make it ourselves. The food, the clothes, the furniture – even the tent; my mother and sisters and I made it together. We took the wool from the goats, we dyed it, we spun it, we wove it, we sewed it like this with a needle and thread; we built the house.

There are a few things, slaughtering animals and cutting meat, which are left to the men; it's *haram* for us to touch it. But even then, if we're left alone, we just take one of the boys, the little ones, and hold his hands under our own on the knife.

I think Bedouin women are different like that; we're tougher than the city girls. If our men go out, they don't tell people they've left the house empty like the men would in town; we still welcome guests – we make them coffee, we cook for them, we make sure they are well rested before they set off again, whether there's a *mahram* around or not.

It's his job to protect you

A woman is weak, *yanee*, weaker than a man. It's not an easy life out here in the desert: you need a man – it's protection. You know, in the old days, people were very ignorant. They used to rob each other, attack each other's villages, wells, tents or what-not. They didn't know any better; they didn't know it was *haram*.

So your father, your husband or your son, this is your *mahram*, and it's his job to protect you, to provide for you. Whether he likes it or not!

He married her without telling me

Before, when the rains came, big groups of Bedouins would gather together in one place. When my husband was a young man, he and his friends were at one of these gatherings watching us children play, and they teased him that this little girl could be his wife one day. He told them they were crazy, but look, that's how we ended up.

It was maybe ten years later that he saw me again, at a well. After that he went to ask my father for permission. The others here like to gossip and say we had some kind of romance, but it's not true. We never spoke, and I never saw him again until our wedding day.

In the old days it was a shameful thing, to meet before you married. I was lucky I even saw him. We married when he was around thirty, and I guess I was sixteen. Our wedding lasted for four days. Life was good then. I gave him a good family.

But when we'd been married almost fifteen years, he went and he took another wife from my tribe – a younger one – without telling me. And I was meant to welcome her into the family.

I was spitting. You cannot imagine! I didn't talk to her for a long time – or him. But in the end, I accepted it. I had to. A man has this right, and what was I going to do? March off into the desert by myself?

Now we live better together. We have twenty-two children between us. They're all brothers and sisters; we're family now. But I keep to my hut, and she keeps to hers. In the end, how well you get along is up to the husband. If the husband is good and treats you both well, there is peace. If he doesn't, well – there's war!

Thanks be to God, my daughter's husbands haven't remarried, and I hope they don't. It's better with one wife. There are always a lot of problems at home when there's more than one.

Anyway, the generations have changed. When I was young, the man's parents chose the girl and she didn't have any say; they would even use force to get her to marry. There used to be a lot of divorce and separation back then, just because they didn't know each other at all. They weren't suited.

Now, the lady and the man can choose each other. They get to know each other first. They even talk on the phone. Thanks be to God, it's better this way, when they both agree. Life moves more smoothly – and they get to enjoy their own love stories.

There was no such thing as niqab

It's true, there are tribes where a woman never shows her face. The Otaibis, the Rashidis out here, the women veil their faces even amongst themselves. Imagine, the children never see the faces of their mothers. My husband thinks they take it off at night for their husbands, but who knows?

In our tribe there was no such thing as a *niqab* when I was growing up. We always kept separate from the men; they gathered at one end of the tent and we stayed at the other, behind this sheet, look. But we never covered our faces; we just wore the *issaba*,[15] it's like a cord.

Since then we've had *imams*[16] to visit us. Now we understand more about Islam – we're more educated, thanks be to God. So now, that's it, I wear it. We all do; even my son's wives are wearing it in front of each other now sometimes. I'm scared

---

15 Traditional headband worn around the forehead, used to secure a woman's headscarf. Previously common in rural, western Saudi Arabia.
16 Islamic leader in worship and community life.

what will happen if I don't. Maybe my prayers and fasting won't be accepted; maybe I won't be allowed into Paradise.

It's not a problem for me; I don't care, I don't mind wearing it. But okay, if I'm honest, and my husband isn't listening, I do miss the breeze on my face sometimes, especially in the evening.

Before the motorways, women drove everywhere

The first time we saw cars when we visited the villages, well, to us it felt just like a plane coming to take us, this roaring machine. The first truck my father bought was like a pick-up; all fifteen of us kids would pile in the back, my parents in the front.

Now with my husband we have like most families: a jeep, a truck for the water tank and a regular old car that stays here by the house. My daughters can drive them all – and they're not automatics mind you; they're all the old stick gears.

My husband taught all six of them and he's proud to say it. Now the girls can drive the water truck to the lakes to fetch water; they can drive the children around; and if anyone in the tribe is sick, they can drive them to the neighbours' or to the closest doctor.

Before the motorways were built and so on, the women would drive everywhere. It was nothing unusual, but the city folk didn't accept it.

I never learnt – I'm too old – but I'm proud of my daughters too. It's important for a woman to know how to drive, or what she can do in an emergency.

We were all Bedouins in the beginning

I know that the city folk look down on us; they think that we're ignorant, that we're dirty, that we're lower than them. If I'm honest, we used to envy them too. I used to look at them and be jealous because they seemed to have everything better than us; they lived such an extravagant lifestyle.

But the fact of the matter is, we were all Bedouins in the beginning. They all lived in tents, with just the light and the heat of the fire, at some point. Now you see them coming to spend their weekends in the desert, camping in the old tents and cooking their bread in the old way. It's in our blood.

I consider myself a Bedouin first, and a Saudi second. The histories of our tribes go back much further than the Kingdom. Our borders, too, extend further than the new national ones. We have a lot to be proud of.

As for the way women live in other countries, how should I know? From what I understand they live like men. Well, they can do what they like, but we will keep our traditions and our Islam.

When we are gone, who will remember?

I wish I could be a girl again. Life was harder then, but it was more fun too; it was easier on the soul. You went to sleep under the stars with a clear head, and you woke up at dawn the same way. You didn't take life as seriously as you do now. Nowadays women have to worry about so many things: money, work, the things they need to buy. Their heads are always whirring.

But life is much more comfortable, that's true. My daughters' lives are good. They live in the city, they watch TV, talk on their mobiles; they have people and machines to help them clean, to cook. They have showers and toilets right inside their homes.

But they are already forgetting the old ways. There are things – our stories, our crafts, the importance of kin and hospitality – which shouldn't be left behind.

Soon there will be no more Bedouins left, no more traditions. There are a few, deeper in the desert, who still live the old lifestyle – just in tents; no concrete houses, no electricity – but there are fewer of them each year. When they and we are gone, who will remember?

WHAT WOULD YOU DO IF YOU
WERE A MAN FOR A DAY?

I'd sit around all day and talk with my friends like the men do. Look at them! That's how it is here, the men talk, talk, talk and the women work. I'd drive in the city and travel wherever I wanted, without a care. The old man never lets me go anywhere.

THE PRINCESS

AMIRA

Princess, aged forty-five, Riyadh

Princess Amira is a senior member of the House of Saud. An active supporter of various charities, she lives in Riyadh with her husband and children.

Half of what you've read is pure fiction

People think being a princess means walking around with a crown on your head or with an entourage. In reality we are very much blended into society. I rarely give my last name or my status – people treat you differently. Often the attention is positive, but still, I'd rather avoid it.

Being a princess doesn't mean you're wealthy by the way. A lot of people here are richer than a princess; I don't own a private jet or anything like that! A princess will do anything anybody else does, she will earn a living if she has to.

Even worse, people associate you with some negative story they've picked up in the press. I can't tell you these things never happen, but when you read those stories you should also know that more than half of it is pure fiction.

We're a big family; you can't have 5,000 people behaving themselves impeccably all of the time. But those stories still upset me. I hate for the whole Royal Family, for all Saudis even, to be tarred with the same brush because of one or two who might misuse their privilege.

It's probably the hardest thing about my position, making sure you're always representing your family right, here or abroad; as a princess, as a Saudi and as a woman.

People still know they can come to us

I think, as a princess, people expect a lot from you. People look to you for help. It doesn't have to be financial; they come to you for guidance too, and I accept that as a great blessing. A house that has a prince or a princess in it, they don't just support their families; they support everyone around them – people who work for them, people who may not even know them.

Our homes are always open. You know, my father's house used to belong to my grandfather, and the gates have never been closed. Bedouins still visit when they have some business to attend to in the city. They'll come to my father's house to eat. There are always places laid out for them to rest in the *majlis*.[17] In earlier days even the Kings' houses were never closed; now, unfortunately, security is more of an issue.

But you'll still find that princesses are very close to the community. Nobody knows who they are, but they are there and they help as much as they can, whether it's in charities or something on a smaller scale. People still know they can come to us, and *alhamduLillah*, I think that's why we've always been supported.

You don't stop working or cease to exist just because you're at home

Personally I love being a woman and I thank God I'm not a man; I think we have more pleasures in life as women. I'm very grateful for the men in my family, that they take on so many of the big, stressful responsibilities in life. They make my life

---

17 Sitting area, often reserved for welcoming guests.

easier and happier; they give me the space for being a woman, for doing what I want to do.

And I should love being a woman – I have quite a brood. My family is the greatest treasure in my life, and I'm a hands-on, full-time mother.

That doesn't mean I don't think a woman should work. I worked before I had children, and for some time after. I was a director in my company. But I realised that my family needed me more than anything or anyone else did, and that I would be the biggest loser if I was working for everyone except my kids. So I quit.

I believe that running a household is a business in itself. You have a company, which is your family; you're taking care of your employees, which are your kids; and you're creating programmes for them and helping them develop.

I always think a mother is a mother, and a doctor, and a psychiatrist, and a caregiver; she has a lot of different roles in her life. You don't stop working or cease to exist just because you're at home. I feel my role is extremely important, just as important as the men's.

For me, being equal doesn't mean that women do whatever men do, or vice versa; it's like comparing apples and oranges. We complete one another.

Having a strong, male figure in your life is very important

My husband is an amazing man in my eyes; all the men in my family are really. They protect me so much. They give me structure.

But I don't believe a legal guardian is always necessary these days, not unless the woman is unable to provide for herself. Although, the truth is, you will find some women who are not so independent who still need a guardian. Some women do struggle to take care of themselves, to be honest with you.

Quite aside from the legal aspect, I do believe having a strong male figure in your life is very important. I respect the way women live in the West, but personally, I couldn't do it. I can't live without a man supporting me. It doesn't have to be financially, but I need a male role model in my life, let's put it that way.

I have a lot of international friends, and when they come to stay with me, when they see my husband, my kids, the way my family is, they say, 'We wish we could have these values. We wish that when we talked to our kids, that they respected us like yours do.' And this, this comes from the family dynamic that we have, where everyone knows their role and what's expected of them.

I don't think any man can treat two completely equally

In our religion it's true that a man is permitted to marry four women, but only on the condition that he treats them all equally. To be honest with you, I don't think any man can treat four equally, or even two; he can barely handle one. I respect that it exists in Islam, and would understand that if a man's first wife is uncaring he might take a second, without divorcing her, for the sake of the kids.

But in my case, no, I wouldn't accept it. Not for myself, and certainly not for my daughters – not a chance.

Hijab is not only my religion, it's my culture

The most attractive thing about a woman is her face, her hair – we all know this. So we don't flaunt these things, we use *hijab*.[18] But it's not only our religion; the *abaya*, the *tarha*,[19] these are also part of my culture, and I respect this enormously.

---

18 Modest code of dress that applies to both men and women, often used informally to refer to a woman's headscarf.

19 Women's headscarf; in Saudi Arabia usually worn together with the *abaya*.

Whether or not you cover your face is a matter of personal choice. I don't always, but if I happen to be wearing make-up or I'm in a crowded place, like a hospital or a market, I'll just pull my *tarha* fully over my face. I feel more comfortable that way, especially in Riyadh where people are a little more conservative. It's simply a matter of not drawing attention to oneself.

Why do we have to be ashamed?

The rest of the world views us the way the media shows us, and most of the time, unfortunately, the media is not complimentary.

I find it very unfair. The West can look to other cultures and respect them — their religions, their customs, their clothes. But once you get close to the Islamic world, the differences are always portrayed as negative.

You go to India and you see women in bright, beautiful saris; you see women in Japan wearing kimonos, and it's a source of national pride. Why do we have to be ashamed of our *abayas*? I love wearing it and I'm very proud of it.

I keep my values wherever I go, but I also try to respect other people's traditions, religions and cultures. I mean, we don't go to Europe and stop women and ask why they're wearing shorts. I would just like others to show us the same respect.

Saudi Arabia is really just like any other country. I always say, 'If the world were perfect we'd be in heaven right now. Nobody would be on earth.' Like any culture in the world, we have the good, the bad and the ugly. But I would like the world to see a little more of the good!

It won't be as easy for my daughters

My grandmother died more than a decade ago; I feel her presence every day. I don't think I'll ever stop missing her. She told me so many wonderful stories; I wish I'd written them down.

But then I always thought she'd live forever. I think you always
do with people you love.

She was a remarkable woman; she came from another era.
She didn't go to school – there weren't any in those days –
but she was highly educated nonetheless. There is a *hadith*,[20]
'Seeking knowledge is an obligation upon every Muslim', and
that knowledge came packaged in the accumulated wisdom
and stories of all the esteemed elders, visitors and scholars who
passed through the royal household, as well as every book that
happened to fall into their hands.

She was taught by everyone around her: her brothers, her
wise aunts – and probably the best tutor of all at that time,
the holy *Qur'an*. The *Qur'an*, by the way, makes no distinction
between men and women when it comes to the virtue of learning. Back then some families even employed blind *muttawahs*[21]
to mentor their daughters in their religious studies.

Royal life was also a lot more luxurious in those days. I
don't mean in terms of fancy furniture or fast cars; when
Riyadh was first established as the country's capital, conditions
were still very basic – the first royal palace was entirely constructed of clay.

But it was luxurious to a different standard. Riches took
the form of occasional packages from far-off India laden with
rich dress silks and the heady *oud dukoun*[22] which they used to
fragrance their clothes and their living spaces. These treasures
were simple, but I think they were more valued in their simplicity. We are often reminded by the older generation to be
appreciative of what we have.

---

20 Recorded saying or deed of the Prophet Mohammed.
21 Deeply religious individuals who practise *Sharia* according to its most literal
interpretation and encourage others to do the same; colloquially used to refer to
members of the religious police.
22 A perfume derived from the dark scented resin of agar trees.

Things have changed enormously since then, and, of course, they continue to change. When I look to my daughters, life's not going to be as easy for them as it is right now. It's getting harder. They'll be living in smaller houses with less help. They'll have to take care of themselves more; you can't rely on your title any more. In fact, it can be a heavy burden to bear if you don't take care of it.

But I admire them; I love the new generation. They are so excited about life, about supporting themselves. They don't drop their names to get what they want. I think they're adapting beautifully.

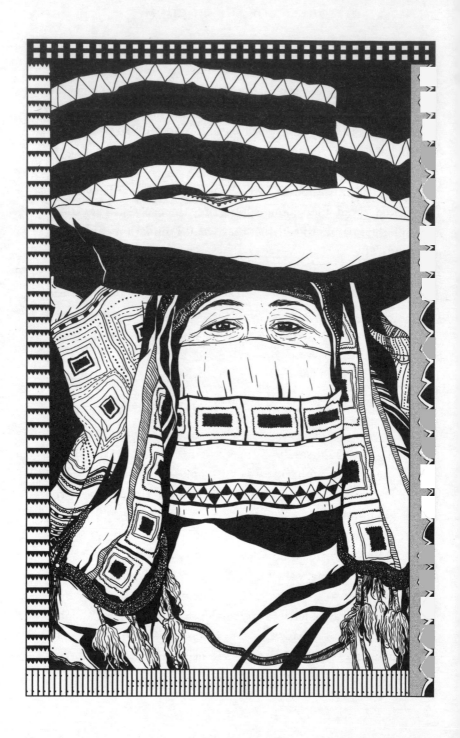

THE MOUNTAIN WOMAN

WAFFIAH

Housewife and local historian, aged sixty-three, Taif

Waffiah grew up in a mountain village near the western city of Taif. As the area has modernised and customs have changed, Waffiah has made it her mission to keep the memories of traditional village life alive. She maintains a private collection of traditional dresses and household items that she happily shows to visitors. She now resides in Taif city with her eldest daughter and her family.

You could smell the perfume in the air

I grew up in a stone house in the mountains, surrounded by rose fields. You could smell the perfume in the air all around you. At dawn, I would harness up the camels to the pulleys of the well and bring water for the animals and the plants; we grew fruits and wheat.

From six in the morning until six in the evening I took the goats out to graze, then I was back to the well to bring water again. I would carry the huge clay jar on my head all the way up to the house to cook and make coffee.

When I was older it was just the same, but with my babies on my back in a basket. I would cross mountains, visit the farm, whatever I wanted. I didn't need permission or anyone to accompany me. There was nothing to fear.

It was hard work, but *w'Allah*[23] it was a beautiful life. I wish things never had to change. Of course, they did; they changed completely. But still, I am very, very proud to come from this heritage, to have Bedouin roots, and to share my culture with others.

A woman is a helper

A man is the head of the house; he has to be strong, he has to lead. But you know, he wouldn't even build the house if he didn't have a wife. An unmarried man rarely comes to anything; he needs a wife, someone to support him. It even says in Islam, a man who has married a good woman has already fulfilled half of his religion. So you can say a woman's role is to be a helper to her husband.

'Instead of money, I'll give you a wife'

I was betrothed to my husband when I was five years old. He was a cousin and completely penniless. He came to my father's farm looking for a job. My father said, 'I won't pay you, but if you work with me for ten years, you can have my daughter; instead of money, I'll give you a wife.'

So that's what happened. He stayed, he worked hard, and when I turned fifteen, we married. I was young, but you have to remember, I had known this man since I was five. He was part of the family, so it wasn't a shock. He wasn't a stranger. I remember it as a happy time.

We stayed at home with my parents for another two or three years; they built us a little bungalow next to the family house. My mother still did most of the cooking, and my husband still helped my father in the fields and the garden.

Later we moved further into the village, then to the town. My husband never became very wealthy, but it's just as well. It meant he couldn't take any more wives!

---

23 I swear it by God.

I still think this traditional way of meeting is best. Parents know better what their children need. Normally a mother will spot a pretty girl at a wedding, then she'll make her enquiries: is it a good girl, from a good family?

Of course they get to see each other too, and he can say if he doesn't want her and she can say if she doesn't want him! But if you marry for love, there can still be problems down the line. I think you take a bigger risk with romance.

There was always a bigger party for a boy

I have eight children: two girls and six boys. I had three of them before we had any kind of clinic in the village. There were no nurses, no doctors, just my mother and an aunt who had helped with other births in the family.

The first one was the toughest. I went into labour at six o'clock in the morning; the baby didn't arrive until 2 a.m. the next day. It was another seven hours for the afterbirth.

There was no bathroom back then, no shower. We kept our water container in the shade of a big tree out on the hill. That's where I had to walk to clean myself up.

In those days there was always a bigger party if you had a boy. They say boys will do more for the family. But, as a mother, really what you wished for was a girl. I think mothers are closer to their girls, and when you're tired, they're always there to help around the house. Girls are better for a mother. But the men are keener on having boys.

I think it's still that way really. My son-in-law was quite upset when his first-born was a girl. They want a boy first so they can be called 'Abu-Ahmed' or 'Abu-Mohammed'.[24] No man wants to be 'Abu-Noura'! But my daughter's second

---

24 'Father of Ahmed', 'Father of Mohammed'; in Arab culture it is common custom for parents to be known informally by the name of their eldest son.

child was a boy, so now he's 'Abu-Hamza', and he's happy, *alhamduLillah*!

I miss the way we dressed before

I never wore an *abaya* in the village. They didn't exist. We wore colourful dresses or brightly embroidered tunics just to the knee, with loose trousers underneath. That's what we wore on the street; that's how we dressed in front of the men.

But in the village, we knew everyone, we were all the same tribe. I think that's why things have changed; now, in the towns, you have people from all over. You don't know who they are or what kind of people they are. You don't know if you can trust them.

A pretty girl would be harassed with so many strangers around, or at least stared at. There might be men with bad intentions, who might want to do something bad to her. If she covers herself, those men won't look at her; she won't be bothered.

We've also learned more about religion since I was young. You know, the wives of the Prophet, peace be upon him, Aisha and Khadija, would cover whenever strange men came to visit; they would pull their veils just halfway across their faces, so they were only showing one eye.

I think the *abaya* has become popular too because it covers up what women are wearing underneath. These days they're all in shorts and leggings like the Western girls. I can't say I like it very much; I don't think it's very ladylike.

Truly, I miss the way we dressed before – the colours, the care that we put into each design. I still have the dresses of my sisters, my mother, my grandmothers. One is at least 160 years old. That's why I keep them here – to show my daughters, so they don't forget. If not, how would they know what their mother wore, what our life was like? There's no sign of it left any more.

You feel like royalty with your chauffeur in the front

Women do drive. Out in the countryside, it's just more practical; they all do it. If you're out in the desert herding the goats or the camels or you need to fetch water, it's much harder to do it all on foot.

But in the city, women don't drive. I don't think they should. We have too much traffic as it is, and in any case, a woman should be treated like a queen. You feel more like royalty when you are sitting in the back with your chauffeur in the front.

A lot of young girls in the towns want to drive these days, but I don't think they've thought about the consequences. What if they break down on the highway, or they're involved in an accident? Men are stronger; they know how to deal with these kinds of problems. A girl is weak; I don't think she'd know what to do.

A woman shouldn't be left alone to fend for herself in the world; it would be shameful for society to allow it. What if she has children? She shouldn't have to take long journeys to places she doesn't know without some form of protection.

Now, the world is so much bigger than it was when I was young. My daughters are grown, they are educated, they want to see the world a little. But if they take a trip somewhere, if they go on some adventure, I know that their husbands or their brothers will be there to look out for them. If they were all alone, I can't even imagine how much I would worry.

To them their religion, to us our religion

I think the West just thinks of us as Bedouins, people who live out in the desert and ride camels. They think we don't understand life, that we're not educated. They think we're ignorant.

But it's not true. Nowadays Saudi women are engineers and doctors and teachers and nurses. They even own factories now, thanks be to God!

I think, in the West, women developed faster than we did here. They're stronger, they're more open than we are. We look up to them a bit really.

There are some things I'm not so keen on – the way they follow their religion, the way they dress, the drinking and so on. But you know, the Prophet told us, 'To them their religion, to us our religion.' So I don't think it's our place to judge.

People are already forgetting

A country that doesn't have a past doesn't have a present. We need to remember our roots; we need to preserve the stories of the times that have passed. But people are already forgetting.

Of course there are some changes I am very grateful for: running water right in your house, electricity, transport, and, thanks be to God, the washing machine!

But, for everything else, I wish we could go back to the old days. The clothes were more beautiful, the food was prepared on an open fire, the women cooked the bread straight on the coals. We had our milk and yoghurt each day from the goats, the camels and the cows. It was all fresh, it was all natural. Not like now, when we eat everything out of tins.

I miss the safety of the village. In those days I went everywhere alone; I was never afraid of anything. As a woman I had to go out to work to help my husband. We were more independent then. We had to be. These days I'm afraid to go out on the street by myself.

For myself, I only wish that, when I die, I am permitted a good death – not too much sickness and suffering, just an easy passing – and a good life in Paradise.

KINGDOM COME

انا اخو نورة

'I am the brother of Nourah'

—KING ABDULAZIZ IBN SAUD,
first king of Saudi Arabia

Princess Nourah bint Abdulrahman Al Saud was an educated woman of remarkable strength and charisma. When the Al Saud family found themselves in exile in Kuwait following the loss of their territories in central Arabia, it was she who convinced her younger brother to return to the land of their forefathers and to continue the fight for a united Arab nation.

Abdulaziz[25] often turned to his sister for counsel during the three decades of struggle that followed. It was in 1932 that he finally succeeded in his dream of unifying the disparate sea of sheikhdoms, emirates, tribal unions and city states that stretched from the Red Sea to the Arabian Gulf and declared a Kingdom in his family's name. He achieved his victory on the battlefield, but he consolidated his throne through his ties with women.

---

25 In the West, Abdulaziz is popularly referred to as Ibn Saud.

In the course of his life, Abdulaziz is said to have married twenty-two times. He chose his brides from every major tribe of the lands that he conquered, and with them, fathered close to a hundred children. Through these unions and the offspring they bore him, he was able to supplant long-standing tribal rivalries with a new common loyalty – drawing together a nation under the eaves of the House of Saud.

In these early days of the Kingdom, life was harsh on women; maternal and infant mortality rates were high, child marriage was common and arduous physical labour was a fact of life. But physical conditions aside, in some ways women were endowed with a status and independence higher than in the decades that followed.

> 'Their work was as much needed as the men's; they were
> farmers together, providing equally for the community,
> so women were looked upon very respectfully.'

> ——LOUJAIN AL HATHLOUL, activist

Older women in many regions recall a time when women walked around unveiled, received male guests in their homes unchaperoned and interacted freely with men in public. But beyond the ties of marriage, Abdulaziz had consolidated another tribal bond that would impact the very nature of his Kingdom, and the role of women in it.

In 1744, his ancestors had formed a partnership with Muhammad ibn Abd al-Wahhab, a religious reformer who aimed to rid Islam of encroaching superstition and return the faith to its original form, as it was practised in its first three generations, beginning with that of the Prophet Mohammed.

It was an interpretation of *Sunni* Islam influenced by the land of its conception: the unforgiving desert plains of the central

Najd region. 'It was never colonised,' explains communications manager Raghad. 'It never had the influence of other countries and cultures in the way that other places did.'

Such origins help explain its isolationist standpoint, which branded not only people of other faiths as *kafir*, or non-believers, but even other Muslims who failed to conform to their unique understanding and practice of Islam – a tension that is still felt by the country's estimated 15 per cent *Shia* minority. Its application of *Sharia*[26] in regard to the rights of women, meanwhile, was almost certainly coloured by the strict patriarchal tribal codes of the region.

When Abdulaziz returned to conquer the peninsula, he renewed this alliance; it was with Wahhabi warriors that he subdued regional revolt and rebellion. Their pact was based on the agreement that for as long as the House of Saud retained political power, the Wahhabi clergy would maintain authority over matters of faith and law; it is a bond that has never truly been broken.

> 'The official title of our King is "the Custodian of
> the Two Holy Mosques". As a Kingdom, we are often
> viewed as the "guardians" of Islam, much like the
> Vatican is with Catholicism; making Saudi Arabia
> a trendsetter to many other Muslim nations.'
>
> —MARRIAM MOSSALLI, blogger

Such deep theological foundations paired with the nation's status as homeland of the Prophet Mohammed and the holy cities of Mecca and Medina confirmed the inseparable union between Saudi Arabia and Islam. Here, Islam is understood

---

26 Islamic system of life and law, based on the *Qur'an* and *Hadith*.

and implemented, not just as a spiritual practice, but as a comprehensive guidebook to every aspect of life, in both public and private domains.

~

As Wahhabi ideals of womanhood spread alongside the influence of the new Kingdom, women withdrew from their fields and study groups and focused their energies on the domestic realm — but no society is static. In 1938, just six years after the country was unified, oil was discovered in commercial quantities beneath the dunes of the Eastern Province. After the Second World War, the exploitation of this massive natural resource started in earnest and the nation's prospects shifted dramatically.

New technologies and the import of foreign domestic workers lightened women's burden in the home; in the public domain more opportunities for travel and education opened to female citizens; the possibility of women driving was subject to official discussion. It appeared that a new trajectory was opening to Saudi women, but it was not to be.

In December 1979, a radicalised former military officer named Juhayman al-Otaybi who believed his brother-in-law to be the *mahdi*[27] stormed the Grand Mosque in Mecca, with demands to overthrow the monarchy and repudiate the West — along with all its customs, technology and expat workers. During the siege that followed, at least 255 died in the world's holiest mosque; hundreds more were wounded.

In the end, the Saudi state won out, but their sense of security was shaken and the events of the Iranian Islamic Revolution next door less than a year prior raised fears that if the support of

---

27 Islamic messianic figure, who it is believed will be present on the day of judgement.

religious conservatives could not be guaranteed, similar scenes could unfold in Riyadh. The state returned to a stricter interpretation of Wahhabism, aided by the growing influence of the more modern, but equally puritan, Egyptian Salafi movement in the country. Once again it was often women's liberties that were sacrificed to the greater good.

It wasn't until this turn of events, less than thirty years ago, that the religious police became omnipresent in both their numbers and their powers to harass, that women required their guardian's permission to travel abroad, that women were formally prohibited from interacting professionally with men and that the colours of Waffiah's traditional dresses (see p. 40) were finally extinguished. 'I was in the South in the early 1980s,' says one female researcher, 'and I have photographs that prove it – there were women wearing colourful dresses and straw hats; they didn't have the *niqab*.'

> 'People don't understand this; they think we're all exactly the same – I always tell them, no, we're like the United States; we're completely different – in the way people talk, in traditional life, in marriage, in everything.'

> —Maha, municipal councillor

Despite the impression now projected through consistency of religion and national dress, the young Kingdom is far from a homogenous landscape. 'Hejazi girls are the toughest,' says student Mona, mischievously. 'Najdis are really Bedouin – they're super conservative so they judge everyone else. Southern women are tight with money; Qassimis are the most beautiful – but that's only because they were invaded by the Turks!'

'You see, we have Riyadh, then we have the Eastern Province and we have Hejaz – it's like three different countries – then if

you go south it's like Yemen,' explains ministry worker Ruba.
Like different countries, prior to unification these areas had
their own rulers and kings and followed very different paths of
development, which in turn have impacted on the experiences
of the women who inhabit them.

In contrast to the untouched, traditional heartland of Najd,
now home to the capital, Riyadh, the Eastern Province has
long welcomed outsiders in the form of migrants and traders.
Later, when oil was discovered in the region, this influx began
to multiply. Foreign female employees of Aramco oil company
were issued with official Saudi driving licences to be used on
their vast compound, where the infamous ban on women driving was never adopted.

As home to the holy cities of Mecca and Medina, the Western
Province – or Hejaz – has hosted countless pilgrims from all
over the world for more than a thousand years. Thanks in large
part to this exposure, it is broadly considered the most liberal
area of Saudi Arabia. In the Hejazi capital of Jeddah, it is not
uncommon to see young women with faces uncovered, hair
loosely wrapped in a coloured headscarf, sharing fruit-flavoured
shisha[28] on open terraces.

Riyadh women, while proud of their heritage, often view a
trip to the coast as something of a weekend escape. 'I told my
mum I was going to Mecca to perform Umrah,'[29] confesses shop
assistant Aasma. 'I lied and said there were no return flights for
three days. I went to do Umrah for three hours; the other three
days I stayed at a friend's place near the sea. We smoked shisha
and went anywhere we wanted!'

～

---

28 Tobacco-based water pipes.
29 Non-obligatory pilgrimage to Mecca.

Since the insular days of the 1980s and '90s, life has changed in every corner of the Kingdom. The traumatic events of 11 September 2001 forced the government to re-examine its approach towards sustaining fundamentalist and isolationist viewpoints at the expense of natural evolution and open debate. At the same time, the Kingdom's gates finally creaked open to the world through its cautious acceptance of the internet, exposing its subjects to a new dimension of information and cultural input.

The media often accuses Saudi Arabia of living in the Dark Ages. But, objectively, the rate of transformation has been remarkable. Just fifty years ago, more than half the population lived like Mama Muna and Hafsa in this chapter, as nomadic Bedouins or rural farmers. Today, more than 85 per cent of Saudis live in modern cities. Like some form of grand-scale sociological experiment, the Kingdom leapt from tent to penthouse in a single bound, bypassing industrial revolution, social restructuring or cultural movements.

Thus, while there are few women today who live in communities like Hafsa, where tribal affiliations are openly used to navigate day-to-day life, Saudi Arabia remains a kinship society, and lines of tribal and familial hierarchy continue to hold, just below the surface.

From this standpoint, Saudis broadly self-categorise into two groups: *Qabili* families claim to be able to trace their lineage back to one of two original tribes on the peninsula; *Khadiris*, on the other hand, either lack such illustrious heritage, or have lost it.

'It's Khadiri *or* Qabili. *It's two, you know, just*
to make it simple. If you're Qabili *you're from a*
higher tribe; if you're Khadiri, *you're lower.'*

—MUNIRAH, doctor

'The old tale says that if a person commits a crime, they're kicked out of the tribe,' explains housewife Afnan, 'and then they're tribeless.' Of course, nowadays, there are many more plausible reasons for an individual to lack tribal affiliation, including migration, intermarriage and even being orphaned, but, to some extent, the stigma persists.

The tribe and family a woman is born into still affect her prospects in many ways; your name and network impact heavily on your level of social influence, or *wasta* as this soft capital is known in the region. '"Vitamin Waw" as we call it,' laughs legal student Wejdan.

Wasta affects the doors that are opened to you and those that are closed in terms of social mobility, bureaucracy, education, employment and even romance. 'I think it's a bigger issue to be addressed than religious extremism right now,' says social worker Lamees. 'It's not looked at, it's not talked about, but it's heavily practised, especially when it comes to marriage.'

But while continuing tribal loyalties may be viewed as a blessing or a burden depending on your position in the hierarchy, there is one area where most Saudi women agree on the benefits of living in a kinship society, and that is the special nature of family bonds.

> '*We are especially close family-wise. Even when we reach eighteen, we stay in our parent's homes — I know that in other cultures, they're forced out! But our parents like having us there. When we lived in the UK there were no gatherings — just work, study, you know. We were a bit lonely.*'
>
> —RAHAF, academic

Provided relationships are healthy, there is a genuine desire for family to be involved in everything, from everyday activities to choosing a husband. Fridays are family day, and women usually spend them at large gatherings in the company of cousins, aunts and grandmothers.

'When I go outside to the West and I see a child being rude to their parents, I can't stand it,' says university lecturer Nadeen. 'Here, even if they don't learn these skills at home, they learn it from the community. It's something beautiful and I don't want to lose it.'

~

But perhaps the most significant legacy of the Kingdom's origins is society's continuing commitment to and pride in Islam. No other religion is acknowledged in the country's official religious demographics. Faith infuses every aspect of public and private life.

Uniquely among Muslim nations, Saudi Arabia has never codified its legal system – refusing to manipulate the law of God into a manmade structure. The King may issue supplementary decrees and civil servants create specific regulations, but these are always subordinate to *Sharia*, which is interpreted by judges on a case-by-case basis.

This literal interpretation of Islamic law includes the implementation of practices which have since been limited or even abandoned in most other Muslim majority states, including women's legal testimony, compensation and inheritance being valued at half of that of men.

But this is not viewed as discrimination; rather it is understood as the simple acceptance of the God-given roles and attributes of each sex. 'Women are more compassionate than men; having another woman with her, to support her in court, it stops others from trying to manipulate her,' says women's rights advocate Aisha. 'A man gets a double share of the inheritance, but he has to use it to support his family, to support his wife; the woman's share is smaller, but it's only for her.'

In public life, shops, banks and restaurants are obliged to close their businesses five times a day in keeping with the ever-changing schedule of daily prayers; arrows attached discreetly to ceilings indicate the way to Mecca, the direction of worship; every public restroom is accompanied by a neighbouring prayer room – even your daily mouthwash is alcohol-free.

At home, the regular rhythm of women's lives is interwoven with small rituals of prayer – often announced by a digital prayer timer – ablutions, blessings, fasting and feasting. Even menstruation has a clear set of rules regarding sexual activity, worship and washing. Women consistently cite their faith as a source of strength, comfort and healing.

> '*Whenever I'm weak, I know there is always God beside me. If I pray, immediately I can feel the change . . . I know then that I am supported.*'
>
> —AMIRA, princess

As the country modernises and previously forbidden cultural practices and social norms creep into the mainstream, more traditional sectors of society have expressed fears for the future of Islam's heartland. Saudi headlines warn of the threat of atheism in the same way that Western publications might report on the dangers of rising religious extremism.

Even if faith, with time, changes shape, Saudi Arabia is unlikely to become the secular state that some fear. 'We do have a lot of atheists now,' says Ruba, 'and I think it's a reaction to the extremism we've seen. People get frightened – but I say let them leave! If you don't find God inside you, you won't find him anywhere else. When they feel that thing inside their hearts, then they'll come back.'

Similarly, Saudis have not lost their devotion to the royal House of Saud, which, as King Abdulaziz's large brood has multiplied, now comprises several thousand members. Seemingly exempt from Islamic concerns regarding the permissibility of portraiture, the faces of King, Crown Prince and Regional Emir smile benevolently from public billboards, school murals and the walls of private homes.

'I saw King Abdullah as leading women's empowerment, and I see King Salman as empowering youth: the first thing he did was put his son in a high position – above the older generation.'

—MARAM, teacher

As might be expected, the faces of princesses are not so publicly broadcast. But, much like Nourah before them, royal women continue to wield significant influence behind the crown, and many of them have used that power to further the cause of their Saudi sisters with less prestigious family names.

Despite their positions as the figureheads of a highly patriarchal system, Saudi women also tend to regard male royals as allies. 'King Salman genuinely cares about the country and the vision that he has for us,' says Nadeen. 'We need to hold onto it.'

The King's vision was clearly laid out in 2016 by his son and now Crown Prince Mohammed Bin Salman in the form of Vision 2030 – a strategy that encompasses economic, business, educational, social and cultural reform. At the heart of this transformation is the participation of Saudi women.

Whether the impetus of this change is to be found in rising efforts of Saudi activists or in the realisation that, both in terms of international relations and a less predictable economy, it is no longer feasible to keep half of its citizens behind closed doors, reforms have been rapid and tangible.

Since 2015, women have gained the right to vote in municipal elections, open their own businesses, attend sports stadiums, concerts, cinemas and gyms, and the ban on women driving – perhaps the most emblematic symbol of women's subjugation – has been dropped.

But embracing modernity doesn't have to be synonymous with Westernisation. 'There's no one template for modernity,' says Hoda, member of the Shura Council.[30] 'Why is it that people are constantly trying to rip up our roots, only to replace them with nothing, except something on the surface that is not really palpable, acceptable or understandable to the majority of society here?'

'I love our traditions. We have a beautiful culture and a beautiful religion – it protects a woman from birth until the end. I don't want us to become just like the rest of the world.'

—SARA, university lecturer

Saudi women want to learn from what women in the West have achieved, but they don't hold up the Western conception of womanhood as the blueprint for their own daughters to follow. 'If you lose your authenticity, you lose your identity . . . I'd love us to be more advanced socially, technologically and everything. But we're Saudi and we should

---

30 The highest consultative assembly in Saudi Arabia's theocratic monarchy, charged with proposing legislation to the King.

always be proud to be Saudi,' says business woman Abeer. 'If we let go of that, we're lost. And we don't want to be lost, not at all. We want to find our own way. We want to shine.'

THE *MUTTAWAH*

KHADIJA

Religious scholar, aged thirty-eight, Riyadh

Khadija is an extremely devout Muslim, informally known in Saudi Arabia as a muttawah. *She graduated in Islamic Studies and endeavours to follow the teachings of the* Qur'an *and the Prophet Mohammed in every aspect of her daily life. Her form of* hijab *is the most conservative, concealing her eyes, hands and feet as well as her body. Khadija lives in Riyadh, where she shares a home with her sisters and parents.*

I admired the scholars

The truth is, I didn't want to study Islam at university. I wanted to do IT; we were all so excited about the internet and new technology. But I found myself drawn to the scholars; the famous ones, you know – the ones who've spent their whole lives studying Islam. We would see them on television and hear them on the radio, and the way they spoke and defended their ideas was so impressive. I admired them, a bit like you might admire a famous actor or actress! I wanted to be like them, I guess.

So I went to an Islamic university. It was very strict, very intensive, and I studied the *Sunnah*[31] for four years. After the *Qur'an* comes the *Sunnah*, the texts that talk specifically about Prophet Mohammed's life, peace be upon him. And the more I

---

31 Collected religious practices established by the Prophet Mohammed.

studied, the more I admired Mohammed; for his patience, his perseverance, the way he treated people.

And it's amazing, because the two books complete each other so perfectly. For every situation in your life, there is an *aya*[32] or a *sunnah*;[33] there are prayers for when you're anxious, for when you travel, for when you are feeling unwell; there are instructions on how to eat, what to eat, how to do business, how to look after the environment. It's like a law book, a psychologist and a medical encyclopaedia all in one.

Now that I understand the texts better, I'm more careful about little things in my day-to-day life. I love watching videos online – I'm very interested in science, in politics, in history (my family will tell you I'm quite addicted to *National Geographic* documentaries!) – but I'm careful not to watch movies or series; I don't want to see women uncovered and I don't want to hear music. In Islam we believe that music negatively affects a person's thinking; it's not the lyrics – though those can be bad too – but the melody, the playing of instruments, that's *haram*.

I truly believe that if you followed Islam in every area of your life, you wouldn't have any problems. You would live in happiness. Even if you were sick or you didn't have a single *riyal*,[34] you would still be happy. You look at the people in Syria now and you think, *How do they survive? How do they keep going every day?* Well maybe that's how: God guides them through.

When Islam is correctly applied, a woman is a princess

God created the body of a woman differently to the body of a man. A man is able to bear more. Of course, you might find a few very strong women, but in general, it's not good for a

---

32 *Qur'anic* verse.
33 Recorded saying or practice of the Prophet Mohammed.
34 Saudi currency; 10 Saudi *riyals* (SAR) is roughly equivalent to £2 (GBP) or $3 (USD) at the time of going to press.

woman to do physical labour, to work long hours or to travel a lot. She's just not built for it.

So it follows that the man should be the one to bring in the money; to take care of his mother, his sisters, his wife and his daughters. I mean, you know how exhausting it is, being a working woman – imagine adding a husband and a baby to that schedule. It's too much.

That's why you have your Islamic rights, to protect you as a woman, so you can be at home with your children. It shouldn't be up to you to worry about paying the bills and settling the school fees on top of that.

In Islam, a woman has complete authority over her own finances. Any money she does earn, she keeps for herself. That's her right. She's under no obligation to support her husband, her household or her children. If she wants to give her money away, that's her choice, but it's a gift, never a duty.

People ask why, in Islam, a man receives twice the inheritance of a woman. It doesn't seem fair. But it's the same logic: a man must use his share to provide for his wife, for his family, while a woman keeps hers to spend as she chooses.

So you see, when Islam is correctly applied, being a woman is like being a princess! Even if you're a millionaire and your husband is poor, you will always be the one taken care of.

Men have been given responsibility for driving

A man works, but a woman sits at home like a queen. It's her husband's job to take the kids to school and bring home the shopping. If she wants to visit her friends, it's up to him to escort her there and carry her home. That's why men have been given responsibility for driving.

It makes sense practically, too. There's already so much traffic in Riyadh, I really don't see that there's any space for women to learn. We also have to remember that Saudi Arabia is mostly desert, and we have huge distances between cities. If a woman was driving alone and something happened, she would be completely alone, and very vulnerable.

It doesn't have to be black

Even if a woman were to walk around naked, the first thing a man would look at, before her legs, before anything else, is her face. Your face is the most important thing, your most beautiful asset, and a man should only look at it if he is seriously considering marrying you.

Islam asks us to cover and wear *hijab* to keep us safe. Maybe only one in a hundred men is actually dangerous, but still – he's one in a hundred.

It doesn't have to be black. We just use black because it's discreet. If you were to choose another colour, like purple, there are many different shades; men's eyes would still be drawn to some more than others. In black, we're all equal. Even if one is a bit darker or shinier than the others, you hardly notice the difference.

Nowadays, of course, a lot of girls cheat . . . They wear heavy eye make-up under their *niqab*s. That's not real *hijab*. In fact, it's even more provocative; some girls have beautiful eyes, but when they take off the *niqab*, they're quite plain!

Your guardian only needs to be there if there is a likelihood of danger

A *mahram* doesn't follow you around everywhere. I didn't ask my father for permission to meet you today. I'm an adult; he knows me, he trusts me, that's it, I can make my own plans.

Your guardian only needs to be there if there is any likelihood of danger. Even if it's only a tiny risk – if there's a risk, he should be there. It's really just for big things, like travel.

A *mahram* doesn't have any say in how a woman spends or invests her income, and he doesn't have the final say in who she marries. If a girl wants to marry someone, for example, and her father says no, she can take her brother, or any other male relative, with her to court and the judge will decide if the man is suitable. If it turns out he's a good man and her father has no real reason to oppose the union, she is free to marry him.

Women are learning more and more about their rights. Maybe in the past a man could get away with saying, 'Oh, but you need your guardian to do that', but now women are very much aware of what they can and cannot do.

An arranged marriage isn't a forced marriage

Your mother and father have more life experience than you; they're wiser. Maybe, when you're full of emotions, you think you know what's best for you, but ten years down the line, you'll live to regret your decision. I'm thinking even of a female friend of mine; a few years ago we got on like sisters, now I wonder why on earth I chose her as a friend, she's so narrow-minded.

But an arranged marriage isn't a forced marriage. The girl has to agree to the match too, and she has to be involved in the process. If a man comes to the house to ask for a girl's hand, the father has to tell his daughter that he came. Even if the father doesn't approve, she has to think it over for herself. When he comes to the house to see her, this is also her opportunity to see him, to see how she feels in his company.

It was different before. The Bedouins didn't even let the couple see each other before the wedding, but this is wrong. In Islam, a man has the right to see the woman he's going to marry.

He doesn't have to be a cousin of course, but it helps if he's close to the family. A man from Riyadh is not the same as a man from Taif, and for her own happiness, it's better for a girl to choose a partner whose customs and ways of life are familiar to her.

People call them religious police, but they're not police

In the past, everyone was a *muttawah*. If you saw someone doing something wrong, in any area of life, you were meant to confront them, to guide them in the right direction. Everybody has this responsibility; this is Islam.

The *hai'a*[35] here, it's just how they've made it official. People call them the religious police, but they're not police. The police carry guns; they follow official legal procedures. The *hai'a* are only here to advise, to set you back on the right path; that's the role of a true *muttawah*.

The problem is that some of the *hai'a* are not properly qualified; they don't act professionally. They're supposed to behave respectfully, but some of them come to work with an attitude; they start shouting orders or intimidating people. How can the public respect people who don't practice what they preach?

They've started to remove them, to cut their numbers and their responsibilities. But I hope they retrain the ones who are left. Better to have an educated *hai'a* than get rid of them entirely.

The word *muttawah* is still applied to anyone who is very devout, who keeps themselves and those around them close to God. My family tease me that I'm a *muttawah*, because of my studies, because of the way I cover! But I don't think I would say that about myself.

They think we're all running off to *Daesh*

I'm sure some people don't even know Saudi Arabia exists, or think it's just a desert with wandering Bedouins and camels! I know there are a lot of negative ideas about us: that our women

---

35 Colloquial name for representatives of the Committee for the Promotion of Virtue and Prevention of Vice, externally referred to as the religious police.

are treated badly; that people only care about money; that we marry off our daughters; that the guys are really chasing girls and alcohol.

Either that, or they think that we are all Islamic extremists, running off to *Daesh*.[36] If they knew anyone who really followed Islam well, they would know that Islam is peace.

Some people have joined ISIS just for the money. Maybe they're drug addicts; maybe they just want to kill. Sometimes it's a renowned preacher who's getting paid, so he tells men to go to Europe and, I don't know . . . blow themselves up. And they're young; they look up to him.

So in Europe all you see is that people here are bad or cruel. I hope at least when you come here, you see you are treated as friends, as family.

As for the West, I see good things and bad things. I love the way women get out and achieve things; they're more motivated. I respect the way they raise their own kids, too – not leaving them with the maid like they do here. True Islam wants these things for women too.

But there are negatives. The fact that a woman is forced to work, often for less pay than a man, and what she does earn has to go to support her family. I believe that goes entirely against a woman's rights.

Now I can see the whole world

My grandmother would say, 'A woman's place is in the home!' Whatever other projects and interests she may have, her first priority should be to take care of the housework, the visitors, the children, the garden, the cooking; her responsibility in life is towards her husband and her children. I still think that was a very good philosophy.

---

36 Also known as ISIL, Islamic State or ISIS.

When she was young, she would be expected to do chores and help her mother from the age of six. Now a child of that age still expects her mother to feed her. I think it was better that children were given responsibilities, that they grew into that. I feel women now are just interested in eating, sleeping and fashion. They don't spend enough time with their families, and when they do, they're on their phones.

I can't blame them for wanting to be connected, though. Now we have the internet, the whole world is like a small village. If I didn't watch the news for a week, I'd feel I'd landed on another planet. So many things would have happened. I might be shut in my room, but I feel I can see the whole world. It's incredible.

WHAT WOULD HAPPEN IF WOMEN RULED THE WORLD?

It's not the role we were made for; you'd turn the world upside-down.

If there was a female president and they woke her up in the middle of the night to tell her there'd been a revolution or a coup, the first thing she'd want to do is put her make-up on. It wouldn't work. A woman is more emotional. Where a man follows his mind, a woman follows her feelings.

God blessed us with different kinds of strength. The man is able to take on hard work and make difficult decisions; a woman is able to bear and raise children. Maybe a woman could not cope with being president, but no man could cope with sleepless nights and a crying baby.

We are equal, but equality doesn't mean being the same.

WHAT WOULD YOU DO IF YOU
WERE A MAN FOR A DAY?

I would take off my veil and my abaya *and I would drive!*
And then I'd be fearless; I'd go wherever I wanted. I'd go
to all the museums in the city, just like I did as a child,
but I'd do them all in one day and I wouldn't have to wait
for anyone.

THE DESIGNER

RANA

Fashion designer, aged thirty-one, Riyadh

Recently graduated from l'Art Pur Fashion Institute in Riyadh, Rana has turned down requests to design contemporary Western fashion in order to concentrate on her first love — the abaya. *She lives in the capital with her husband and their two young children.*

Why should men design what I wear every day?

For me, design is a passion. I started nine or ten years ago, just creating *abayas* for friends and family, but in good-quality fabrics with good finishes.

At that time there weren't many Saudi or regional designers around. All our *abayas* and traditional clothes were designed by Indian or Yemeni men; men who didn't know our culture, who didn't know what's comfortable for a woman to wear.

I thought, *This is crazy!* Under my *abaya* I wear clothes from designers all over the world. Why should these men design what I wear every day? That's why I started. I wanted to show everyone that a Saudi designer could produce something beautiful, something wearable. I wanted Saudi women to start designing for Saudi women.

Now all the international designers have started making *abayas*. Everyone's seen the Dolce & Gabbana collection! But still, they don't know our market. Honestly, when I see their designs, I see the same *abaya*s that the Yemeni and Indians were making for us. I think you have to come from inside to do it well.

It's more challenging to create modest fashion – even in haute couture, even for international designers. It's very easy to make people look at you if you're revealing a lot; it doesn't matter if what you're wearing is well-designed or not. But to create something decent, and at the same time very fashionable – these are the classic pieces. You can wear them anywhere and you always get compliments.

We don't get bored of the *abaya*

I have never covered my face and don't design *abaya*s with *niqab*.

As far as I'm concerned, the religious obligation is to dress modestly and to cover your hair; this is *hijab*. But the *niqab* – even the *abaya*, this in itself is not a religious garment; this is our culture. This is tradition. It's not something I wear when I travel abroad.

Another misconception is that it has to be black. Again, this is tradition, not a religious requirement. When I first started designing, you could only buy black, so I went wild; my first two collections were very colourful. I had to be careful about where I exhibited at that time; not everyone appreciated my flamboyance.

Hijab is all about your own personal principles; how much you cover depends on you. Your faith is more about the inside than the outside. You might see one woman who's completely covered and assume she's very religious, and another who is revealing more, but in fact the second could be more pious.

But the *abaya* in itself is quite a beautiful garment. We don't get bored of it; you always feel you are well dressed.

We have more space to be creative

I'm really glad I'm a woman. Women in Saudi are so strong; everyone depends on you in so many ways – at work, at home, with the kids. We are really seen as the pillar of the household.

I feel that women are more creative than men; I see it all the time in my work as a designer. I think in Saudi in particular, we have the great advantage of being . . . looked after. This leaves you with a lot more time and energy to follow your passions, without the pressure of having to provide. It gives you so much freedom to be creative, to explore new angles, to concentrate on design.

In this respect I think that men carry a far heavier burden here. In our culture and religion, it's always his responsibility to pay the bills. It doesn't matter if I have my own job, if I'm earning a great salary; I am under no obligation to support the household.

After you're married, a lot of things change

I was introduced to my husband by his sister; we had a formal meeting and several phone calls, and then, we agreed to marry.

So what happens is, you get married, but it's just the paperwork. You stay in your house, he stays in his. But once it's been formalised like this, you can go out together and get to know each other as much as you want before the wedding. Then you have your big day, you go on honeymoon, and then you come back home together.

My arrangement was pretty traditional, but these days social media and travel have changed everything. People are meeting online, or they're studying together abroad; they join a summer course or whatever, they meet as friends and get married later.

I have no regrets about the way I did things, though. Sometimes people in the West, they meet naturally, they fall in love, and they still end up getting divorced. I've also known couples who have met traditionally and stayed together, and they're so happy.

The fact is, after you're married, once you're in the same house and take on all the responsibilities, a lot of things will change. It's all about getting to know each other in the period before getting married.

Polygamy, though – that's a tradition I don't support, not any more. In the *Qur'an*, Allah said, 'Yes, you can take a second, a third, a fourth wife, but only if you could be completely fair to all of them,' and, of course, you can't. Even with your children, it's hard to treat them exactly the same. How could you be completely equal with your wives?

It happened in the time of the Prophet because there were a lot of wars; a lot of women were widowed. It was always for a reason, not just for pleasure.

Nowadays, I can only say I approve of it in certain circumstances. If the first wife can't have children, or if they have many children but have serious issues as a couple, it's better for him to get another wife than to divorce her, than to abandon her. I think even in the West, people could appreciate this.

It depends on your relationship with your guardian

Male guardianship goes beyond culture; this is a requirement of our religion. Your *mahram* should accompany you when you travel and he should be there to support you.

You only run into problems if this is abused, and this really depends on the relationship you have with your husband or father. If a woman is having difficulties with her husband, he may refuse her permission to travel; he can use this to manipulate her.

It can be extremely difficult for a woman if her husband dies while her children are still young. It's very confusing for her to have to go to her little boy to legalise papers or get permission for something. This, I really don't agree with.

In other countries, having a driver is associated with royalty

People look at us and see that we haven't been able to drive, and they think, that's it, we have no life. I think women should be allowed to drive, for sure; we should have the option, but it's not on my checklist to go and get a licence.

To me, having a driver is a luxury. In other countries it's something associated with royalty; here, most ladies have this privilege. We don't have to worry about parking; we don't have to get into the car when it's hot. Just yesterday I had an accident; I was able to call another driver and go home, while my driver had to wait around in the sun and the heat for over two hours.

That's the thing: I wouldn't want to be in that kind of situation myself. I think that's why it's taken so long to change the law. Our community, they're afraid for women. If you were alone, for example, and your car broke down, anything could happen; you could be assaulted. The idea has always been to protect us.

For me, I find the roads scary enough as it is. It's very luxurious to have a driver; why would I want to change?

It must be tiring to be a woman in the West

Whenever I see Saudi women represented abroad, they seem to show images of poor ladies, sitting on the floor, completely covered; or they put her in the desert with a camel! They think we're miserable, that we have no rights, that we are a nation of housewives, trapped at home, cooking.

I would like people outside to know that we are very happy! That we're nothing like the images you've been presented with. I'm a mother, a friend, a sister, a daughter, a designer; I go about my daily life like any other woman. I go to work, I come back, mostly the maids will take care of lunch, the nannies look after the kids. I don't feel restricted.

I really believe that women are stronger here than anywhere. We are very much depended on and we are very much supported.

I think it must be tiring to be a woman in the West. It seems that career is the most important thing; you have to make it on your own, you have to prove yourself. I can't even imagine my husband telling me – 'I'll stay home and you go out to provide for me and the home.' I wouldn't feel feminine.

I think, as a woman, it's very nice to always be taken care of.

We are rediscovering our roots

The Kingdom is changing so fast. For me, even in the past five years, we've seen far greater change than the ten years before. My mother's life was far simpler; she could sew clothes for herself, she could do domestic crafts, as a hobby. But to study, to make it as a professional designer, that simply wasn't an option.

In the future, I would like to see us becoming stronger in our own identity. Right now, all the restaurants, the fast food, even the workers, it's all imported. I think about how, when I go to Italy, for example, the restaurant owner, the food, the hotel staff, the babysitter – they're all Italian. It's a very authentic feeling.

I want that for Saudi. It's starting to happen, when you see small coffee shops opening, traditionally themed restaurants. We are rediscovering our food, our roots. I think these young Saudi businesses are so important.

THE JOURNALIST

MUNIRAH

Newspaper journalist, aged thirty-four, Riyadh

Munirah is a journalist at a newspaper in Riyadh. One of the first women in her family to work outside the home, she overcame huge familial resistance to establish herself in her profession. She works with young people and runs internships for other aspiring female journalists. Presently single, she resides in the capital with her parents.

I decided I wouldn't give up

I had a lot of issues with my family. The first time they saw my name in print, my brother went to our father's office, took a gun and held it to my head. If my mother hadn't intervened, I think he might have killed me there and then.

And it was all because of my name. Because once it was out there, in black and white, people would know that I was his sister, that I was a journalist, and that therefore I worked in a news office, probably with men.

This is the thing they object to. Nowadays women work, often we are expected to work, but as teachers, as professors, only in places that are not mixed. One of my friends wanted to study to be a nurse, but her family took her file from the college because they didn't want to risk her working with men in the future.

When I felt that gun against my head, I was so shocked, I couldn't even cry. I just couldn't believe my brother was capable of this. But at the same time, it was an important moment for me, because in those few seconds I decided I wouldn't give up, that I would challenge everyone to prove myself. It was awful, but it made me stronger. After surviving that, there was not much anyone could say to dissuade me.

And *alhamduLillah* things have changed since then. I've worked hard, I have proven myself, and my family has kind of grown with me. My brother took a scholarship in the US; he saw a bit more of the world and started to understand that there are different ways of living.

When I was asked to give an interview on TV, my father was so proud, he called all of his friends and told them to turn it on. He was saying, 'That's my daughter on TV!' Even my brother says he's proud of me now!

I wanted to explain the issues that women face

I got into journalism because I wanted a space to express myself; I wanted to explain the issues that I – and other women – face. I thought if I could show people what we experience, and what we need, I could make things easier for others.

As for the freedom we have, it really depends on what kind of newspaper you work for. If you write for a government-owned paper, you can't write just anything. But in private newspapers like mine you have wider parameters. I don't feel restricted in my work.

And I don't feel that I am any less valued than my male colleagues. We work in different offices so there's no need to cover, but we report on the same kinds of stories, and we deal with each other respectfully.

Of course I would like things to keep developing and opening up here, but I don't have any interest in trying to challenge the system itself, not directly. My goal is to educate the next generation. That's why I always have interns; I'm always working with kids, with young people, teaching them how to express themselves as journalists. They will be the ones to make the big changes here.

For girls it's different; you have to fight

It's not better to be a man or a woman. I'm very happy to be a woman. But it is harder to be a girl. When you're a boy, everything comes easily to you; there's no challenge. For girls it's different; you have to fight. But, you know, I don't see this as a negative. I want to face this challenge; I want to feel the value of the things that I make. Nothing is given to you here; it's all earned.

The things is, women have fewer opportunities, so if you give a woman a chance, she'll seize it! And what she produces will be better than anything a man can make. The things I'm doing right now, I don't believe anybody could create but me.

I can't think of a job that a woman shouldn't do. Now we have doctors, engineers, artists, female policewomen in prisons. Perhaps we're not ready for female soldiers yet; I don't think a war zone is a suitable environment for any woman to be in, even less so if she is a mother.

Your partner should make your world bigger, not smaller

I'm still single. I just don't think I've met 'the one' yet. I was almost engaged once but it didn't work out between our families . . .

If it happens, though, I want to get married to someone I know, not someone my family chooses. I want a man who is independent, confident in himself, dreams big, and has high respect for women! Your partner should be someone who helps you grow; someone who makes your world bigger, not smaller.

I'm also not sure I could accept being a second wife. If you choose a man who is already married to another woman, he always goes back to the first wife in the end. If I'm the first wife, I suppose I don't mind so much about the others. I believe he'd come back for me.

Men have taken this part of the scripture for their own interests

Two years ago I got this amazing opportunity to travel to America for my work. (You know how excited I am to travel!) But my family refused, so I had to turn it down. This is where we feel the guardianship. Legally you just need one signature, so as a single woman I would ask my father, but in practice your brothers also have to agree. Mine didn't want me to go. Thank goodness they have their own kids to worry about now – they are too busy to care whether I travel or not!

You know, the guardianship, it exists in Islam, but it's only for very specific things. Here they've made it into a general requirement for women. It was never meant to be this way. Men have taken this part of the scripture and used it for their own interests.

If a woman knows how to take care of herself, how to behave, there is really no need for her to have a guardian at all.

'Cover your face!'

In the beginning, you cover because your family wants you to. You reach a certain age and your brother, your mother, your father, they all start with this, 'Cover your face, cover your face!' So it's true, in the beginning I didn't want to wear the *niqab*; it was an obligation. But now I wear it out of choice. To me it's just part of the culture; it's not a problem.

Sometimes I'll uncover my face at work with the men, if that's more comfortable. Also for travel, if I went to Europe, for example, I would take it off. I know that it's not usual for women to cover there, and I don't like to stand out. I'd prefer to respect the local culture.

Driving isn't the biggest issue

I would like to drive. I've never tried, but I'm going to learn as soon as I can. Can you imagine how much easier it would be? Just taking yourself to work or to the supermarket, without having to wait for a stranger to take you?

At the same time though, while needing a driver is an inconvenience, it's not the biggest problem women in this country face. I know it's an easy target for foreign media, but sometimes I think they are more upset about it than we are!

Saudi women have great strength

When you're actually here, in the country, you can see that women live very well. But I know that outside they say the opposite. I would like to change this view, and especially the idea that we are weak. Saudi women have great strength.

From what I see of the rest of the world, I think Western women are very independent. I respect that a lot, that they depend on themselves. I know they dress differently to us, they drink and so on, but that is their own business. We should allow people to live as they wish. The most important thing is to keep an open mentality, to accept other people and our differences.

My mother lived in a different world

I don't even know how to describe the change that's happening here. My mother lived in an entirely different world. Just since the millennium, I feel my life has changed completely. I'm able to support myself as a professional, as a journalist.

I hope to keep working with young people. I want the kids I mentor to keep growing more confident and more creative as they get older. I want them to know they can make a difference.

We have such a young population here; the more invested they are in their country and how we develop, the better it will be for everyone.

Personally, my dream is just to travel! The whole world! Look, I have my plan right here: I'll go through Algeria, Ankara, Rome, Switzerland, London, Canada, then back to Riyadh.

I've never left Saudi Arabia. In the past my family – most families – would never accept it, for a girl to travel alone. But the world is changing, and my family is changing too. I'm older now; they see I can handle myself. In a way, they have grown up a lot too!

And if I am lucky enough to have daughters, I hope they'll be just like the interns I have at work here: so confident and open-minded. When I see them I have so much hope for the future, for all of us.

THE RUNAWAY

AYA

Student, aged twenty-four, Jeddah

Aya is a medical student in her final year of studies. Three years ago she undertook a scholarship programme in Canada. The move required her to seek drastic measures to leave the country without her father's permission. She has since returned to the Kingdom to resume her studies at a different university, where she has launched a new student association.

If you don't have a guardian, find a husband

It's not how I dreamed I would get married. It was a small wedding here in Riyadh. I didn't tell any of my friends; only my close family knew what was happening, and my mother did not give her blessing.

But I didn't marry for love; I married for my education. In my second year of university I won an amazing scholarship in Canada, but as a girl, I needed permission from my guardian to accept it, and my father isn't around.

It's stupid. You know, a lot of Saudi boys just take a scholarship just to get out, to drink, to have sex; they're not studying. If a girl applies it's because she really wants to work, but they make it so much harder for us.

But you know what they say: if you don't have a *mahram*, you'd better find a husband. And that's what I did.

I found him online. There are websites for this, for marriage, for women who don't have a guardian. He was twice my age, but he lived in Canada, he had money and he told me he wanted to help me with my studies.

With time he won me over in other ways too; by the time I married him I thought it might even be a love match. But once we got to Canada, he wasn't the same. He was very controlling; he knew my father wasn't in the picture and I didn't really have anywhere else to turn.

He used to use prostitutes, mostly men. I think he married me to hide that he was gay. He wanted me to give him children. Thankfully I didn't get pregnant. We didn't live together for most of the marriage.

After a year, I decided to get away; even then, divorce was a struggle. It was hard for him to explain why he was divorcing a young woman. He needed an excuse; he needed me to be bad or crazy or both, so once I got back here, he started putting in calls to the *muttawah*, accusing me of anything to get me arrested.

It was a very hard time, but I don't regret what I did. That marriage made me a lot stronger; I figured out who I was. And if I hadn't left Saudi, I would never have had my eyes opened to the world.

We're taught to know, not to learn

I go to university here now, but it feels like high school. Every day it's exams, exams, exams: multiple choice, fill in the gaps. We're taught to know, not to learn.

When I was studying in Canada, I had to do research, I had to give the professor my opinions and back them up. I wrote essays, I made reports. Now I just read what's in the book and write it down. Since I came back, I've failed every semester; I just can't do it under this system.

When I get home late from my internship, the neighbours

are more interested in what I might be up to, out of the house at night, rather than the grades I'm getting.

We need better education. We need people to start thinking for themselves. People have become so lazy, they're happy to have everything done for them. Have you ever seen a Saudi doctor in a good position? Why are we bringing people from outside and paying them more instead of improving our own system?

Women especially need better education. If a woman's not educated, how will her children turn out? What kind of environment will her home be? If she doesn't know how to challenge them or make them think, how will she raise all these professionals we say we need?

If you want to change a country, if you want to build it fast, you have to educate the women. If you are keeping her as if she is nothing, then trust me, nothing will happen.

Women could do so much

Women here, we're just used – for cooking, for cleaning, for bed. Women are for babies, that's it. They've lowered us to nothing, really nothing.

And we could do so much. Men only have one responsibility – go out to work and bring home the money. A woman you'll see pregnant, going to work and studying all at the same time. Then she goes home, acts like it's nothing, cooks dinner and looks after her husband, too. Tell me which one is more powerful? And yet we don't even acknowledge the woman as an adult.

Without a guardian, you're nothing

Without a *mahram*, you're nothing. You're absolutely nothing.

My father walked out on us when I was three years old; he hasn't done anything to help my mother since. Where does he get the right to decide if I can travel or not?

A woman doesn't need a guardian. I don't believe God gave a woman that much power just to have her sit at home and follow orders. Women are sensitive; if you show her love, she'll follow anyway, without any need to control her. That's the way it's supposed to be.

The problem is we've been 'protected' like this for so long, now we're dependent on them. We haven't grown up like other women: exposed to men, to different situations – learning what's appropriate and what's not.

Women here don't have that knowledge. I knew a Saudi girl in Canada who became a kind of call girl. She thought she'd found freedom. If women here are suddenly left without anyone to guide them, I'm afraid they won't know where to draw the line.

She'll believe the first man who tells her he loves her

It usually starts with a phone number. That's how girls and boys start talking. Then he'll tell her how he's fallen in love with her, how it's okay for her to come and meet him, because he's her man, he loves her and he'd never hurt her. Then after he's had sex with her, suddenly she's 'garbage' and he doesn't love her any more.

She doesn't have the knowledge or the experience with men to defend herself – she'll believe the first man who tells her he loves her. The man has nothing to lose, but the girl loses her virginity. And then who can she go to for help? Her family could kill her for this.

So some girls stick to other girls. It makes sense. They're young, they're full of energy and hormones and they have nothing to do. They only have the mall, if they're allowed to go out at all.

Arranged marriage is meant to be safer than dating and all that, but so often, there's no real feeling there. They just don't know each other. He tells her to do her 'duty', to clean the house and have babies; she's just there for his money. It's like a job. Then, at the weekend, she goes to her family, he goes to his friends.

I think you need to know someone really well before you marry them. There is someone I'm talking to. We met once at a party, and since then we've spoken every day. He's always there to support me. He's married already, but I can see his first wife doesn't really care.

Sometimes I don't understand him; his messages are so confusing. But I think he's trying to train me in some way, to shape me to be a better person. Recently he disappeared completely, but it's because he wants me to stand on my own two feet. That's a real love, no?

We wear *hijab* to blend in

My belief is that the purpose of *hijab* is to protect you. So yes, I wear *hijab* and *niqab* here because I don't want to be followed home. It's not comfortable to walk around with everyone staring at you like you're naked.

But when I'm travelling, no, why would I? We wear *hijab* to blend in; if I wore *hijab* in Canada I would actually *attract* attention, so there's no point in wearing it. One of my aunts went on a trip to Japan; she made the whole trip in *niqab* and an over-the-head *abaya*. Imagine, she's the only one in the mall all dressed up like this. It doesn't make any sense; you're not thinking any more about why you're wearing it.

I think you just need to use a little logic about what's modest for the place you're in. You wouldn't go to church wearing a crop-top and shorts – it's the same thing. Just respect where you are.

Using a driver isn't safe

Many times I've been in the car with a driver, and they've been looking at me in the rear-view mirror and playing with themselves. It isn't safe, but I need to go out, or how will I work? How will I study? So I pay 3,000 *riyals* a month to be driven around by strange men. Where is the Islam in this? How is a woman not allowed to drive, but you're forcing her to be with a man she doesn't even know in the car?[37]

But suddenly having women drive is going to cause a lot of problems too. If you're just walking alone on the street here, think about how many men watch you, how many men follow you. Now imagine you're behind the wheel of a car. It's not safe.

We take your bad habits and call it modernity

People here get tattoos, they pierce their noses and dye their hair stupid colours, they drink every night of the week and then they say, 'I'm Westernised now, I'm open-minded.' They take your bad habits as fashion and call it modernity.

They don't know that if most teenagers in the West got a tattoo, their mums would kill them, or that you call people with rainbow hair and too many piercings punks or hippies. You should see the way the girls here turn up to university; it looks like a music video.

Sometimes I think people in the West follow Islam better than we do. The Prophet Mohammed told us to be polite with people, to smile, to look after the environment, to work hard and take responsibility for our actions. You are not Muslims, but you understand better what Islam wants. It's sad, but we in Arab countries often don't follow our own teachings.

So people outside have a horrible impression of Islam. And

---

37   The driving ban was officially lifted in June 2018.

I don't blame them. How can they know that Mohammed was kind and gentle with all of his wives, that Islam teaches us how to live and how to love, when all they see is us? Islam is more than just covering your hair and praying five times a day.

The government can't move faster than society

We have fancy malls with all the brands, nice cars; we have better Wi-Fi than I had in Canada. But in a lot of ways I think we need to go back to basics; we need to build our society first.

People think it's the government that's oppressing us, that they're holding us back, but the government can't move faster than the society – it's the same as anywhere. They can't pass new laws if the people don't want them.

King Abdullah[38] wanted to give women the right to drive, but there was too much opposition. The government gave women the right to vote, but they didn't use it; they gave more legal rights to women, but they don't have the courage to use them yet.

If the government didn't care about us, there wouldn't be 10,000 Saudi students studying abroad on state scholarships right now.

And I think that's how they're trying to change things, because this new generation is coming back with an education, with an open mind; they're ready for the changes, they will accept new laws and new ways of doing things.

---

38 King of Saudi Arabia 2005–2015.

A WOMEN APART

ألا لا يخلون رجل بامرأة إلا كان ثالثهما الشيطان

'When a man and woman are alone,
Satan is the third among them'

—Hadith

'We are raised with the story that Adam was made from the earth, and Eve was made from his rib,' explains teacher Mariam. 'So we are only a part of a whole, easily bent, and from the left side, under the heart.'

In Saudi Arabia, men and women are respected as quite different beings, each divinely imbued with their own strengths and weaknesses and corresponding responsibilities to society. In their differences, they are divided: into the world of women and the world of men. Each one orbits the other, but the two rarely coincide.

Walking through any public space in Saudi Arabia, it is hard to escape the notion that one has inadvertently stumbled into a carefully orchestrated game of chess; with men robed in white, women in black and neither straying too far from their designated paths. It is far from the only nation to encourage segregation of the sexes, but it is unique in the extent to which the system has been institutionalised. From the doctor's waiting room to the queue at McDonald's, public life is distinguished by these monochromatic divisions.

The practice stems from the belief that the free mingling of the sexes prompts an inevitable decline into immorality. 'I read a study a couple of years ago that in foreign countries, there are far more affairs because of the mixed environment,' says nutritionist Ashwaq. 'In Saudi the rate is much lower, because we're not together.'

The result is a world divided into 'singles', meaning men, and 'families', comprising women, children and sometimes their husbands. In restaurants, the custom manifests in separate signposted entrances and eating areas. In many, the 'families' sections are divided into private, curtained-off booths, where women can remove their veils and enjoy their meals safe from the prying eyes of waiters and other women's husbands.

Banks, phone service providers and government offices regularly offer separate 'ladies' branches', usually identifiable by their blacked-out doors and windows, and staffed exclusively by women. Where services are not segregated, the fairer sex almost always takes priority.

> *'I feel like it's a privilege to be a woman. When*
> *you go to a bank or an ATM, they treat you*
> *differently — you never have to queue.'*
>
> —MAHA, municipal councillor

Even within the home, gender divisions are not entirely dissolved. While members of the nuclear family will of course mix freely, male and female guests will generally be welcomed through separate entrances to be entertained in corresponding parlours, decorated according to the respective tastes of the lady and gentleman of the household.

Children, of course, exempted by their innocence, can traverse this divide, and male and female cousins will play uninhibited until adolescence, when girls are firmly withdrawn from the fray, usually at the onset of menstruation.

Segregation in schools starts earlier, however, not only on moral grounds, but on the assumption that girls and boys have different needs. Accordingly, girls will only ever be taught by female teachers and boys will only receive instruction from men. The only exceptions occur at university level. If an appropriate female specialist cannot be sourced, female students will either observe the class from a shielded balcony, or the male professor will lead the group via a one-way video link.

~

Such rigid division might seem highly restrictive to outsiders, but it would not be true to say that segregation is simply a custom created by men and enforced on women. 'I like it better here, with just girls around. I'm comfortable,' says student Hanan on her university campus. 'In Kuwait or the Emirates, there are always boys and girls together, and they always wear *hijab*, so girls never even bother brushing their hair. It's not nice.'

In women-only spaces, femininity is celebrated: perfume and incense are liberally diffused; carefully groomed hairstyles are revealed; voices, muted in public, are raised in debate, songs and laughter; 'girly' is not a derogatory term.

Separate, they point out, doesn't always mean inferior. While in the Wahhabi-Salafi revival of the 1980s and '90s, the line of segregation pushed women firmly into the domestic sphere, nowadays it's hard to find a restaurant without a family dining section, and thanks to women's increased disposable income,

velvet-draped women-only coffee shops and candlelit spas now
vie for business in every city centre.

*'We want to uncover, we want to relax, just us
women. Islam gives us the right to that privacy.'*

—JAMILA, Islamic studies graduate

Nonetheless, social engineering on such a scale inevitably leaves
a mark, with critics claiming that men and women who have
grown up in total ignorance of one another don't always find it
easy to interact, and that women's naivety with the opposite sex
can also leave them vulnerable. 'Any girl who meets a guy, she
thinks he's in love with her,' says law student Wejdan, 'because
he says something nice and he's the only guy she's met.'

The impracticality of collusion between male and female
spheres can also lead to practical difficulties. Sometimes these
are merely inconvenient. 'I want to go to the police station
without being questioned at the door and being asked to wait
forty minutes while they see if the head of the police station
will allow women in,' says women's rights campaigner Hussah.

Occasionally, they are fatal. In 2002, fifteen girls died in a fire
at a Mecca school. Overcrowding played a role in the tragedy, but
there were also allegations that local *muttawah* had frustrated the
efforts of firefighters access the building. In 2014, a female student
at a Riyadh university died of a heart attack after male paramedics
were delayed entry to her campus. In both cases, rationale for the
obstructions appears to be rooted in the fact that the students and
teachers within might not be appropriately veiled.

~

'These small ones, they're just for dress up,' says designer
Lamia, stroking a rack of miniature embroidered *abaya*s. 'They

like to be like their mums.' Contrary to the claims of certain sensationalist publications, little Saudi girls spend their childhoods much as elsewhere – clothed in bright floral dresses and Disney princess costumes, wrestling with their brothers, and occasionally trying on their mother's veils, like a grown-up pair of high-heeled shoes. Only after puberty will it become a regular feature of their wardrobe.

The word *hijab* in Arabic simply means 'cover', and can be used in the context of a screen, partition, cloak or veil. Multiple connotations have translated into multiple interpretations, resulting in the many different ways *hijab* is worn worldwide. In Saudi Arabia, historically women's clothing varied from region to region, and while always modest, it often incorporated bright colours and embroidery.

Since the conservative reform of the early 1980s, however, *hijab* in the country has become synonymous with a particular set of garments originating in the central Najd region: a black, loose-fitting cloak worn over the clothes known as an *abaya*, a light headscarf or *tarha*, and a fine face veil or *niqab* revealing only the eyes. The *abaya* is mandatory for all women, including female foreign workers, but the religious police will often berate Saudi women who appear in public with their heads and faces uncovered, too.

But whatever its form, it is agreed that the purpose of *hijab* is to protect. 'There are always good and bad men,' says academic Rahaf, 'and, you know, men appreciate beauty; that's how they're designed. Some of them abuse this; they'll follow you – these stupid things they do.'

> *'When you deal with a guy and you're covered, he will look*
> *at your inner beauty; he will be dealing with your brains,*
> *not your body – he will never look at you as an object.'*

—NADEEN, university lecturer

Women's hair is viewed as a particular source of temptation. 'Here it is considered something sexual,' explains Rahaf. 'If you have your hair out, you're much more beautiful than without it; you look totally different.' By concealing it, a man is forced to focus on the matter at hand.

The form this fabric barrier takes, however, is not so uniform as it first appears. In coastal regions and more cosmopolitan families, *hijab* may comprise simply a *tarha* and button-up *abaya*. For more conservative women, and especially in central areas, over-the-head *abaya*s with *niqab* are favoured, and for the most pious, may be accompanied by black socks, gloves and a veil that covers even the eyes.

Seasons and contexts also affect *abaya* choices; light, breathable summer fabrics are replaced by draping wools and velvets in the cooler winter months. And while young women may favour discretion and simplicity in crowded areas such as malls and *souq*s, students will often make the short trip from the car to the university gates flaunting *abaya*s with gem-studded shoulder pads, gothic spikes and trailing tassels.

> *'You thought they were all the same? Ohhh,*
> *that explains it; we were wondering why you*
> *all came over in grandma* abaya*s!'*
>
> —HUDA, international employment
> agency HR manager

Saudi Arabia's rising generation of fashion bloggers and home-grown designers are keen to reclaim the garment – not as a symbol of oppression, but of cultural pride. 'I would really love to see the silhouette of the *abaya* internationally recognised,' says renowned fashion blogger Marriam Mossalli, 'in the same way one would immediately recognise a kimono, kaftan or poncho regardless of context. I think it has that potential to become an international garment, styled in a non-traditional manner.'

The movement has not been missed by high-end brands with an eye on Saudi Arabia's luxury market. In 2016, Dolce & Gabbana launched its first line of *abaya*s and *tarha*s, setting label-hungry Gulf women back $3,000 per twinset. Carolina Herrera followed suit with its own collection in 2017.

Despite the international fanfare, Saudi fashion royalty remained nonplussed. 'Stefano Gabbana actually blocked me on Instagram,' sighs another well-known style blogger. 'What he had initially produced was so dated . . . It had nothing to do with what Saudi women actually wear or how we wear it. Look: the cut, the cheap lace – it's just horrible.' For now, there appears to be more excitement around home-grown designers.

At present, the high street *niqab* market is dominated by one particular domestic Islamic fashion brand. Walking through the mall, you find yourself surrounded by women with the familiar text logo embroidered just above the right brow: *Bedoon Essm*, meaning 'Without Name'.

~

In Saudi Arabia, a woman's name consists of her given name, her father's name and her family and tribal names. Women of 'high' *Qabili* tribes will proudly recite not just their father's names, but their grandfather's and great-grandfather's up to six or seven generations past. Her family name and tribe are her birthright and will not be supplanted by her husband's when she marries. However, they will remain largely silent treasures.

Women are rarely addressed aloud in public, and almost never directly by non-related men. A woman's name is as private to her as her physical appearance, and broadcasting it openly may be considered disrespectful or even provocative.

It is not uncommon for wedding invitations to welcome

guests to celebrate the marriage of a man and his bride, without his new wife's name actually being mentioned. In everyday conversation, men tend to refer to their female relatives as simply 'my wife' or 'the family'. The result is that colleagues, close friends, and in some cases even brothers, not only never meet each other's wives, they may never even learn their names.

'We kind of had a rota going in our office,' says Faisal, who works in a ministry in Riyadh, 'for when we were going to the supermarket at the mall' – the idea being to avoid the awkward eventuality of bumping into a co-worker and being forced to introduce, or ignore, each other's spouses. 'There are some tribes, further south, that will actually refer to their wives using the neutral pronoun, like "It's cooking dinner."' He adds, 'It's awful, but it's true.'

Of course, regional and generational differences play a part in how strictly this code of discretion is adhered to. 'Now, if a man is less than thirty years old, it's different,' says teacher Mariam, 'but for my brothers and my father, the name of a woman is still a secret.'

> *'I wouldn't like to say the names of my sisters out*
> *loud, not at school. Maybe I would when we lived in*
> *Jeddah, but not here. They might think bad things*
> *about them. They would think bad things about me.'*
>
> —MOHAMMED, fifteen, Riyadh

The arrival of the internet has played an important part in weakening the old taboo. Now, a woman who chooses to can spread her own name; activists and public figures openly share opinions under personal accounts. Family and societal pressures are still present, however. 'The focus in media and social media is still on male artists,' says artist Lama, 'because maybe women, they don't want to be famous; they don't want people to talk about them and their work.'

In Saudi society, privacy is held as a fundamental right – a value demonstrated by the high walls that surround most homes. But perhaps it is this very penchant for secrecy that makes hearsay all the more irresistible. In a culture where reputation is so decisive, anonymity can be seen as the simplest protection against rumour and gossip – especially for women, who in kinship societies tend to serve as the primary vessels of family honour.

~

The concept of a *mahram* exists in all Muslim societies. The term refers to any male who by kinship a woman is not permitted to marry, and in front of whom she is not obliged to wear *hijab*. 'With your sons, brothers, father, husband, your sons-in-law, your nephews – they're all fine; you can uncover,' says housewife Fatmah. 'Other men; that's *haram*.' From these close relatives she is guaranteed financial provision as well as protection when travelling.

In Saudi Arabia, the word *mahram* is used almost interchangeably with the word *wali*, meaning guardian. It has come to be accepted as an equally valid religious requirement that a woman should have a legal guardian, although there is far less evidence for its existence in Islamic scripture.

'All the schools of religious study agree: the *wilayah* is a guardianship for minors and the mentally ill and so on – people who cannot make decisions,' confides a member of Shura Council. 'But it has been taken by tradition beyond the religion because of the cultural representation of women.'

The result is there is no age of majority for female citizens; all women live as wards of a male relative. At first this will be her father; later she will be passed to her husband; then potentially to a brother or even son. As a result, adult women are still unable to travel abroad, renew their own passports, choose a husband or leave prison without the consent of their *wali*.

But that doesn't mean that all women view male guardianship as a constraint. To some, it represents privilege. 'Women in Saudi Arabia live like princesses,' says teacher Hoda. 'They are served in the beginning by their fathers and brothers, then by their husbands. You don't need to work; my husband brings me everything I need.'

This sentiment is not limited to women who have never known more independent lifestyles. 'I feel safe here because I know that, in my country, I'm going to be taken care of, no matter what,' says university lecturer Nadeen, who was educated in the UK. 'I know I have a safety net to fall back on. If I don't have my father, I have my brothers, I have my uncles – somebody in the family, a man, is going to take care of me. Financially, they are responsible; they have to provide for me.'

But the line between care and control can be a fine one, and when so much authority is concentrated in male hands in a deeply paternalistic society, frequent misuse of guardianship becomes a near inevitability.

> *'A woman's guardian is somebody who's going to take care of her, for life. It's something I see as very positive. The problem is some people abuse this right.'*
>
> —SARA, university lecturer

Although, perhaps those at the greatest disadvantage are those without any guardian at all. 'I'll give you an example of a friend of mine who just got divorced and was removed from her husband's guardianship,' says one high-flying female professional.

'Suddenly she's floating around in society because she's not stamped to anybody; she had to go to her son, who will be her guardian now. We're talking about a woman in her fifties.'

For those, like Manal (see p. 159), who have no surviving male relatives, there has been some relief. Since 2013, such women have been able to apply for their own identity cards and can now appeal directly to courts and government offices for travel documents and other services.

In the country's current climate of reform, there has been a general move towards a dismantling of guardianship as a legal construct; a woman no longer requires male consent in order to accept employment, receive medical care, start a company or open a bank account.

Regulations might be changing, but culture will take time to follow suit. In a country where women's citizenship was often only recorded in the dependents section of her husband's 'family card' identity document, along with his children, until individual IDs became the norm in 2001, the concept of guardianship runs deeper than the bureaucratic need for signatures and permission slips.

In more conservative households, it is understood that a woman will inform her guardian, not only when she travels abroad, but every time she leaves the home. And while legally a woman only requires one *wali*, the reality is that other male relatives will often chip in to support or veto a woman's decisions. 'Your brother has the right to tell you if you're free to go out or not,' says journalist Fatemah, 'not in the legal way, but as your family. You're not free to do what you want if your brother doesn't accept it.'

Similarly, while no longer legally bound to do so, many hospitals, schools, employers and landlords still honour the wishes of the guardian over those of their female patients, students, workers and tenants. 'The law, we have already. We have it by

CEDAW[39] – the international agreement,' says doctor Afnan, 'but it's the implementation; anyone who does not apply it, they need to be held accountable.'

~

The dissolution of the formal regulations that legitimise such practices must be considered an important step towards women's autonomy, however. It's a move that is being mirrored in changes to restrictions on freedom of movement, participation in business, and the way women choose to dress.

In early 2018, Crown Prince Mohammed Bin Salman unexpectedly announced that, 'The decision is entirely left for women to decide what type of decent and respectful attire she chooses to wear.' If true to his word, it may mean an end to the days of women being followed and verbally harassed on the streets by members of the religious police over a coloured *abaya* or an exposed lock of hair.

It is likely, though, that most will keep their *abayas* buttoned for a while longer, whether due to family pressures, respect for a tradition they have witnessed through their grandmothers, mothers and sisters, or simply their own conviction of faith. 'There are lots of girls, young girls, who don't cover any more,' says nurse Alyah, 'but they don't think about the future, about eternity, about what they would earn in Paradise. *Insha'Allah*,[40] God will guide them.'

There are also questions of comfort and habit. When one women's university in the capital took the decision to ban the wearing of *abayas* on campus to reduce the risk of male interlopers, many young women were discovered to be wearing their pyjamas underneath.

---

39 UN Convention on the Elimination of all Forms of Discrimination Against Women, ratified by Saudi Arabia in 2001.
40 'God willing'.

It's true that the traditional garment is frequently voluntarily abandoned when travelling abroad, but that doesn't necessarily indicate a sense of envy for a more Westernised mode of dress. 'Maybe we like their outfit, it's nice, but I don't think we really want that,' says art agent Nada. 'Like, I'd wear it to my friend's house, but I wouldn't wear it on the street. For me, I like to be appropriate; I like to wear appropriate clothes.'

> 'In the media, in movies, we see Western women as people who maybe don't care about themselves very much – always exposed. But I've been to London and I've seen people are actually very decent. Look at Queen Elizabeth. She doesn't wear hijab, but she's very careful with her clothes. That's self-respect!'
>
> —HUDA, teacher

In terms of the physical separation of men and women in the public sphere, there has been less challenge to the status quo, especially outside of the major cities. Nonetheless, it should be acknowledged that Saudi Arabia's ability to maintain such elaborate systems of segregation and gendered facilities stems not only from religious conviction, but also from their economic capacity to do so.

The complete isolation and often economic inactivity of one half of society was only made viable by the excesses of the nation's oil boom. As the nation starts to tighten its purse strings, the luxury of maintaining its women in harem-like seclusion may not remain so high a priority.

THE TEACHER

IMAM

High-school teacher, aged thirty-five, Dammam

Imam is a high-school science teacher, mother, housewife, unofficial community agony aunt and firm patriot. Born in the Eastern Province, she moved to its capital five years ago after marrying her second husband. She has one young daughter.

My first marriage only lasted a year. The day we married, my family gave me around £3,000 as a gift. My husband stole it on our wedding night, and, well, it only got worse from there.

He refused to divorce me so I went to the court. I told the judge, 'He doesn't pray, he doesn't fast, he lies, he steals.' The judge looked in my husband's eyes, and he could see I was telling the truth, so he agreed to *khula*.[41]

Anyway, it was eight years before I decided to try again. I didn't meet either of my husbands before I married them, but the second time I did my research!

For me, I don't need to meet the man, but I want to know everything. Not only about the man, but also about the family. How do you say it? The apple doesn't fall far from the tree.

Because, you know, a man will lie to you. At the beginning

41 Divorce instigated by a woman whereby she returns her dower in return for separation.

he's all springtime and roses, and women are sentimental; we believe it all. This is nothing to do with being Muslim or non-Muslim – this is the nature of women. And often, after marriage, well, things aren't the same.

But if you know his family, if you do your research, if you know how his father treats his mother, you can get a good idea of how this man will be as a husband.

Romantic love? I don't see the benefit. I know that's how it is in the movies and the love songs, but when people marry for love, is it always successful? Of course not. Better to ask about him.

I don't want to be the same as a man

Life is completed by opposites, not equals; everything needs black and white. Men and women are like this. I don't want to be the same as a man. I see how European women do everything for themselves. The man can just take what he wants; in the end the woman is only there for enjoyment. I prefer to divide things, half and half.

A man, for example, can't control the home. Men are the same everywhere in the world, I'm telling you – they love themselves. They're not capable of giving like we can. Women give to their families non-stop, from dawn till dusk. You know, the *Qur'an* doesn't give women any instructions on looking after children; it's already written in their hearts.

And, really, it's the most important role. In our culture, a mother must always be cared for. If your father ends up living alone, fine, but not your mother. You should live with her, look after her, give her some kind of allowance to live on.

You know, one of the Prophet Mohammed's followers once asked him who you should most love and obey in life. The Prophet replied, 'Your mother.' The man asked, 'Then who?' He answered, 'Your mother.' The man asked, 'Then who?' The

Prophet answered again, 'Your mother.' Only on the fourth time did he answer, 'Your father'!

So, no, I don't agree that a woman can take any job. Working part-time, being a teacher, this is fine; it's good to keep a little independence. You never know what the future holds. But a woman is the heart of the home; she is the warmth, she is the rest. If she's away too long, it hurts her children; it hurts her husband.

I wouldn't want one guardian; I'd want four

A man should look after a woman. Here, as a woman, you have to live with a man and the man protects you. If I hear a noise in the night, my husband doesn't let me get out of bed. If I have a big decision to make, he helps me.

When I see how women live in other countries, I always think how hard it must be, doing everything on your own. I wouldn't want to live without a man. If I was living in a rougher area, I wouldn't want just one; I'd want four!

In the past, yes, it was difficult for some women with the legal restrictions. But things are getting a lot, lot better, *alham-uLillah*. Now a woman can go to court, the banks have opened women's branches, she can manage her own affairs more.

Girls and boys need different kinds of attention

I don't like mixing girls and boys in the same classroom; they're different. Boys want to be in a competitive environment; they like being communal. But a girl, no – she wants the teacher to take care of her only; they need different kinds of attention.

Then, from the age of twelve, they just think about sex. Boys start to see girls in a different way, and they learn quickly, you know! They learn how to play with girls' emotions, and then the girls – they're tired, they're upset, they can't focus on their studies. And the poor teacher is trying to teach while all of this is going on. So, no, it's better not to mix.

But what they study is just the same: the same subjects, the same textbooks, the same hours. Of course there are a couple of differences: the girls have some cooking, some sewing, they don't do sports.

There's nothing in the *Qur'an* to say a woman shouldn't do sports by the way; it's more to do with the clothing. A woman shouldn't wear anything too short, too tight. That's why we don't have a history of women's sports; it's just not in our culture.

Happiness doesn't come from wearing or not wearing an *abaya*

When Allah made the man and the woman – Adam and Eve – he made the man attracted to the woman, not the woman attracted to the man, so the man wants the woman; wherever the woman goes, with her breasts, with her hips, you find the man following behind! So Allah protects her with *hijab*.

And for me, it's a lot better. Look at me in my leggings. If I went out like this now, all the men would be clawing at me, right? And when a man first looks at you, he doesn't really like you; he just likes your body. If you agree to give it to him, he's very happy; if you don't, you can be sure he won't cry about it – he'll just look elsewhere.

Men will tell you you're beautiful, just to get what they want. And we women are all the same, whether we're eleven or fifty: we like to hear it. Even if I know I'm ugly, even if I'm ugly with no teeth and one eye (or no eyes!), if he tells me, 'You're beautiful,' I'll believe him.

So *hijab* protects me from all this. I don't want any man seeing my backside; then he'd be interested, he'd try to flatter me, and, really, where's the benefit for me?

The *niqab*, I only wear in Riyadh; if I'm outside I don't bother. If you're in a country where everyone's uncovered, it's fine to show your face. But if you're in a place where all the women cover, then you should wear the veil. Because even if you're ugly as sin, you're the only one the men will see . . .

I know some people say Saudi women aren't happy because they're veiled. Some Saudi women themselves, they watch Hollywood movies and believe that in these places women are really happy. Of course they're not. Why would they be happy? They have the same problems as everybody else.

Girls think if they take off the *abaya* they'll be happy too. But happiness doesn't come from wearing or not wearing an *abaya*! It comes from the conditions you set for yourself; it comes from your heart and your mind.

I don't think it's safe for women to drive

You know, driving is not a dream for me.

I just don't think it's safe for women to drive. I mean, I know they do; the women in Bahrain and Kuwait all drive. But a woman can't protect herself; if her car breaks down, if she blows a tyre, she's stuck.

It's better for men to drive, especially at night. It's hard driving in the dark, and going to the petrol station – I swear, those places are dark and creepy everywhere in the world. A man here wouldn't let you go on your own; he'd lock you in the car while he fills the tank and brings you whatever you want from the shop.

I'm happy to have a man drive. I call my driver, I take a taxi, I order an Uber; I go wherever I need to go. But then, it's true, I can afford it. If I couldn't, then yes, I would have been one of those women pushing for the law to change too.

They imagine we're closed and miserable

I know people think we're no good. I know because when someone sits down next to me on a plane or anywhere outside, I can see they're uncomfortable. They think we're criminals, that we're oppressed and uneducated.

When someone talks to me abroad, they can never believe I'm Saudi; they imagine we're all closed and miserable. Then of course they ask me if I have oil in my house; as if I could run it from a tap in the bathroom! I don't blame them, okay? They're foreign; they can only go by what they see on the television and what they hear on the news.

And it goes both ways. When they watch movies, 99 per cent of Saudi women feel that women in other countries are happier. But when they actually go and see how people live, they find out that, no, they're not happier.

My family told me that when they went to America, they didn't see any women on the streets after 6 p.m. People are afraid of guns! Here, I come home from parties at one or two o'clock in the morning and I'm not afraid of anything. It's safer.

When we travel, I see the way people drink, the way men want to grab at you on the street and I thank God we don't have any of that here. I'm not naïve; I know some people drink behind closed doors, but that's not my business, as long as it doesn't affect anyone else.

I don't know how I would control my children if I lived in the West. The heart loves freedom, even when it's not good for you, and I think my children would love freedom more than they would love what their mother had to say to them! I don't want freedom. What would I do with it?

Thanks be to God, here I have everything I need. There's nothing I can't do – nothing that matters anyway.

Our lives seem to change every six months

Life was so much less complicated before. It was safer, too. When I was a child no one locked their doors; we knew everyone around us.

Of course there have been a lot of good changes since then. Now we have schools, we have electricity, we travel. When my mother was young, your husband was your be all and end all. Now that's not the case.

I can't imagine how life will be for my daughter. Something new happens to change our lives, it seems, every six months; it's happening faster than I could make it up. So, for her, I have no idea – maybe she'll live on the moon!

WHAT WOULD HAPPEN IF WOMEN RULED THE WORLD?

In every country where a woman becomes president, the country starts to fail. Even when a woman is a manager, she's not really happy – and neither are the women who work for her. Women are emotional; men, by nature, are more level-headed. Living through your emotions is no bad thing by the way; life needs emotions too. But for the big responsibilities, where you need to be clear-minded, I prefer to have a man in charge.

THE GENTLEMAN

WAAD

Photographer, aged twenty-six, Jeddah

*Registered female at birth, Waad is biologically intersex and has iden-
tified as male since puberty. In strictly gender-segregated Saudi society,
he continues to inhabit the female sphere in which he was raised. He
currently works as a professional photographer and resides in Jeddah.*

It's just not accepted here, the way I am

I don't think I've ever worn a skirt; I grew up with my dad so
it was easier to avoid the dresses, the girly stuff. I was always
a tomboy, a bit different. But then when I was about thirteen,
things started . . . changing. My voice got deeper, I had all this
hair on my face. They did a blood test, and yeah, it came back
male. It was scary, but it was also kind of a relief.

I was seventeen when I tried to get the surgery. You know,
this is okay in Islam, because it's not really a change, it's just a
correction. But a *muttawah* found out. He told everyone I was
a girl and started harassing my mother, my family. We tried
another hospital but it got out again; somebody wrote about me
in the news. So the hospital cancelled everything: my hormone
treatment, the surgery, everything. I had to accept that I would
need to find my own path here. Nobody would help me.

I know some people would say that it's sinful – that I wear
men's clothes, that I date girls – and that I should be locked up.

My family did too in the beginning; they didn't want to accept my diagnosis. Now, I just don't talk about it any more. They think I've forgotten, that I'm happy being a tomboy. I have to keep a lot of secrets!

It's just not accepted here, the way I am. The *imams*, they don't understand and they worry for us, the ones who are different. They want to take care of us; honestly, I can understand this. And the older generation, they think they have all the answers, that they know all there is to know. But we are a very young country; we are learning a lot.

But you know, I try to look on the bright side. There is a reason for everything in this life. God creates us, and as for the way I am, he writes everything for us while we are still in our mums' tummies. Everything he writes, happens. We can't stop it. So I have to live my own way.

I'm a lot more comfortable dressed as a man

Usually I'll wear an *abaya* on the street; my ID still says female so it's safer that way. And of course if I'm out with girlfriends I have to; I don't want to make any problems for them. I never cover my face though. I feel claustrophobic enough here as it is; I don't think I could breathe in a *niqab*.

But, sure, I'm a lot more comfortable dressed as a man. Sometimes I'll go out in jeans. So far no one has said anything. Even the religious police, they've seen me and not noticed a thing.

I do think women should cover though. It's safer for them. You know how the boys are here: they're not used to seeing girls. Even if they see a girl in a bin bag, they're gonna go after her!

And it's not just because it's the law here; it's written in the *Qur'an* that they should wear the *abaya*, they should wear *hijab*. There are many different types of Muslims, I know, and different interpretations. But in the real religion, the right religion, according to the *Qur'an*, the *abaya* should be worn.

For me, though, when I go out without one on, I'm not breaking the rules. This is just the way I am.

I'm the only guy at all-girls' parties

The big advantage to my situation is that I get to meet girls! My friends always joke that I'm the luckiest man in Saudi Arabia: I'm the only guy at all the girls' parties.

And so, yeah, I've had a looot of girlfriends. I've had relationships with younger girls, with married women. Once there was even a pregnancy scare. Sometimes it's a headache, *w'Allah*!

But it's not like that for most guys here. You know, the religious police, if they catch a guy and a girl together, they force them to marry. If they refuse, they send them to jail. Anywhere, even if you're sharing a coffee in Starbucks! They go crazy on Valentine's Day.

So you get a lot of girls dating girls. You walk into any girls' university and it's so obvious. They're all holding hands, kissing in the bathrooms. In the past they used to punish them, but now it's too much; they can't handle it. So they just ignore it.

It's worse in the male universities actually. You know, when you see the boys there, you'll be shocked. You would never see your son again if he was here, trust me on this! It's really bad. There's rape even, and the guy can't tell anyone about it; he just has to go back to them, day after day.

But all this is because boys and girls can't meet each other, you know. They're not thinking; they just follow their emotions. Personally, I think homosexuality is wrong. It's forbidden in the *Qur'an*; there's a divine punishment for this. I read some study, that 89 per cent of gay people in America don't even want to change their sex. They just want to stay as they are and be gay. I don't really get that.

If two men or two women fall in love, I think they should try to stop it. I mean, in the end, it's up to them; they can do what they want. But I can't say that I like it.

If girls suddenly got all their freedom now, it would be such a mess

It's so much easier to be a boy here! Girls aren't really allowed out, but boys can go wherever they want; no asking for permission, no guardian. I know it's a hassle for travel, but sometimes I think it's better that the girls still have to have a guardian.

Girls have a lot more to handle with the religion, too. They have to wear an *abaya* when they go out; they have to surrender to their families in a lot of ways. It's difficult for them to be free like us.

You know, when they get out on their own, even the boys, they go wild – it's hilarious. They just want to do everything, experience everything in the world. They don't care if it's right or wrong, they just want to do it. They'll drink, they'll do drugs, anything. So sometimes, honestly I prefer that we have *mahram*s, so things don't get completely out of control.

Of course they should have their freedom, but it's really difficult because it's not something they've had from the beginning. If they suddenly got everything now, it would be such a mess! They would want to try everything, good or bad. It's like when you have a bird that you've never let out of its cage; once you open it and it has its freedom, it can never go inside the cage again.

They think if women drive, Saudi will become like the West

It's not true that we think driving will damage a woman's ovaries! We saw the video of that *imam* speaking, it was hilarious.[42] Even here in Saudi Arabia it was a big joke; no one knew what on earth he was talking about. Come on! You see all the women outside of Saudi Arabia; the Kuwaitis, they have like ten children each, and they drive. It doesn't make any sense.

They just don't want women to drive here because they think Saudi will become more open, more Western. They're afraid.

You know, I've done it though. Sometimes I'll take off the *abaya*, put on a *thobe*[43] and *shemagh*[44] and drive around the city. So far nobody has stopped me. I once broke my collarbone coming off the back of a motorbike on the beach here. I have no regrets though; I want to try everything!

In my self-portraits, I am a man

Photography is really my passion. I'm never going to stop doing it. It makes me free. I can work with men and women in the same space, I can play with my own image; in my self-portraits, you can see I am a man, the same as any other.

I have lots of friends who are artists. It's amazing the talent we have here now. The portraits they draw, it feels like you can just reach out and touch them.

People say it's forbidden in Islam to draw human figures or faces, or even to take photographs. I don't really understand this. If it's *haram*, why do the religious police take photos of you?

---

42 Video clip that went viral in both East and West, featuring a prominent Saudi sheikh who claimed driving was dangerous to a woman's ovaries and led to children being born with 'clinical problems'.
43 Men's traditional long white tunic.
44 Men's traditional red and white checkered headdress.

I don't know, I am not God to judge this. In the end, people can believe what they want. I'll keep on working.

It's not as tough as people think

People think Saudi is such a tough country; we're so restricted, women have to wear *abaya*s, they can't travel, they can't do what they want. But really, it's not that dramatic. I know a lot of girls who are really happy with the way things are. Sometimes at the mall I tell them, 'Come on, take off your *niqab*, it's okay; your brother's not here, your husband's not here,' but they say, 'This is our religion and we have to do it.' They accept it themselves.

Of course we see Hollywood films and American TV and the girls like it. They say they'd like to live that way if it wasn't *haram*, of course they would. But because it's forbidden, they choose not to. They follow their faith first.

We can't judge the West though; everyone has their own way of life. There are so many religions, we can't tell them to put on an *abaya* or take it off. It would be very wrong of us.

In the future, I want to live outside

Oh, my God, life has changed so much. My mother and grandmother didn't go anywhere. They just sat at home, cooked, washed dishes, cleaned clothes. But now women work, they go out, they hold meetings, they have projects, they open restaurants, malls; they vote, they're on the Shura Council. It's a whole new story now.

But for me, in the future I want to live outside; I'm already saving for my escape! I'm thinking about Canada; my friends said maybe they would accept me there as a refugee. I can't live my way here, not openly, so it will be easier for me there. I still want the surgery, but after they rejected me, I don't want to risk it here again.

I hope one day I'll get married, to a nice girl. Not a Saudi;

they're too narrow-minded. I'd like to have an apartment, family, kids. And I'll find a job, even if I'm just a waiter. I like to work; I'll take whatever God gives me.

There is nothing impossible under the sun; I'll keep doing whatever I want for as long as I am breathing.

THE REBEL

MAYSA

Primary school teacher, aged twenty-eight, Dammam

Maysa is the daughter of a Saudi father and an American mother. A child bride turned wild child, she refuses to conform to the expectations society has of her, as her short skirts, exposed hair and illegal tattoos testify. She now works as a teacher in Dammam, where she lives along with her husband, her two children and her girlfriend.

I wished I was a boy

I often wished I was a boy. Especially in my father's house, because I have five little sisters. I wished I was a boy, not just for my sake, but because then I could protect them. I could be their *mahram*; they wouldn't need husbands, they wouldn't need to marry like I did. I could be their 'yes' and their 'no'.

We're raised to believe a woman needs a man to look after her. And I guess it's true; I like to have a man I can depend on. Maybe it's just so conditioned into me, but when I see how, in the US, for example, a man can be a house husband, I don't think I could respect a man like that. My God, if I was going to work every day and he was looking after the kids, what do I have breasts for? I wouldn't feel comfortable; I wouldn't feel like a woman.

Suddenly, we were expected to be Saudi girls

I was eleven and a half when my mother left; our parents divorced and she moved back to the US. So my sister and I actually had to raise the younger ones, and we did everything: we potty-trained them, we took them to kindergarten, we talked to them every day in English so they wouldn't lose their language.

It was a trauma – and at the same time, our world started to close in. Suddenly we were expected to be Saudi girls; we lost all our mother's American friends, we weren't allowed to go out, we weren't allowed to speak to people. We weren't allowed to visit friends unless my father knew their mothers; of course, he knew that it was impossible in our society for him to meet their mothers. I was moved from my international school to a local school. The girls weren't exactly welcoming. It was a very lonely time.

And then this guy kept coming to the house. My father's family marries very early, and this man was asking about me. My dad told him, 'No, she's too young!' But he kept coming. He hadn't even seen me. In the end it was me who said yes. In some way I was just looking for a way out; once you're married, you usually have a little more independence than when you're under your father's roof.

I was fourteen when we married. Little did I know I was marrying a man even more closed-minded than my father! I got pregnant in the first four months, and again a year and a half later. This wasn't what we'd planned. This was based on his decision, because when you're married, he can tell you, 'I don't want you to take birth control.'

So I had two kids before I was really grown myself. And I would just do what they did. When it was bedtime, I slept with them; when they woke up, I got up; when they went to school, I went to school.

I was desperate to keep up with my studies. He came from a wealthy family, so he could have helped, he could have hired a nanny, but he didn't. He just said to me, 'You're a mommy now. That's your job now.'

At the same time, he could be very lavish. When it was my birthday, he would reserve the whole restaurant. But in the end it was all about control; nobody was allowed to see me. I wasn't even allowed to speak to the waiters; I would just point at the menu in my gloves.

It was the same at home. I wasn't allowed friends over; he deleted their numbers from my phone. I couldn't paint my nails, no mascara, no coloured bags. And then there was the violence.

I lived in his house for ten years. When we finally divorced, I made a promise to myself: if I got married again, I would get to know the man first.

I got my tattoos, I uncovered my hair

I hardly recognise myself from that first life. I was a very 'yes' kind of person back then, very quiet – can you imagine? When I started meeting people again, I made girlfriends and they built me up, they made me strong. I got my tattoos, I uncovered my hair and dyed it pink! I started to figure out who I was.

My second husband is older than me: he's fifty-eight. So I accept him as a companion, but it's not like I miss him when he's not there. And . . . I'm not the first wife; I'm number two. But that kind of makes things easier, because in Saudi, if you're the first wife, you have a lot more responsibility.

His first wife, she's like a *muttawah*, *masha'Allah*,[45] and I respect that. As he says, she's the mother of his children and he wants his children to have that kind of conservative upbringing.

But with me he has this – I don't want to call it a double life;

---

45 'God has willed it', used here in context of praise.

his first family knows about me – but it's different. We have a lot of fun. He's mellow, easy-going, we travel non-stop together, we drink. He's very Americanised; he doesn't care if I wear a bikini when we're abroad.

You see, you can live very well here if you know how to play the system. If you're a smart lady, if you know how to dress and present yourself, you're gonna get any man out there. And once there's a man you want, you know how to cook a good *khapsa*,[46] you can live exactly the way you want.

If I veil or not, this is between me and God

Oh, my God, I'm in trouble with the religious police all the time. My *abaya*'s always open and I don't cover my hair. I've had a lot of looks: purple hair, rainbow colours, all the piercings.

Whenever the *hai'a* see you at the mall it's, 'Cover, cover, cover!', and when you don't they get really aggressive. I just talk English to them; I never let them know I'm Saudi. If I did, they would take me down to the station and call my husband.

My father still gets upset with me. He'll beg, 'You're a mother of two, you're a wife of two! Control yourself!' But I won't cover for them, not when they speak to me like that.

I don't believe that veiling myself has anything to do with faith. I don't think I have to cover myself in order to prove something to my creator. Ultimately, how I dress, if I cover or not – this is between me and God.

My daughter is twelve now, so she's starting to feel these pressures. If she decides to wear a *niqab* because that's what makes her feel closer to God, I would accept it. But if she wanted to wear it just to please other people, then no, I would not be supportive. Not one bit.

---

46 Traditional dish of chicken and rice.

Driving is going to be tough at first

I don't want to drive. I'm going to be honest, I'm too comfortable. The streets are a headache here, and the way people drive – they scare me!

I think it's going to be tough at first. I get followed a lot by guys as it is. How's it gonna be when they're chasing me and I'm trying to drive? People here really need to get used to the idea of women not covering their faces, of women being okay to drive. Maybe in two or three years, when everyone is chill with the idea, maybe then I would learn to drive.

You have this man who gets to decide where you can go and where you can't

It makes me angry. I already have two children who are almost as tall as me – what do I need a guardian for? But you have to; you have this man who's in charge of all your paperwork, who gets to decide where you can and can't go. And I'm not just talking about leaving the country – even in the household. That's how it is.

I still fight with my dad about it. Once, when I was divorced, I decided to take a trip across the border to Bahrain, but I didn't get permission. I got stopped at the border and they called him. He was so mad at me, but I said, 'Dad, you have a choice: you can tell these nice gentlemen I have permission to travel, or you can drive 500 kilometres across the country to collect me from the police station.'

I find it heartbreaking. We should have a little bit of faith in our girls, especially the father, the guardian, who should have faith in who he's raised, as a daughter.

He chose me based on the way I walked

My first husband wanted me because his mother saw me dancing at a wedding. She thought I was pretty. A guy gets to choose his wife based on what his mother sees – and then he gets to spend three minutes with you to make a decision for life.

And so that's what happened. I came into the room and he chose me based on the way I walked, the way I served his coffee. If it was three minutes, but you walk in and say, 'Hi, how are you? I'm Maysa!' – that I understand, but just walking in with a tray?

It was a huge wedding; I don't know how I coped with it. I was scared, very scared; I remember shaking. But, actually, I was more afraid of my second marriage than my first. Perhaps because the first time I was a child; I didn't really know what I was getting into.

I agreed to be the second wife on the condition that there were no secrets. I've never met his first wife – our houses are far, far apart – but I was sure to obtain her permission and to let her know that I would never do anything to threaten her household.

And something I've realised in the last couple of years is that even after she's married, a woman often takes a girlfriend. I never felt anything for girls until I was divorced. But then I met someone, and we got really close – abnormally close.

I thought, *I've seen this on TV, I've read about it, I know this kind of relationship exists.* It was hard for me because I wasn't used to being affectionate with girls. I mean, I wasn't even allowed to have female friends for ten years with my first husband. But it's more than a physical thing.

I mean, my husband takes care of me, and we have a lot of fun together. But my girlfriend's the one who provides the emotional support. I can really talk to her. You have a bad day at work, you come home and talk to your husband and he says, 'You're lucky I let you go out to work!'

But with her we're just totally in sync; you're there for one another, and it's completely reciprocal. So my husband would never let me pay for dinner; but with her, I'll buy lunch, she'll cook dinner, we talk – it's perfect. It's wrong I know, but it's a feeling you don't have otherwise.

I like breaking people's expectations

When I see the things the Western media says about us – that we're terrorists, we're Bedouins – it makes me so angry! And then I go to parties here and they start insulting Americans back, and I'm just furious! I'm a halfie; I'm an American and a full-blooded Saudi. It's very upsetting for me how wrong both sides get it.

I have to admit, though, I like it when I get to break people's expectations. I'll post things on my Facebook or Snapchat: parties with the girls, hanging out with boys. People are so shocked. They say, 'Oh, my god, your hair is green! You're wearing shorts! You're smoking in the house!' I don't know, they think the religious police are crouching in the garden, ready to jump through the windows and arrest you at any moment.

I don't want us to lose our soul

The change is so fast. I mean, just look at the difference between my 'first life' and my 'second life'. It's amazing what's happening, but at the same time, I don't want *everything* to change. We shouldn't become Dubai. I don't want us to lose our soul.

But my daughter's gonna have more freedom, I'm sure of that. She's been raised in her father's household; but still, I see that she's shining. I'm so glad, and I hope maybe it's because I'm still in her life. If I had picked up and left for the US, I don't think she would be the person she is today.

THE FIRST WIFE

JAMILA

Housewife, aged fifty-seven, Taif

Jamila comes from a village near the cool mountain city of Taif. She is the first wife in a polygamous household and a mother of nine. An illiterate child bride from a Bedouin settlement, her standard of living has changed enormously since she reached the city, but many traditions have stayed the same.

I never guessed he would be my husband

I was twelve years old when I married my husband. I wasn't scared; I didn't know what there was to be scared of. I was only a child.

His father and mine were brothers. As children, boys and girls play together, so of course I had met him. I never guessed he would be my husband though!

But then, when I was twelve, *Baba*[47] died, and then there wasn't much choice. My parents had divorced when I was small and my mother had moved away. My five sisters and I were effectively orphans. So my family arranged for us all to marry cousins, to be sure we'd be looked after; I wasn't the youngest.

But getting married doesn't mean you become a wife in every way, not when it happens at that age. I had my first child when I

---

47 Colloquial term for father.

was eighteen. I have four girls and five boys, and now they are all grown and starting to have families of their own, *alhamduLillah*.

Women don't marry as young as they used to. My oldest daughter married when she was twenty-one. It's better that way; at twenty-one you know what you're doing, you're better prepared. Being a wife and a mother in your teens isn't easy. It's very tiring; it's a lot for a young girl to take on.

He takes it in turns to visit us

Look, nobody *wants* their husband to marry another woman. It's not something you dream of when you get married, and no, it wasn't easy to hear when mine came to me and told me he would be taking a second wife. We can laugh about it now – she's part of the family – but she reminds me I was quite furious and not at all welcoming when she first arrived.

It wasn't easy when he decided to marry a third either, but I accepted it. I accepted it because God has told us clearly: a woman may only take one husband, but a man may take four wives.

Really, I think I have been quite lucky. My husband chose wives from our family, so these weren't strange women coming into my home. They were my cousins; I had known these girls all their lives. The second joined our family when she was around twenty, the third when she was sixteen.

You know, often it happens that a husband doesn't tell his wife that he's taken another wife at all. It's *haram* to do it that way; it goes against our religion, but it happens all the time. And then, when she eventually learns the truth, of course it causes a lot of pain. I am grateful I was spared that.

But we three, well, we all know about each other very well; we live in the same building! Our husband owns the block, all four floors. The ground floor is for guests, and then each of us has our own floor with our own apartment.

Each year we take turns to redecorate a room. You can see my living room is full of colours and flowers, but the second wife's is covered, covered, covered in pictures of London, Tokyo, New York. She is always dreaming of travel.

It's better this way, that we all have our own space and then our husband takes turns to visit us. We're all equal; there's no hierarchy here; no first wife, second wife, third wife. We have a good husband, *w'Allah*; he knows how to treat us fairly.

It's not like this in every house. In some homes all the wives are piled in together, and a lot of families fight – you can imagine!

But in the end, we do end up spending a lot of time together. We visit each other's homes for coffee, to talk, and the kids run in and out of all of our apartments all day. They play, they fight; they're all brothers and sisters. In the end, we are all one family.

People say it's not so common now, houses like ours, but I can't say I've noticed any difference. Maybe we have more divorces now. But you still see plenty of men with two wives, three wives, four. A man only stops at one if he doesn't have the money to support any more!

But my husband always says he couldn't handle a fourth. And eighteen children is enough for any man, I think. So, that's it, our family is now complete.

As guardian, he has to provide for us all

My husband is my guardian. He's also guardian to the two other wives, all the children, and the grown-up daughters who aren't married yet. He has to provide for and protect all of us; it's a big responsibility. I don't envy it.

It's important to us, that a woman has a guardian. Without him how would she look after her children? What would happen to her if she had to travel everywhere alone? We would worry for her; it wouldn't be safe.

Overall, we have it a little easier than the men

Men and women, we're not the same – you can see we're not the same. So it makes sense that we don't do the same things.

It's the man's job to go out to work and bring home the money, to travel long distances, to take you to the hospital or anywhere you need to go, and to bring the things we need here at home. A husband has to provide.

A woman's role is to take care of her home and to be a mother. We have to go through pregnancy; we have to raise children; we have to cook and clean for the whole house – it's a lot of work for us too. But I think, overall, we have it a little easier than the men. We get to be more relaxed at home most of the time.

Of course we have the odd 'house husband' too. Not often, but sometimes if a man is out of work, his wife will take a job to pay the bills. I think that's okay; we all have to help each other. But in general, it's better if the man is the one supporting his home. People will respect him more like that.

In any case, a man is always the head of the household; it's up to him to make all the big decisions. But then it's up to his wife to keep him to them. That's one advantage of living in a house with three wives: we can all work together to hold him to his word!

After my children finished their homework, they would help me with mine

I've never been to school; I've never sat in a classroom or read a book. I grew up in a little village. We were a Bedouin family really. We learned our prayers, we memorised *Qur'an*, thanks be to God, but we didn't do maths or learn to read. I spent my childhood running after goats and helping Mama in the house.

I learnt to read when I was forty years old. I looked at my

clever children around me, all nine of them reading and studying, and I wanted to understand what they understood. There was a ladies' course at a mosque in the city, so I started going every morning. And there we were, a room full of housewives and grandmothers wrestling with numbers and our ABCs.

Then, in the evenings, after my children finished their homework, they would help me with mine. It was my oldest son and my daughter who taught me how to read. I could finally do it; I could see what they saw; I could read the *Qur'an* properly. I never really got the hang of the writing though. I started too late.

But now, look at my daughters, *masha'Allah* – they've done everything; three of them even went to university. I'm so happy that they've learned something more than I did, that they were able to do what was impossible for me.

I would feel naked without it

I wear *abaya*, I wear *hijab*, and of course I wear *niqab* – you have to here. You wouldn't see any good woman in Taif with her face on display.

But I don't just wear it because I have to. I want to wear the veil; it's my choice. It's an agreement we make with God. It's not uncomfortable for us; it's something we wear every day, like shoes. And to be honest, I think I would feel naked without it.

I don't see any need for a woman to drive

Sometimes we'll go on a family picnic or a barbecue out in the desert. That's when the women drive. I never learned, but the other wives and the older girls, they all know, *masha'Allah*. They go racing around and the men have to wait.

Here in the city, it's not allowed. But really, I don't see any need for a woman to drive. We have drivers, we have taxis. If women started driving too, where would all the cars go? We would have huge traffic jams. Plus women would start leaving the house more; if that happens, they might start meeting men, and that leaves the door open to all sorts of trouble.

I hope people see that women are well looked after here

I really don't know what other people think about my country. I hope they see it's a good place, where people follow their religion and take good care of their families. I hope they see that we women are well looked after. You know a girl can walk on the street here and it's no problem; nobody harasses her. I've heard it's not like that in every country.

But really, I don't know how things are in other places. I've never been outside, I don't know those people, so how could I judge?

Maybe one day when all the children and the grandchildren are a bit bigger, we'll go somewhere. *Insha'Allah* our husband will take us abroad. His second wife will never forgive him if he doesn't!

What else is there to want?

Saudi Arabia is getting better and better all the time: better hospitals, better streets, better buildings. And now we have phones, we have internet; I couldn't have imagined these things as a young woman. Maybe we'll have other new inventions too. Now we have Vision 2030; God willing, the future will be even nicer.

But for myself, I don't have any great ambitions. There's nothing more I really want. I love my life as it is: my home, my family, my children. Thanks be to God, I have a good life here. What else is there to want?

I hope my daughters will have good lives too, that they will marry well and use all of their wonderful studies. And I hope that their husbands marry only the once. I wish that for them. It's an easier life.

AFFAIRS OF THE HEART

أنا عنكِ ما أخبرتهم

لكنهم لمحوكِ

تغتسلينَ في أحداقي

أنا عنكِ ما كلمتهم

لكنهم قرؤوك في حبري وفي أوراقي

للحبِّ رائحةٌ

I hadn't told them about you,
But they saw you bathing in my eyes,
I hadn't told them about you,
But they saw you in my written words.
The perfume of love cannot be concealed.

—Poem, Nizar Qabanni

'Oh, my gosh – at the red lights; that's the easiest,' laughs kindergarten teacher Reem, explaining how more adventurous men and women make contact in the country's capital. Strict traditions of segregation that prohibit social interaction between unrelated men and women have engendered a creative approach to courtship; phone numbers have long been shared via balls of paper launched through open car windows or recited in hushed whispers in supermarket aisles. Later, Bluetooth made the process more discreet, with couples connecting invisibly at malls, in supermarkets and at the traffic lights.

For although pre-marital relationships are forbidden by law, and the concepts of 'girlfriend' and 'boyfriend' are absent from Saudi culture, young love is a hardy perennial that has ways of blooming – even in the desert, where dating is a risky business. Couples who meet for a restaurant dinner know they chance being caught by, or reported to, the *hai'a* and having their romantic evening end in a family scandal or a jail cell.

The arrival of social media has facilitated the dating process enormously. Entire love stories now spark, flourish and fizzle out without the couple in question ever having met in the flesh. Most meet over Snapchat or Instagram, although apps like WhosHere and even Tinder also exist in the region.

> *'Before social media, you'd always run into the problem of cars chasing you. Now that's not happening because men and women are meeting each other online. You aren't harassed on the street nearly as much as you were in the past!'*
>
> —AMANI, filmmaker

Of course, some girls and boys do still find one another in person. 'One girl will have a boy who she knows and the others will ask her, "Did you go out with him? How was it? Did he try to hurt you?"' says Reem. 'Once they feel safe, the others will meet up with him too. That's how they make connections.'

Women have reason to tread carefully. At school, female students are well instructed in the predatory ways of men, and warned to steer clear until the ink is dry on the marriage contracts. These words of caution are reinforced in the playground by tales of former pupils who got into cars with 'boyfriends', only to have their mutilated corpses recovered from the desert. While some of these cases have been confirmed, others have sprawled into urban legend.

Horror stories aside, there is a very tangible fear of loss of reputation or, worse, virginity; while boys may entice them to it, women who date are rarely considered wife material. And if things move beyond her control at a secret rendezvous, she can expect little social or legal protection. 'She can tell her family, and they'd probably chase the guy down and give him a beating,' says engineer Rawan, 'but she has to be prepared that the same punishment they give to him is going to be coming for her as well.'

'A lot of men think of a woman like a candy. If anyone's touched it, if it's already been opened, it's no good for anyone else to eat. It's trash.'

—AASMA, shop assistant

In order to maintain respect for their faith, their families and their reputations, most avoid pre-marital encounters altogether. 'I believe if you're raised in a certain way, if you have conviction in your values, it's not difficult to avoid these things,' says nutritionist Ashwaq. 'I know it's not the right thing to do. For me, getting to know a man is something that happens when you're engaged and not before.'

For some young women, though, there are other ways to satisfy their need for affection and intimacy, while keeping men at a safe distance.

~

While Waad's case (see p. 113) is highly unusual, he is far from the only one to be wearing men's clothes under his *abaya*. The term *boyat*, formed by adding the Arabic feminine suffix '-a' or plural '-at' to the English word 'boy', is used to describe the small but visible minority of young women who take on the role of men in the closed world of Saudi women.

Boyat cut their hair short, they wear men's clothes and perfumes, and often, they date other women. In student canteens, you will find groups of girls, hair cropped and slicked back like 1950s teddy boys, their arms draped around more traditionally feminine girls, flaunting false eyelashes and glittering accessories.

These same-sex but gender-exaggerated couples behave much the same as any other beaus: they bring each other flowers, they go out to eat, they sometimes have physical relationships. Of course it's perfectly normal to find gay, transgender and non-gender-binary communities in any populace, but in Saudi Arabia, it appears that 'situational sexuality' is also at play.

It is a behaviour often witnessed in closed, single-sex populations, from traditional *harems* to prisons and boarding schools, where individuals who would usually identify as heterosexual form partnerships as a means to secure companionship, protection or social mobility. In a strictly all-female environment, with no outlet for romantic affections or raging hormones, it's not hard to see how the conditions for such liaisons might emerge.

These relationships, while often accompanied by intense emotions, are not always indicators of genuine sexual preference. 'I wasn't popular before,' Nora, aged twenty-seven, tells me. 'There was this really beautiful girl in the class, always surrounded by people; I wanted to be like her. I cut off my hair, and suddenly she wanted to be my 'girl'. I was part of the cool crowd. She wanted to do more, so I did. But I was never really interested in all that. Now I'm married; I have two children.'

For some girls, a *boya* may be viewed as a 'safe' boyfriend, providing the companionship and affection of a boyfriend, with none of the associated risk of ruined reputations or pregnancy; she may even be invited over for a movie or a sleepover without arousing too much suspicion.

From the *boya*'s own perspective, her behaviour can be seen as a form of defiance. Dr José Sánchez García, one of the only academics in the world to study the phenomena, explains: 'In a society where gender is so rigidly defined, they're looking for their own identity; they're acting out against the only role their culture is offering them – being a wife and a mother.'

He believes it also serves as a strategy for girls to secure the same privileges and freedoms as their brothers. Teacher Maysa agrees: 'Often she's the oldest girl, maybe she doesn't have brothers; she's had to be the "man" at home; she's had to hold it together. She doesn't want to go back to being a girl.'

> *'It's a double rebellion – think about it. On the one hand she's rejecting societal gender expectations; on the other she's defying the norms of her culture. She's not dressing like a Saudi male; she's dressing like a Western man.'*
>
> —DR JOSÉ SÁNCHEZ GARCÍA

But if the *boyat* are sheltered by the female sphere, it doesn't mean they are universally accepted there. 'I don't like to talk to them; I don't like to look at them,' says student Ghaida. 'I guess they want attention, but for me it's disgusting – and it's *haram*. If God made you a woman, why would you try to make yourself a boy?'

Indeed, it is perhaps unexpected, in a kingdom like Saudi Arabia, one of eight remaining countries in the world to enforce the death penalty for homosexuality, that such deviation from accepted gender norms is permitted to exist.

In other Gulf countries, including the United Arab Emirates, there is evidence that girls who transgress in such ways are being routinely institutionalised and forcibly 're-educated' in the womanly ways of dressing, cooking and sewing. As yet, Saudis have largely preferred to turn a blind eye.

Saudi codes of gender segregation and modesty in dress prove helpful in this approach. Not accustomed to seeing women uncovered beyond their immediate families, few men are even aware of the *boyat*'s existence in their communities. To the extent they are publicly acknowledged, they are labelled tomboys. It's a phase to be grown out of – with time, with marriage.

~

There is still no minimum legal age for Saudi women to marry, although it is now rare for judges to approve matches for girls under the age of sixteen. Families and women themselves increasingly value further education over young motherhood, and most now tie the knot for the first time in their early twenties.

Given the risks and pitfalls inherent in dating, family arrangements remain the most popular way of securing a spouse. While women in the West might balk at the thought of their parents picking their future husbands, and even joining them on their first date, to many young women it is viewed as a positive aspect of close family ties.

> '*I would want my mother involved, honestly. Your parents would want what's best for you and they're older; they have more experience; maybe they can see something you can't.*'
>
> —NADA, art agent

And, as they are quick to point out, a love match is no guarantee of a happily ever after. 'I mean, if that was the case, you wouldn't see people all over the world getting divorced, people who knew each other beforehand,' says one senior princess. 'Sometimes, arranged marriages work very well actually.'

It is still tradition that a man – or his family – seeks out a bride, and not the other way around. But few see this as an issue. 'Even for you in the UK, maybe the couple meet and get to know each other and everything,' says teacher Mariam, 'but the real, final decision is still with the man, isn't it? He's the one who asks the question.'

Who he asks the question to will be influenced not only by a woman's beauty, brains and reputation, but also, to some extent, by her name. There are many stories of women who have had to renounce a love match or even been forced to divorce, after establishing a home and family, due to perceived 'genealogical incompatibilities' between families.

The desire to maintain tribal lineage and traditions means that life partners are often sought close to home. Consequently, when women take their vows, more than half of them will do so with a man who shares a common ancestor; more than a third will be a first cousin. There is no taboo around such close marriages, and choosing a partner closer to home may be appealing for other reasons. 'When you think about it,' says blogger Nouf, 'it's probably the only man outside her immediate family she's ever got to know, at least as kids, so it's normal she'd feel safer with him.'

'It's the first thing you do, the first thing: "Hi, how are you? I'm Heba Al Qahtani, what's your family name? Are you from the tribe from such and such? No? Well, okay, alright, nice to meet you", and then let it go. Because you might

fall in love with him, and he might fall in love with you,
and it won't work out because Mama and Baba say no.'

—HEBA, HR assistant

If a pairing is deemed promising by both sides, a meeting
or *showfa* is arranged at which the potential bride-to-be may
appear, unveiled, and usually exchange pleasantries with her
suitor, chaperoned by her father. Islamically, both parties must
agree to the union – a condition that was reinforced by a ruling
from the country's Grand Mufti in 2005.

Once the big decision has been made, there are other details
to be agreed upon. Unlike Western brides, Saudi women have
a hand in writing their own wedding contracts. Much like a
prenuptial agreement, the contract allows each partner to make
certain stipulations for married life; for a modern woman, this
might entail ensuring the right to finish her education, keep her
own salary and to be purchased a suitable family home. It will
also contain the terms of her *mahr*, or dower.

A groom-to-be must present his new bride with an offering
of gifts and money, traditionally partly offered in the form of
weighty and elaborate gold jewellery. 'My *mahr* was £15,000; my
mother's was £21,000,' says Huda, a teacher from Taif. 'We're
middle-class. If you're from a higher-class family, they have to
give £100,000 – and diamonds!'

The traditional purpose of a dower is to secure a woman's
financial independence; if at any time she finds herself abandoned, widowed or divorced, the family gold is her insurance
against hardship. Men, however, complain that demands have
increased to the point that they are having to take out hefty bank
loans – or delay marriage altogether.

Although officially married once the contracts have been
completed and signed in the presence of an *imam*, her father

and the groom, a woman will seldom move in with her new husband right away. An engagement period, known as *milkah*, follows, the length of which is determined by regional and family tradition. During this time, couples who may never have had a conversation before taking their vows often have the opportunity to get to know one another a little better in the presence of their families – and, nowadays, frequently in private via covertly exchanged cell phone numbers. Only then will they reaffirm their commitment through a public ceremony.

In a society where family is everything, these wedding celebrations tend to be extravagant affairs. Traditional dress has been phased out, and now the vast majority of brides celebrate their big days in Western-style white gowns and matching tiered cakes. Not all traditions have been abandoned though, and gender segregation remains in force – meaning the bride and groom will celebrate most of the first day of the rest of their lives together in separate rooms.

In any case, it is broadly agreed that more fun is had on the female side of the festivities. While men sit and talk, the women party until the early hours. The dress code is red-carpet glamour, with trailing bespoke gowns – only momentarily concealed in a flurry of black veils when the groom is presented to the room, rarely before midnight. Male guests won't catch a glimpse of the bride at all.

Music and dancing then continue through the night, with single women dominating the dance floor; the mothers and grandmothers sitting on the sidelines take advantage of the opportunity to scout out potential partners for their own sons in the next room.

~

While new matches are being made, however, almost as many fall apart. Approximately 45 per cent of Saudi marriages now end in divorce – a rate similar to that of the UK. Under *Sharia* law, men and women have equal right to demand a separation when a relationship breaks down, but the rules of engagement are somewhat different.

Men maintain the right to divorce their wives unilaterally. Once his decision has been made, all he need do is formalise the paperwork. For a woman, the process is a little more demanding. She must go to court and demand *khula*, or paid separation.

For her request to be met, she must first gain her husband's consent, or else convince a judge of his neglect or wrongdoing; she must also return her dower. The increased demands made on women are often attributed to differences in the way men and women respond to problems in a relationship.

> *'A woman lives through her emotions. If she could divorce her husband with a word, she'd do it the first time she caught him smiling at another woman; or if she was pregnant, or on her period, or her child was grouchy. Men are less erratic; they're better at making long-term decisions than we are.'*
>
> —IMAM, teacher

Whatever the process, divorce is as painful and messy as it is for women anywhere in the world. In the past, divorced women were also faced with stigma and often isolation, but attitudes are changing. 'In the old days, a divorce was a scandal,' says one businesswoman, 'but not any more. I mean, if she works, she takes care of herself, she might even get married again and make a life for herself.'

And there can be a silver lining: divorced women are increasingly permitted to circumnavigate the restrictions of guardianship with regard to travel and work, and do not require parental consent to choose their next husbands. 'It's like this: if you're not married, your dad has to sign for you; if you're married, your husband has to sign for you,' explains photographer Waad. 'But if you are married and then divorce, this is the open way to do whatever you want.'

~

Even successful marriages take work, but it's an altogether different set of challenges when there are more than two in a union. Saudi women are no more immune to jealousy than women elsewhere in the world, and few relish the thought of sharing a husband. Nonetheless, polygamous family structures remain a little-opposed fact of life, with government statistics suggesting that around 20 per cent of married men have more than one spouse.

> 'People ask, "Why can't a woman marry four?" But a woman can't break herself that way; for her babies, yes, but not for her husband. Men are different; a man can divide his heart into a thousand pieces. But a woman, no, she cannot; for a man she gives it all.'
>
> —MARIAM, teacher

In the present day, polygamy has become so conflated with Islam as to be considered a product of the religion. However, the roots of the custom in the region go back millennia; the holy Qur'an is credited by Muslims with regulating and humanising the previously unchecked polygamous practices of the Arabia Peninsula, rather than encouraging them.

It was the sacred text, as revealed through Prophet Mohammed, that limited the number of wives a man could take, and introduced strict rules as to how these women be treated. The Prophet himself married at least nine times over the course of his life, but it is stressed that he did not do so for personal gratification.

His wives comprised divorcees, wartime widows and orphans. It is argued that by choosing women from these vulnerable – and less desirable – groups, he set an example to other men, while offering the women in question shelter and protection in the unforgiving environment of the time. In short, polygamy was an act of compassion, not of lust.

Women today continue to provide examples of when polygamy might be viewed as a pragmatic solution; it is often cited as a more merciful alternative to divorce when a wife is infertile or the relationship has broken down, but the couple has children. 'I know some wives who are really sick and ill, and they would actually tell their husbands, "Please marry!"' one princess tells me. 'It happens, but it takes quite a sacrifice from the wife.'

> 'In the beginning, things can be pretty . . . political,
> especially when they're all having kids around the same
> time. But as they get older, and the husband gets weaker,
> they tend to gang up on him and take control!'
>
> —HUSSAH, women's rights advocate

Of course, dynamics between wives vary from household to household. While in simpler times they may have been obligated to share the same tent or home, nowadays it is more common for a man to establish multiple households – either on different floors of the same building, or in different houses altogether. In modern polygamous family structures, many wives and their children have the option simply never to meet.

But together or separate, Islam places one very clear stipulation on the polygamous husband: all wives must be treated equally. If a man is to remarry, he must have the capacity to be

fair with his time, his resources and his affections. Men's fail-
ure to keep to this primary condition is the principal source of
women's opposition to the practice. 'There are very, very few
men who could be fair just to two women,' says Mariam, 'and if
you cannot be fair, you should only take one; it's in our *Qur'an.*'

Their argument is illustrated by the custom's frequent abuses;
although marital etiquette demands that a man inform, and ide-
ally seek consent from, his existing wives before remarrying,
the modern practice of maintaining separate households and the
increased ease of travel mean that some men are able to conceal
their new families in another home, another city or even abroad,
for months, sometimes years. Other men are accused of using
their conjugal rights to justify extra-marital sexual relations,
taking an additional 'wife' for a matter of weeks before sum-
marily divorcing her.

In any case, the days of the four-wife family may be num-
bered, not so much due to moral objections as to economic
constraints. Saudi Arabia's days of oil-funded excess are coming
to a close, and as salaries decrease and household bills multiply,
the prospect of supporting multiple households, and perhaps
dozens of children – who now expect higher education and
international travel – is no longer such an appealing option.

As men's financial standing becomes less assured, women's
economic independence is on the rise, and with it, the power
to say, 'No.' The right to an uncontested divorce should a husband remarry is an increasingly frequent condition on women's
marriage contracts.

It's an evolution supported by the fact that today's generation
of marriageable women have grown up in a far more globalised
world than their mothers. Having spent their teenage years
swooning over *Twilight* novels and Hollywood love stories,
their ideals of love and romance feature strictly one man and
one woman.

Despite women's increasing rejection of the practice, no broad-based or cohesive call has ever been made to abolish it. Unlike driving rights and guardianship, the right of a man to take more than one wife – although not encouraged – is clearly confirmed in the *Qur'an*.

The result is that most women accept the validity of polygamy, but simultaneously have little personal tolerance for it. 'It's something in our religion and I respect that. I'm not a scholar; it's not my place to challenge these things,' says academic Rahaf, although she adds, only half-jokingly: 'But I can tell you my opinion: for me, I would kill my husband!'

THE DOCTOR

HALLA

Doctor, aged fifty-eight, Jeddah

Halla is a family doctor and supporter of women's rights, especially in the fields of public health and domestic abuse prevention. She volunteers as part of a charitable programme against violence in the home and trains other women to do similar work. She lives in Jeddah near the homes of her four children.

Saudi women are no 'queens'

It's a man's world, no question. Just the fact that a woman can't travel; can't rent an apartment under her own name – the obstacles against her speak for themselves. Saudi women are no 'queens', whatever people may try and tell you.

But while men have been taking it easy and living like kings in their homes, women have been investing a lot in their education and development. The women here are not spoilt; they take life very seriously and they've had to strive to accomplish their goals.

It's created quite a social imbalance. Men have been taken by surprise; they don't really know how to deal with a woman who's educated, who's mature, who's ambitious. When they marry, I think in the back of their minds they're still thinking of their mothers; they're not anticipating what a modern woman is, or what her expectations might be.

But now, women are becoming more economically independent, so as soon as he begins to become a liability, or he starts threatening with the second wife, she thinks, *Why do I need to deal with this?* It's contributed to a very high rate of divorce.

I've always wondered why men are awarded this 'natural' status of authority anyway. It doesn't make any sense. I often think men are more irresponsible, aren't they? With money, with raising children, with being available, with everything.

I wasn't raised to be an educated professional

Both my mother and my father thought my ambitions were ridiculous. They raised me, really, to be barefoot and pregnant in the kitchen, not an educated professional. I had to fight a lot. In any case, I think with me the drive is so deep you could have dropped me in a Maasi village and I would have come up with something to rock the boat.

Now, of course, we have so many female doctors, I'm just a drop in the ocean. The change we've seen has been unbelievable; the hospitals we have now are fantastic. As for the women I see, they have a very similar spectrum of ailments to women in the West, really. Of course we've noticed differences with changes in lifestyle, changes in diet.

For sure there are more women now who are becoming anorexic and have eating disorders, and it's not addressed. People just say, 'Oh, it's a fashion to be skinny,' but it's more than that. I think it happens mainly because she doesn't have power over her environment; the only power she has is her body. So you tend to see a lot of obesity or anorexia, and not so much in the middle.

And another major issue we're seeing is with the thyroid. We have a lot of thyroid cancer, thyroid problems, imbalances. They've done research on it, and found that stress can really exacerbate underlying thyroid problems. Therapists always say this is the place where your voice comes out. It makes you wonder if there isn't a link between the two, between the thyroid and repression of voice.

The conditions for violence are there

I don't think you need to be a specialist to realise that domestic violence is a problem here. We don't even have any statistics to figure that out. But legally, if a woman doesn't have a voice, if she can't leave her house because she can't drive, if she can't access medical care without the help of her guardian, and if he has total, unquestioned authority over her, then by culture, by default, she's already placed in an intrinsically abusive situation.

We may not have our own studies, but there are enough statistics out there to say that closed societies suffer from these kinds of severe internal problems. Why should we be immune?

On top of the violence, we have reason to believe that sexual abuse within families is really quite endemic. Just sit down and think about it. You don't even have to be a professional to see that the conditions are there.

And it's an incredibly complex issue. I spent the longest time pushing for prevention and trying to raise awareness, only to find all my efforts falling flat on their face because the mother herself has been abused and she can't recognise it when happens right under her nose. Psychologically, she blocks it out because she has been traumatised herself.

I think it carries a different dimension to anywhere else in the world because the men are the ones who are supposed to be the protectors, they are the controllers. But then they use their own strength against you. And especially in a society where virginity is everything; a woman's sense of worth and value is completely taken away.

It's hard to know even where to begin. But I keep going because I see this as my role; as a doctor my purpose is to help people, to reduce suffering. So, professionally, that's my mission now: how do we tackle sexual abuse in the home?

The face veil makes total sense in the desert

One of the nice things about getting older is that you aren't harassed as much; the *muttawah* leave me alone more these days. I rarely cover my hair, and I certainly don't cover my face.

The face veil is something that was practised by the Prophet – to protect his wives – and it was reinforced by upper-class women at the time. From there, the Bedouins adopted it, and they never gave it up.

It made total sense for them. Think about the black grease American footballers wear under their eyes to reduce glare – you see more clearly through that black rectangle out in the desert. It's useful, too, with all that sand and the dust storms, especially when you think women were doing most of the outdoor work; they were the ones herding the goats, grazing them.

So it became part of the culture. But as for it being a religious requirement – no, not at all. Even the obligation to wear *hijab* and dress modestly is controversial.

I think polygamy is on the way out

My husband was a cousin. I married him because he was liberal; he married me because he felt sorry for me.

I was striving to be educated. I desperately wanted to get to Europe to complete my education and my parents wouldn't send me. So he married me and took me abroad. In the culture we live in, everything I am today, I owe to him.

Things will be different for my daughter. She has so much more independence; she can live alone, she can even marry outside the country if she wants to.

The way the economy is going, I think polygamy is on the way out, too. I love that, now, when a husband comes and threatens his wife and says, 'If you don't do this or that, I'm going to take another wife!', she says, 'Go ahead, you won't find another one like me.' And it's true: women are not willing to serve and give as they used to.

Personally, I think the whole practice should be abandoned and polygamy should be made illegal. These days men are only doing it for their own pleasure, which defies its purpose in the religion.

It's bad for families. It breaks family ties; it causes women to go into deep depressions, which leaves them unavailable to raise their children, and it makes fathers unavailable as they divide their time. Even economically the children suffer – they're not going to be given the best of schools, they're not going to be given the best of anything.

I believe the level of destruction it causes the family is far greater than the benefit it affords to any particular man.

Guardianship has nothing at all to do with religion

My husband has absolute authority over me, 100 per cent. As a married woman, I can't even hire the driver that I need in my own name; it all has to go through him.

Fortunately, I have a reasonable husband, but you can see it leaves the woman in an extremely vulnerable position. You give a man physical, mental and emotional power over a woman – total control – and I don't care where he's from, in one way or another, he's going to be abusive.

And if she dares to voice it, to exercise her legal rights, the judge will say, 'Listen to your husband.' If she manages to get into a shelter, the only way she can get out again is for her guardian to come and collect her. Her guardian, who is her abuser.

It's purely a mechanism of control. Guardianship has nothing at all to do with the religion. And that's where women have great leverage; they can't be attacked for trying to remove this, because in the *Sharia*, it just doesn't exist.

Every country cares about how others look at them

The coverage from the Western media has all been extremely negative, and I thank God for it. Change only comes about because, whatever they may say, every country cares about how other countries look at them. It builds pressure internally. And you know what? It works.

But I don't think this change necessarily means following the West. Arab culture is rich in so many wonderful things – in generosity, in hospitality, in helping others, in the friendship and ties that exist between women. We have enormous potential in things we haven't shown, that we haven't even begun to focus on. I think that we need to look at our heritage and our culture; it's from there we can grow, we can bloom.

We have a young population; they're educated and they're ready for change

When I started out working, there weren't so many women in the public sphere; the word 'empowerment' was still taboo. At that time, you know, it was still the oil boom; women didn't need to work.

Now it's a whole different story. The younger women have all the influence now, and I love their attitude. They're breaking the culture; they do a lot of things we were never able to do. Partly it's down to their sheer number. We have a young population; they're educated and they're ready for change.

But at the same time it's left us in a pit of chaos because there was no transition from one generation to another, from one culture to another. Suddenly there's no normality any more. The lines between right and wrong have become much harder to navigate.

It's left women especially vulnerable. Now maybe she wants to go out dating. Okay, fine, dating is good, but she hasn't had

the culture to prepare for it; she doesn't have the tools to protect herself. She'll walk down a dark street without any sense
of fear, and that, to me, is dangerous.

You see, social evolution was never considered in the development plan. We focused on buildings and economy and
superficiality, but refused to deal with social development;
we were never given the opportunity to grow and develop
in that way.

For the longest time, almost twenty-five years, women were
intentionally preoccupied with the subject of eyebrows. At
every female gathering you went to there was this discussion
about eyebrows. It was completely ridiculous, but it worked in
focusing women's attention on trivial concerns and away from
the bigger picture of social development or civil movements.

The result of all this is that we live in pretty homes, we enjoy
a very modern way of life, but we have become deeply discon-
nected from – and almost incapable of handling – our own
culture, which should be at the core of who we are.

But whatever way things turn, in ten years you'll see a whole
different face to this country. And that's what it's going to take
for women – a new era – to finally secure our rights and elevate
us into humanity as equals.

THE SECURITY GUARD

MANAL

Security guard, aged thirty-four, Dammam

Manal's parents died when she was very young. She was left in an orphanage and finally taken into an adoptive home where her experience was not always one of care. Having left this household and later divorced an abusive husband, Manal has now joined the ranks of Saudi Arabia's first generation of female security guards at a city university. She has two sons and a daughter.

I could be the first Saudi policewoman

When I was younger, I wanted to be a doctor. I wanted to finish my studies and go to college. But my mother, my adoptive mother, said she was afraid for me, that it wasn't safe for a young woman to be single and without a *mahram*. That it was too easy to fall into sin.

I was fifteen when she came to me and told me that she had found me a husband. I was completely distraught, but I knew there was nothing I could do. In the end it wasn't my decision to make.

My new husband's family lived in a small community, over 1,000 kilometres away in the south. They were Bedouins; they lived in houses, not tents, but the culture was the same. In some ways Bedouin women are more independent than city women – they have to be – but they are also far more cut off.

Where I came from in the east, a woman doesn't need to cover her face, and she can spend time with her male cousins. But there you couldn't go out with the men. You stayed at home and you covered your face.

My husband's mother was Jordanian. I never understood how she survived in that place. In Jordan, there's no *abaya*, no *niqab*, you come and go as you please. But life there in the desert, it was very hard.

But now I am back in the city, I have my own papers, and I don't need a man for anything. *AlhamduLillah*, here at last I feel we are equal.

I still hope I'll return to my studies one day. I don't know, maybe it's too late for me to become a doctor, but I could still be the first Saudi policewoman! Why not? I have a gun and I know how to use it; the Bedouins taught me that much. Sergeant Manal. I know I could do it. I wouldn't be afraid. I'm strong, thanks be to God.

My husband would never have let me apply

I love action! I adore action movies, series, anything like that. So I was curious, I wanted to see what this kind of work was like, what a security man does. So when this university started training women for the female campus, I signed up.

If I had still been married, my husband would never have let me apply. My family weren't happy about it. They didn't like the hours, they didn't like the work, they didn't like the fact I was wearing trousers.

But now they see that I'm respected, I'm good at what I do and I'm supporting my children, so they let me be. I like to think that maybe they're even a little bit proud. Maybe.

It's more work than I expected and we are always training, but I really enjoy it. Okay, maybe I don't enjoy the physical training so much – I think I liked that part better in the movies – but the rest! We have a French security woman who comes to teach us: first aid, how to extinguish fires, how to handle someone with a gun, terror drills, everything.

But, thanks be to God, until now the action has been very small – girls fainting, girls getting into physical fights, students with students, students with teachers, teachers with teachers! – nothing too dangerous.

We see them getting in cars with boys

I also chose to work at the university for my daughter. I didn't get to study, but she will; she'll join next year. I wanted to see, you know, what the girls are like, what they're capable of, what's demanded of them.

Of course, now I am also an expert on all the rules they have to follow! They're not allowed onto campus with balloons, cakes, flowers, things like that. If they do, they have parties, somebody gets jealous and it always ends in a fight. So, we don't want any of that drama.

We also don't let them leave the campus before midday. If their fathers are there to collect them, okay, but with the driver, no. Even then, they shouldn't leave until they've finished classes. There's a drive-through restaurant nearby, and sometimes they sneak out there to eat and come back. Or we see them getting in the car with boys. We can't stop them, but we tell them, 'Please, don't do that. Think of your father and mother.' It's not safe.

A third of my salary, just to get to work

My monthly salary is 3,000 *riyals*. From that my driver takes 1,000 *riyals*. That's a third of my salary, just to get to work. With what's left I have to support three children. It's nothing. And they're big now, *yanee*; they want everything.

And I know how to drive; I love driving. I used to drive in the south when we lived with my husband's family. When you're in the desert, you have to be able to do things for yourself. All Bedouin women know how to drive. *Masha'Alllah*, my oldest daughter, she's seventeen, she's a better driver than me.

But still, part of me is nervous about women driving here. Saudi men, they're not the same as in England. They'll follow you, they'll harass you. I'm happy my daughter will be able to drive, but I admit, I'm a bit afraid for her too.

It doesn't say anywhere I should cover my face

I put on the *niqab* for my husband. I'd never worn it before. I was so angry with him. I told him, 'My God only asks me to wear *hijab*. It doesn't say anywhere I should cover my face.'

He insisted. He told me, 'It's in the *Sunnah*, it's God's will.' The truth is he was jealous. He didn't want anyone else to see me.

Now he's not around any more, but I haven't stopped wearing it. That's it, it's just my habit now; I don't mind it. It's quite comfortable for me.

I still don't believe it's the will of God though. Three years ago I went to Jordan, and I just wore my *abaya* and my headscarf; I didn't cover my face. I don't think I'd wear it anywhere outside of Saudi. It has more to do with the culture here than with religion. It has more to do with the men.

The men here are not the same as the men in Jordan, in the Emirates, in America. There, they can see a woman uncovered, without an *abaya* even, and it's nothing to them. But here, just a face and they go crazy. Because we are always separate, unfortunately our men have no idea how to behave around women.

My adoptive father could never be my guardian

We have a saying from the Prophet Mohammed, peace be upon him, that when a man and woman are alone, Satan is the third person in the room. That's why we let the *mahram*, a relative, take that place. In Islam, it's a positive thing, but in the law, it can be very difficult.

My parents died when I was very small. I don't remember them and I don't know how it happened. I was put in an orphanage. My adoptive mother already had one daughter around my age, but she wanted a companion for her, so she came and she took me home.

My adoptive family took care of me, they raised me. I don't want to say they were bad, but if they were good, they wouldn't have made me marry at fifteen.

It was very hard for me. In Islam, your *mahram* must be your relative by blood or by marriage, so my adoptive father could never be my guardian; I had to wear *hijab* in front of him, just like any other man.

That's why I was married so young, but it didn't make things easier. When people say, 'Oh, but your husband will take care of you,' it makes me angry. Not all husbands are the same. I used to beg him, I'd do anything to make him come with me, to the bank, to the ministry, to the supermarket even. But he couldn't be bothered. He would tell me, 'Go ask my brother,' but his brother was not a *mahram* to me.

There was no joy on my wedding day

My husband was twenty-six, I think. I wasn't allowed to meet him. He came to the house once, to look at me, but that was all. There was no joy on my wedding day; I was miserable and afraid. I was a problem and I had been solved, that's all there was to it.

My husband wasn't a good man. He smoked, but it wasn't just tobacco in his cigarettes; it did something to his mind. He never worked; all he cared about was smoking and money. He was always asking me for money. He would threaten that if I didn't give him more he would hand me over to another man. I had a part-time job at a local primary school and I gave him what I could, but it was never enough. I was always being threatened, screamed at, beaten; he would even yell at my family.

I stayed with that man for twenty years. Even his own sisters said they didn't know how I did it. But I did it for my children. I was terrified that if I left, I would never see them again. That's often the way it goes when you divorce.

But in the end, it was my daughter who told me to get out. 'That's it, Mama,' she said. 'Go, we're big now, we'll be okay.' She gave me the strength to leave. And now, miracle of miracles, they've come back to me. The truth is their father doesn't even have money to feed them, so for now, he's left them with me.

But now, *khalas*, I'm free! The law changed, maybe two years ago, and now women who don't have a father or a husband can look after themselves. After the divorce I applied for my own ID card, and that's it! I can work, I can open a bank account, I can apply for my own travel papers. Otherwise I would have to go to my son, and he's only fifteen. But, thanks be to God, from now on, I am my own *mahram*!

I don't think I would marry again. I have my boyfriend, just a companion. We talk a lot; he's very kind to me. But I won't go soft over him and I don't allow him to be anything more than a friend. I'm free now, and I'm going to stay that way.

Things are getting better for us women

My mother's world was so closed; she knew nothing about the world outside. Now, with technology, with travel, we are so connected, we know it all. I look at my little daughter and see that, *masha'Allah*, already her mind is broader than mine. She whips out an iPad and teaches me things I never knew. *W'Allah*, she already knows more than I do. I want her to study, I want her to finish college. I want her to do whatever it is she wants to do, not what I want her to do. I want her to tell me her plans, but I will never stop her.

I want her to meet her husband before she marries. I want her to know his mind, I want them to talk. She will have this freedom. Thanks be to God, things are getting better for us women. For the men, perhaps not so much. They ask what we're up to, going out and about without our guardians; they don't like us going anywhere without them. But, thanks be to God, we women are very happy. For us, we're starting a new chapter.

WHAT WOULD YOU DO IF YOU WERE A MAN FOR A DAY?

I would take off my abaya, *I'd jump in a car and I'd drive all over Saudi Arabia. I'd go all the way up to Jordan! Everywhere! Of course I don't mind wearing the* abaya. *It's just, it would be quicker, easier, you know?*

THE FOOTBALLER

MASHAEL

Health and fitness coach, aged twenty-nine, Jeddah

Mashael is one of a new generation of female sports and fitness professionals. Football is her passion and she is an active member of a local team. Due to a history of cultural resistance to women's participation in sport, she is largely self-trained, but through her enthusiasm she has inspired countless other women and girls to take up the sport. In addition to her training schedule, she currently works part-time as a personal trainer at a new women's gym.

She used to play against the wall

I've always loved sport. I was a very active kid, you know? I tried tennis, basketball, horse riding, ballet, karate – you name it. But it was always a struggle, finding somewhere girls could practice. I never found anywhere that would let me play football.

I find it a bit sad that girls can't find a healthy environment to gather as a team and play. Football is a competitive sport, right? How can you stay motivated when you have to practice on your own?

One of the girls on the team, she's extremely talented. She used to play with her brothers and cousins, but when she turned twelve her parents said, 'You're too old to be mixing with boys now, enough with the football.' And so she stopped. She spent a year playing by herself in her room with the ball. She used to play against the wall.

Eventually she heard about us, that there was this league for girls. The day she joined she actually cried, she was so happy. Today she's a real leader in our activities; I don't know what we'd do without her.

It's not just football; I think that each person, anywhere in the world, has a type of sport or fitness they can fall in love with. And when they discover it, you'll find them committed to it, and it changes everything – their health, their motivation, their work performance. It's not all about becoming an athlete. The girls at the club, we see them become more confident, more outgoing. It changes their lives.

The main mission of the club is to create a healthy environment for Saudi girls to play football, regardless of media pressure or social acceptance. And I think we've achieved that. Now we see girls and women playing from ages five to forty. Girls get married, have babies and come back to play. A whole community has grown up around the sport.

So we're enjoying ourselves; we're playing, we have a league. What more do we want?

We coached ourselves

It started at university. We had a three-hour break between classes. Too short to go home, but long enough to kick a ball around. For a group of us it became something more. We started training every day; we became a team.

We had no coaches, no one to show us how to train; there are no PE classes or sports teams at girls' schools here.

And this was back in 2009; we didn't have smartphones, Amazon or YouTube. Whenever we travelled, we would just try to find DVDs with training sessions or coaching guidelines to sneak back, and then we'd all sit and watch them together. We figured it out for ourselves.

And the more girls heard about us, the more who wanted to

join. Football is the biggest sport in Saudi Arabia, and it's not just boys who follow the leagues. One of the women's teams started spreading the word that they were having a league of their own. And you know what? Eight teams sprang up in the city in a month.

Today there are hundreds of girls playing on regular teams in our city alone, but we still work by word of mouth. We play on private land, on farms, in fields. We tried going public once; we let a local newspaper write an article about us. It was a disaster. Ninety per cent of the comments were abusive. So we went back underground. We've been playing in secret for the past ten years.

But, really, we don't care about the publicity; we're making it on our own. You know we've even played against a couple of national teams in the region; teams that have huge support, funding, excellent coaches – and we've won.

If you meet a successful Saudi woman, you know she's ambitious

Nowadays, I think women are more privileged than men. We have women in the Shura Council, and both public and private sectors are obligated to hire a certain percentage of women; a woman can visit all the government offices and take care of her own business.

Men, though, still have the same obligation to provide; they still face the same restrictions. Single men aren't even allowed to enter shopping malls on their own.

But getting here hasn't been easy. Honestly, it's not that hard for a man to reach his goals in this country, but a woman doesn't get there without a fight. So you'll find women here are more determined to prove themselves; if you meet a successful woman in Saudi Arabia, you know she's ambitious.

You see it even at school; girls' grades are much higher than boys'. They're both smart, but girls have that motivation; they know they need to work twice as hard to make it in the world. I mean, that's my observation here in Saudi, but I think it's probably true around the world, right?

I think women are capable of doing any kind of work; I believe a day will come soon when you will find Saudi female soldiers, female police officers. God may have made man physically stronger, but you give a woman the same task, and trust me, she will find a way to get the job done!

Guardianship is supposed to be a privilege

The idea of having a guardian was always to protect the woman, not to oppress her. If a woman was in any kind of trouble, her male guardian would be contacted, and he would be responsible for taking care of the situation – financially, legally, whatever it is. The idea is to save the woman any suffering. It is supposed to be a privilege.

But it doesn't always work like that. There are girls whose parents have died, who don't have brothers, so a cousin or an uncle she's never met before suddenly becomes her legal guardian. And he can make life very difficult for her. Unfortunately, there are men in this country who take advantage. They like showing authority – being 'the man' – and they abuse the whole system.

Personally, I don't think it's necessary. Especially, if you take a woman over forty, what does she need a guardian for? And as a woman gets older, who is supposed to fulfil that role? Her son?

Men want women to drive

Of course women should drive. There's no Islamic reason for the ban. If you look back to Prophet Mohammed's time, women used to ride camels, and how is that any different? It has nothing to do with religion; it's never religion. It's always tradition and culture.

Islamically speaking, it's better for a woman to drive herself than to be sitting in the car with a stranger every day.

It's easier for the men, too; right now they have their wives and daughters calling them all the time, driving them crazy asking, 'Bring the groceries, take us here, collect us from there.'

If you get a group of people together, I assure you, 80 per cent of the men would tell you, 'We want women to drive,' and 80 per cent of women will tell you, 'We don't want to drive.' It's women who are privileged, *not* to drive.

I never have to think about what to wear

I don't cover my face; I never have. In Islam, there is nothing that says that you should; your hair, yes, but not the face. In fact, when you pray, it's forbidden to cover your face. If you go to Mecca, the holiest place you could be, your pilgrimage is not accepted if your face is veiled.

Of course we have our traditional dress, the *abaya* and the *tarha*. People think it's so oppressive, but honestly, I love it. I never have to think about what to wear; I don't have to get up an hour before going to work just to get dressed and fix my hair. I just cover my hair, cover myself, and go. I'm up and out in twenty minutes!

If ever we had a FIFA national women's team and I was lucky enough to be selected, I would play in *hijab*, like other Muslim countries do. That would be my choice. If I'm going to represent my country, I'm going to do it in the best way possible.

I get asked the stupidest questions

Outside, they see me as oppressed. They see me as ignorant. They see me as uneducated. Whenever I travel, I get asked the stupidest questions!

But if you asked me, 'Where do you want to live?', I wouldn't want to live anywhere but here. I had the chance to travel, to study abroad, and I chose to stay here.

I love Saudi Arabia. I see how, in other countries, when a girl reaches eighteen, that's it, she moves out, she goes to another city. I'm thirty and I still have dinner with my family – my parents, aunties, grandparents – every single night. I love the family atmosphere.

Maybe foreign women have more freedom, but I think we are more privileged. If you were in the US, you would go and get your own groceries; here, your husband or your son would go. Some people might see it as oppression, but it's also privilege; you're giving men more responsibility to do the things you'd rather not do.

We're not oppressed; we have everything. It's just that we're wearing an *abaya*, and I happen to like it.

I'm just waiting for the day we get to prove ourselves on the pitch

Change is happening, but it's gradual; it's a step-by-step process. When you introduce drastic changes – you try to change everything at once – it doesn't tend to last.

It's human nature, to resist change, right? We had the same fight for women's education, maybe forty years ago. Of course it makes sense to have educated women in your society, raising your children, but people were afraid of the change. It's the same thing with sport for girls.

I really hope that with Vision 2030, with all the new initiatives, that we are going to see real development. The Saudi lifestyle isn't so healthy in terms of exercise; we travel everywhere by car, we don't really walk. So if girls find a sport that they love, why not encourage them? Why not help them practice? As for myself, I want to stay in Jeddah. I'm happy here. I want to keep serving women's sport in Saudi Arabia. The teams here are already starting to open up, to show themselves on social media, so more girls can find this community.

I have strong faith in the new generation. I think they're making great changes; they're showing the world that we're educated, we're capable. I'm just waiting for the day we get to prove ourselves on the pitch too!

And, more broadly, my real dream is for each and every Saudi girl to find a place to play a sport that she loves.

WHAT IS THE MOST REBELLIOUS THING YOU HAVE EVER DONE?

Just playing football! And, well, probably travelling with the team. Whenever we travel to another city for a match, we are very careful to move in small groups and not to carry anything that would identify us as a team, just to avoid the abuse from religious men at the airport. Our kit is all hidden under our abayas, nobody has any idea . . .

THE HOUSEWIFE

Fatemah

Housewife and entrepreneur, aged sixty, Hail

Fatemah is descended from regional royalty, but her fortunes changed after an ill-fated marriage from which she has not been able to escape. Now a mother of eleven children, with little support from her husband, Fatemah's entrepreneurial spirit has kept the family going. Her home-cooking business has clients all over the city.

I can make ten different dishes with that flour

You have to try the *msabeeb*,[48] they're delicious with butter and a little sugar! Just like pancakes. They're my speciality. They're simple to make and you can cook them fresh in front of people. That's very important; the customers like that.

I take my little cooker with me to all the local fairs. I started at Janadriyah, you know, the Saudi national festival, but now I go to the horse fair and the cultural shows too. They interviewed me on national television once!

Some customers will call on me directly at home. They'll order 100, 200, even 1,000 *riyals*-worth of food. I can make ten different dishes with that pancake flour; then there's *mataziz*,[49]

---

48 Regional equivalent of pancakes.
49 Traditional stew of meat, dough balls and vegetables.

jereesh,[50] and vine leaves. I grow peppers here to sell in the garden, henna plants too; people come to buy the powder.

If I stayed at home, how would we eat?

I started my business, oh, it must be fourteen or fifteen years ago. I had to. I had small children and their father wouldn't help. *Wouldn't* help; not *couldn't* help, I would like to point out. He's a wealthy man, but very selfish.

So I started thinking, *What can I do?* No one would employ me – a woman with eleven children and no high school diploma – but I thought, *Well, at least I can cook.*

At first my husband was delighted because he got a share of the profits. He said I was free to run my business, as long as I gave him a 25 per cent cut. I told him, 'I'll give you 50 per cent, just don't stop me from working!'

But then he saw I was becoming successful; I was making my own money; I was getting a little too strong. He lost his temper; he forbade me to go out and said I had to give up the business. But I didn't listen. I said, 'You give me the money instead. I'll happily stay at home!' But he refused, so I kept flipping pancakes.

If I stayed at home, how would we eat? How would I clothe them all?

But, *alhamduLillah*, with ten *riyals* here, ten *riyals* there, I've managed to keep us going. You see the car? I paid for it. The driver and the housemaid? I brought them here too. I've kept us all, in spite of him.

My husband ruined me

If I had known what my husband would be like to live with, I would never have agreed to the marriage. I came from a

---

50 Traditional dish prepared with rice, milk and spices.

good family; my mother was a princess in our region. We had everything we needed; I could have had a very good life. But my husband ruined me.

I was twenty and he was a cousin, the son of my father's brother. I never met him before our wedding day; it was all arranged by the family.

I refuse to do this to my own daughters. When my girls were engaged, I let them swap phone numbers with their young men. They should have the opportunity to talk, to get to know one another before they commit to a marriage.

I didn't have that opportunity. I married a male, but not a man. He was wealthy when I married him, now he's wealthier still. When he resigned from the oil company, he got a huge bonus – several million dollars – but we never saw anything from him.

Whenever he's here, he's abusive. He yells and screams about everything. He doesn't pay for food. He even shuts off the electricity and the gas because he doesn't want to pay for it.

Look, I'll show you what he did. He didn't want to pay the water bills, so he put a big lock on this door so we couldn't fill the storage tank. We lived here for six months without running water. No taps, no showers.

Can you imagine? With eleven children . . . In the end I went out and found a workman myself, a Pakistani; I brought him to the house and he broke down the door with a crowbar. Then I paid for the water lorry to come.

Then, four years ago, he got bored with us and took another wife, back in the village. He didn't even tell us; we found out through other people's gossip. He has a son with her now; he's two years old.

Islam says take four wives, but if you cannot be fair with all of them, take one. He's not fair with two; he stays there one month, then here for ten days. I tell my daughters – and

I tell my sons, too! –just marry one. One is enough to be comfortable.

But I'm not angry any more. Why be angry with a man I want to divorce me anyway? He was never good to us; why would he suddenly be good to this new woman? Of course he's not. At least now he's not in the house as much. It's better for us that way.

It made him feel like a man to have all these sons

Look at my belly – it's halfway to my knees! I was pregnant thirteen times. Two babies died in my womb, but I raised eleven: five boys and six girls. I love them all, I want good lives for them all, but of course that's not what I chose; I didn't want that many. I was so exhausted, but it wasn't up to me.

It was my husband who was always demanding, 'I want a baby, I want a baby!' It's his pride, you know; it made him feel like a man, giving his name to all these sons. But once the baby was born, he always ran away.

He's like a rabbit, that's all. He enjoyed the act, but he never wanted to help raise the child. He never did anything in the home; he never felt any responsibility at all.

And so here I am in a house full of losers. I have two boys still at home, not working – one of them with a wife and a baby on the way; three girls still at home, not working. Not one of them is at university. The girls who are working are just working in shops – 2,000, 3,000 *riyals* a month. We thank God for it, but it's not much.

I'm sixty years old. I wonder when it will be my turn to have someone to look after me.

A guardian is meant to provide

I need permission from my husband to get a job, to do many things. It's written in the *Qur'an*: men should be the leaders of women.

It also says, if there's anything a woman needs, her *mahram* must provide it. It's written very clearly in our religion. But look at me: my husband is a rich man, and I am still poor. Now it's *Ramadan* and we don't have a thing in the house. He likes to call himself a religious man, a *muttawah*. He's a hypocrite.

Even if I had the money, I can't go anywhere. I'd love to travel, to Britain, France, Italy. I dream of visiting my daughter; she's in America. My sons would take me, but my husband's the one who has to sign the permission papers.

If only he would divorce me, my sons would become my *mahram*s. I have five. But he won't. And if I try to get *khula* from him, I'll lose our home. The house belongs to him. And then where would my children live?

A woman does everything better herself

In this country, a man is everything. But, you know, being male doesn't necessarily make you a man. There are plenty of males here, but not so many real men.

In the end, a woman does everything better herself. She cooks, she cleans, she carries her babies, she gives birth, she takes care of her children, and then she goes to her job too; she's always working.

Look at me – I look after my kids, I look after my home, I bring in the money, I supply for all my family's needs. I'm more than a man; I'm a man and a woman combined. It's not easy, but what else can I do? We have to eat.

I admit I hoped I would find a better job. I'm not ignorant. Most women my age can't read or write, but I went to school until I was twelve; I knew it was important. But it's not easy for a woman to find good work here.

But I don't think there's anything a woman cannot do. I'd like to work as a security guard. You let me know if you hear of anything! If the government started opening up the police force to women, I'd go for it; I'm a policewoman at home half the time anyway. At least that way a woman could get herself a little *wasta*,[51] and a decent pay check, too.

If a man sees a woman, he might feel the need to do something with her

This is Islam. It's *haram* for us to be uncovered, to show our faces in public. If a man sees a woman, he might feel the need to do something with her, you know. When men and women mix, the devil puts impure thoughts in their heads.

I don't know if you've heard, but it happens a lot these days – young women escaping their family homes and moving in with men. If the police catch them, they take them back to their parents, otherwise anything can happen; they're getting pregnant out of wedlock!

Sometimes their families won't take them back. Then they get sent to the state women's homes. We have a lot of them now, full of girls. It's the devil's work.

I used to drive the truck

I can drive – all the women in my family can. I used to herd the sheep on the farm with a truck, even while I was pregnant. But that's out there, in the village. It's not accepted here in the town, and there's so much traffic it doesn't appeal much anyway.

I used to have to ask my sons to take me out, but now I have the driver I'm a lot freer. Luckily, my daughters all have different schedules, so we don't squabble over him too much.

---

51 Social and professional influence accrued through name, connections and the lending of favours.

I think women are the same everywhere

I should hope, outside, they view us as heroes; we should see all women as heroes. They're working, cleaning, having babies, raising their children. I think women are the same everywhere.

Maybe they do some things differently, abroad, in the West. Maybe they have good men who go to work while they stay at home. I have no idea; I've never been outside to see them. The furthest I've been is Bahrain, and it's almost the same as here.

I'd like to go to Britain though; I think my business would do well in Britain.

Life was better before

Nowadays people have everything: more food, more cars, more development. But there is no happiness.

It was better before, *w'Allah*. When I was living in my father's house, I could come and go as I pleased, without asking – anytime, anywhere. I would put some *laban*[52] in a coke bottle in a plastic bag with some dates and that was it. When I was hungry, I would just make a hole in the sand and line it with the bag. That was my bowl. When I was thirsty, I would milk the goats and drink. It was simple, but it was beautiful. I only wish I'd had a camera, I'd show you!

I swear my mother and my grandmother lived better than I do. They stayed in the village, and weren't burdened with more responsibility than they deserved.

That's all I dream of – that one day I can go back to my village. As soon as all of my daughters are married, that's what I'll do.

God willing, they'll marry rich men – millionaires, billionaires! And they'll bring them drivers and housemaids and everything they need. God willing, they won't be like me.

---

52 Traditional strained yoghurt.

HEALTH MATTERS

من يمتلك الصحة يمتلك الأمل، ومن يمتلك الأمل يمتلك كل شيء

*'One who has health has hope, and one
who has hope, has everything'*

—Arabic proverb

Dr Halla's (see p. 151) grandmother died in childbirth, aged twenty-seven. In 1960, a Saudi woman's life expectancy was just forty-six years. Almost six decades on, women benefit from free, universal healthcare, and that number reaches into the high seventies. 'I can give birth now and not be afraid of dying, you know,' she says. 'Our lives are so different, you just cannot compare.'

In such a highly family-oriented society, maternal and paediatric care are prioritised and infant mortality rates have dropped by more than 90 per cent in the past fifty years. Thanks to vaccines, clean water and accessible clinics, women no longer fear losing half their children before adulthood, as Mama Muna (see p. 11) did.

In fact, women are choosing to have fewer offspring altogether; with growing educational opportunities and the prospect of a professional life outside the home, most young women today recoil at the thought of reproducing the fourteen-child households of their mothers and grandmothers.

> *'My dream is to have three or four children; a small family. I don't want ten; it's too tiring. I don't think it's fair on the children either — how do you give them enough attention? Four is enough.'*

—ASHWAQ, nutritionist

The right to choose has come with the growing accessibility of birth control. Once outlawed in the country due to their perceived interference with the will and blessings of God, the use of contraceptives gradually became accepted during the 1980s. Nowadays, both barrier and hormonal methods are freely available in pharmacies, often without prescription, giving women the power to space out and limit their pregnancies — a privilege universally correlated with improved physical and psychological well-being of both mothers and their children.

When the continuation of a pregnancy poses danger to the physical or mental health of a woman, abortion is religiously and legally sanctioned. Nonetheless, the procedure does require the formal consent of both the woman and her male guardian, as well as three physicians, even if her condition is life-threatening.

∼

There was a time, not so long ago, when a woman required her guardian's permission for any inpatient medical procedure — including to give birth in a hospital. The vast majority of these requirements were revoked by royal decree in 2012, but laws are changed faster than habits, and not all health providers have thrown away their consent forms.

Informally at least, a women's role in relation to men can still impact the healthcare they receive. Many doctors and nurses refuse to give a woman an internal examination if she is unmarried; the preservation of her hymen being considered as important an aspect of her physical well-being as potential illness.

It is a health system that remains highly gendered, with the obligatory segregation of the sexes extending into the country's modern hospitals and doctors' offices. It is an arrangement women are largely comfortable with, allowing them to be examined and treated mostly by female physicians. However, the prioritisation of same-sex care-givers over qualified practitioners can put women in a vulnerable position, especially in rural areas where female specialists may be in short supply.

Paramedics have reported incidents of being harassed by female patients' guardians, or barred from treating them altogether; to date, there is no regulation that allows the paramedic to override such resistance. In 2014, a male doctor who had attended a woman in labour was later shot by her husband in a misguided attempt to protect the family honour.

～

Traditional and religious ideas and practices which far outdate the relatively recent incursion of modern medicine still exert an influence on women's healthcare. Older women especially are apt to forgo early medical intervention in favour of traditional treatments including herbal remedies and prayer.

A 2012 survey conducted at a university revealed that almost half of students and their professors believe that epilepsy is the result of an individual being possessed by *jinn*.[53] There are still

---

53 Hidden spirits or demons, the existence of which is acknowledged in Islamic texts.

reported occurrences of religious healers exorcising women by physically beating such evil spirits out of them.

Perhaps the most reviled of all religiously legitimised procedures practised on women – female genital mutilation (FGM) – while respected by some as *Sunnah*, has never been widely performed in the Kingdom; the procedure is banned in all hospitals. Nonetheless, local researchers and health professionals attest that FGM still forms part of local custom in certain pockets of the country – notably in coastal regions influenced by migrant communities, and in the far south, bordering Yemen.

> *'I remember my youngest aunt's circumcision. I thought how lucky she was to receive the ceremonial care and attention. Much later in life I became aware of socially mandated violence toward women.'*

—MUNA AL YUSUF, author

Beyond these more overt manifestations of traditional belief and practice, Saudi women continue to be afflicted by a curious number of culturally specific ailments, developed through daily life and habits. Simply choosing a husband can have serious consequences for the health of her family.

In Saudi Arabia, the rate of newborns affected by birth defects is one of the highest in the world. It has taken the country time to acknowledge that the root of the crisis is consanguinity, caused by a preference for marriages between cousins.

To tackle the problem, the government has launched an impressive public education campaign, and blood testing of engaged couples for the most commonly inherited blood disorders is now mandatory before a marriage contract can be signed. The move has been met with considerable success; the results of the tests are not binding, but the number of couples voluntarily calling off their wedding before the big day increased fivefold within five years, and young women now talk openly about the issue.

Another health issue to receive much coverage in local media is widespread vitamin D deficiency. Despite living in one of the sunniest nations on earth, studies claim that between 70 and 80 per cent of the female populace suffer from a severe vitamin D deficiency, a malady with symptoms including depression, fatigue and hair loss; usually veiled and spending more time in the home, women's skin is rarely exposed to natural light. In addition, almost half of all women of child-bearing age are estimated to be anaemic, a health issue that has broadly been attributed to poor nutrition.

Diets in general have changed dramatically in recent decades. With the exploitation of natural resources, the nation's fortunes transformed, and before Saudis had the chance to develop their own catering industries, international fast-food chains flooded the country's towns and cities, supplanting simpler local cuisine. With these changes of lifestyle and eating habits have arrived so called 'diseases of affluence'. Around one in five Saudis is now affected by diabetes, one of the highest rates in the world. Approximately 70 per cent of the population is now overweight.

And these excess kilos are not evenly spread. Rates of obesity in women are 30 per cent higher than in their countrymen, a problem that brings with it a host of other associated health issues including heart disease and infertility. The significant gender bias is put down not only to the flasks of sweet tea and plates of dates and chocolates that adorn women's coffee tables and provide centrepieces to their professional and social gatherings, but also to their largely more sedentary lifestyles.

Wherever you are headed in Saudi Arabia, it is unlikely you will arrive on foot. With large open expanses between settlements and summer temperatures that regularly top fifty degrees centigrade, with the arrival of cars and air-conditioning, Saudis have sagely put their desert walking days behind them. Cities are not designed with the pedestrian in mind. Sidewalks are rare, and shops and services are usually gathered in temperature-controlled covered malls.

Walking has become such an anomalous activity that, in 2016, medical student Alaa Alanazi launched a silent protest in support of another young woman – detained for running away from her family – by simply refusing to use her driver, and instead walking to her classes each day and encouraging others to do the same.

But it is women, whose worlds more frequently orbit the domestic sphere, whose movements are most limited. While their grandmothers before them were necessarily encumbered with arduous physical chores, with urbanisation and the arrival of home appliances and domestic workers, women's status as the more delicate sex has been enshrined, and strenuous physical activity is not encouraged.

The sweaty, competitive world of sports in particular has always been considered an undignified arena for women. Even the matter of the clothing required to practise sport is controversial, as was the case in most Western countries until relatively recently. Tight-fitting modern sports clothes are hard to reconcile with the navel-to-knee level of *hijab*, which is meant to be observed even in the presence of other women.

It is well known that women now break such codes among themselves, but society still finds it harder to condone in the public domain; at single-sex swimming pools, which have only recently started opening for women, many simply dive in fully clothed.

*'In our religion, tight clothing is not allowed; it's not
supposed to be anything that parts the thighs.'*

—NAILA, teacher

The combined result of these religious precepts, cultural norms
and popular ideas of femininity is that, for many decades,
women's participation in sport was effectively prohibited by
omission. Female spectators were banned from entering the
unruly environment of sports stadiums and local government
refused to provide licences for female gyms to operate. Physical
education classes have never been taught at girls' state schools.

As usual, innovative ways were found to circumvent such
restrictions; the high walls of private homes have been useful
in shielding many private clubs like Mashael's (see p. 167), as
well as smaller-scale activities. A number of illegal gyms were
opened, but with monthly membership fees in excess of 1,000
riyals, they remained inaccessible to most women.

*'The government is spending a lot, like billions and
billions of dollars every year, on obesity, diabetes;
different diseases that accrue from not having a
healthy lifestyle. And with females, it's even double
because they don't have locations to practise sports.'*

—DONIA, basketball coach

When enterprising Princess Reema bint Bandar made it her
mission to open a women's spa and gym in the country's capital,
she did so by disguising the front room as a seamstress's workshop and launching her venture under a tailoring licence. It is
said that the sewing machine has never been moved.

But finally, with the desire to modernise and the increasing costs associated with preventable illness, the rest of the ruling family has come around to her way of thinking. In 2016, Reema was selected to head a new female department in the nation's General Sports Authority.

In her first year on the job, the long-standing ban on girls' sports at schools was finally lifted, although, to date, the classes themselves have yet to commence. 'They are trying to do everything too fast, so it looks good,' says teacher Naila, 'but we don't have a gymnasium, we don't have any sports teachers yet.'

> 'Since Princess Reema was appointed [to the Sports Ministry], we have an Instagram account, we started going out in public.'
>
> —EBTISAM, student football club captain

Other actions had more immediate effects. In 2017, the government began granting licences to women's gyms for the first time – provided that they were running activities aimed at health and weight loss and steered clear of competitive sports. In early 2018, women finally entered sports stadiums for the first time to cheer on their favourite football teams.

New female gym facilities have already proven highly popular, serving not only as venues for exercise, but often as active social hubs. Both of these roles help in supporting not only women's physical health, but also their mental well-being.

~

'All the studies show, we have the same rates of mental illness as any other country and we need to be prepared for that,' says doctor Afnan. But despite the country's massive investment in public health care, mental health resources have arguably been neglected. Only 4 per cent of the generous national healthcare budget is currently allocated to mental health care, and treatment is not always cutting-edge.

'I had to leave my first therapist,' says masters student Alanoud. 'There were a lot of things I couldn't talk to her about, like boyfriends and stuff. She would advise me to read the *Qur'an* and recite certain prayers; that was her treatment plan.' With little in the way of therapeutic care, many turn to pharmaceutical solutions; many antidepressants are available over the counter.

Following a global trend, women are disproportionately affected by depression, and the disorder is now one of the primary causes of disability among Saudi women. As elsewhere in the world, the women at highest risk are those without employment, those in ill health, and those who suffer from an abusive home environment.

～

Violence against women in all its forms occurs in every nation on earth. 'You can't say that Saudi men are tough with their wives, that they don't treat them right. No,' one princess told me, 'we have exceptions, but Saudi men are just like any other men in the world.'

But where any other women in the developed world might have certain social and legal recourses to turn to should they find themselves in an abusive situation, Saudi women unfortunately find themselves in a more vulnerable position.

Saudi society is closed by nature. The high walls surrounding most properties are a physical reminder of how highly privacy is valued, and especially around the worlds of women. 'There's a fear of reputation,' says engineer Rawan, 'because if she goes out and she talks about it . . . then people are going to be talking about her. There are going to be rumours.' In a 2014 survey of Saudi women, 81 per cent agreed that family problems shouldn't be disclosed to outsiders.

'We all acknowledge that certain things happen amongst ourselves, but we have this thing that "the secrets of the household don't leave the house". It's a cultural thing . . . you just have to put on a happy face . . . It's bulls***.'

—HAYA, photographer

Added to this is the highly paternalistic nature of Saudi culture, which sees a man as responsible for the women and children of his household; women may not leave their guardian's homes and live independently without his consent. Young women who attempt to run away from unhappy home lives may be reported to the police.

When caught, there is little procedural clarity as to what comes next. Some are charged with *aq al-walidayn*, disobedience to parents, and are imprisoned. Others are given the choice of being returned to the family home or taken to a state shelter.

The words *Dar al Raeya* are usually pronounced in hushed tones. These 'care homes' or shelters were created to protect women who found themselves in situations of extreme family violence, or who had been left destitute. They exist in every major city, but facilities are basic, and the buildings have been likened more often to detention centres than to centres of care.

'They're like prisons because you can't leave,' says social worker Lamees. 'You can't go out shopping; you cannot even go out to the garden.' Rumours of institutionalised physical and sexual abuse are rife, but hard to verify – the women interred are also denied access to social media or visitors beyond their legal representative, should they have one. There is another resemblance to prisons: once interred, a woman cannot leave without the consent of her guardian; often the very abuser she ran from.

Imbued with a sense of natural authority, and with little fear of repercussions, those men with a tendency toward aggression have little incentive to curb such impulses. In a separate survey, this time of Saudi men, 30 per cent admitted to having used violence against women in their families, mostly for answering back or perceived immoral behaviours.

Honour killings, although not so widely reported as in countries like Pakistan and Bangladesh, do happen in Saudi Arabia. 'I'll even take you further,' says doctor Halla. 'There's no law against a father killing his own children.'

The root of this statement can be found in the country's refusal to adopt a written penal code, relying instead on the direct case-by-case application of *Sharia*. The result is that Islamic judges wield an enormous amount of individual authority in how the law is interpreted and applied.

> *'I'm telling you, there's no specific law. In the UK, you have one law, one right, one thing to do. Here, if the police are nice to you, okay, they would help you. It depends on the circumstances; it depends on who's involved.'*
>
> —WEJDAN, legal student

Rape, while Islamically punishable by lashings or even death, is often even harder for a woman to prove than elsewhere in the world. If she does bring a case to court, she will also need to demonstrate that she herself was not in violation of gender segregation rules when interacting with the accused. If the perpetrator is a spouse or a family member, the battle becomes yet more insurmountable; legal sexual contact is simply that which occurs in the context of marriage – there is no age of consent and no acknowledgement of marital rape.

Aside from the social stigma and legal difficulties associated with divorce, there is another reason that women may stay in abusive relationships. A father's perceived ownership of his children has long extended to custody rights. Traditionally, a mother would maintain care of her sons until they were seven and her daughters until they reached the age of nine. After that, unless the father revoked his rights, they would become full-time members of his household.

In the spring of 2018, these regulations were amended, making it easier for mothers to gain long-term custody of their children – provided there is consensus between parents. If not, it would appear that, in practice, paternal rights still carry the most weight.

Thereafter, if a mother wishes to see her children and she is no longer on good terms with the father, the only venue for visits to take place is at the local police station. 'I cried when they told me,' says philanthropist Suhaila. 'I can't imagine a parent who would only see their child at a police station. Where are we living? It's traumatic for everyone involved; the police are trying their best, but they're not trained to handle these situations.'

Suhaila now works with a charity that provides a safe space for families to reunite in more homely surroundings. As is often the case, it seems that for real change to be instigated, it will need to come from women themselves. And some have started to do just that.

It was educated and influential women who returned from their studies abroad and employed their privilege to found the government-endorsed National Safety Program in 2005, which has increased public awareness of domestic abuse as a social ill, and united and supported the efforts of scattered organisations and charities.

The same women were involved in the drafting of the Regulation to Protect Against Abuse passed by the government in 2013, which recognised violence against women and children in the home as a crime for the very first time. It also made provision for the opening of more flexible women's shelters and domestic violence helplines.

> 'The Prophet Mohammed never raised a hand in
> anger to a man, woman, child or even animal.
> This is the example that was set for us.'

> —WEJDAN, legal student

The regulation still has limitations; rather than automatically removing women or children from an abusive situation, social workers are advised to prioritise maintaining family ties, meaning victims are often returned to the home after a short period of mediation or after the abusive relative has signed a pledge vowing not to repeat his actions. But its very existence is an important step in acknowledging that the problem exists, and its incompatibility with declared Islamic and family values.

With education and improved communication, more and more women are gaining awareness of the rights guaranteed to them both by their government and their faith. 'If a woman opens the *Qur'an* and reads it, she will find that her rights are in there, all of them,' insists Princess Amira. Legal student Wejdan agrees: 'I've been studying everything, and there's a lot women can do – they are free to go to court if they want – they just don't often have the courage yet.'

In 2016, lawyer Nasreen Alissa gained international recognition for her contribution to this field when she launched the app *Know Your Rights*, a platform designed specifically for women that offers free legal guidance for a myriad of different situations. Since becoming available, the app has been downloaded tens of thousands of times across the Kingdom.

As in many areas, new technology and means of

communication are gradually helping women gain access to support, information and each other. Women are breaking taboos of revealing their faces or other parts of their bodies to publicly expose their bruises on social media accounts. By doing so, they seek not only to find a way out for themselves, but also to assure other women that they are not alone, and that what happens behind closed doors need not stay there.

THE STUDENT

QAMAR

Student, aged twenty-one, Abha

Qamar is a third-year business administration student at a Riyadh university. From a highly conservative family, she arrived at university shy and fearful of foreigners. She has now secured a university internship, and is an active member of on-campus music and theatre groups.

In my family, girls are more loved

Most of the girls here would like to be boys because boys get more freedom. But I like being a girl; in my family girls are more loved than boys. My father drank a toast[54] every time he had a daughter, but he said he couldn't face it after the boys. He says boys bring trouble.

I think girls are better than boys, too. We're more peaceful; you don't see us fighting like they do. We can become mothers, which is way more than any man can do, and we are much better dressed.

Not all the girls at university come to class

I think pretty much all girls here go to university now. Even if a girl's father or brother tries to stop her, the police will help her get there. If she wants to.

---

54 Referring to juice or coffee; the consumption of alcohol is prohibited by law in Saudi Arabia.

Not all the girls at university come to class though. Some of them just come to hang out, you know; to talk, to eat. Maybe 30 per cent of them are like this. I guess they come because there's nowhere else to meet their friends.

I always go to class. I'm not always sure I know what I'm doing, but I go! Although, to be honest, what I really come for are the clubs. There's this new activities programme in the student centre; they have theatre, films, a choir even. I don't think these things were even allowed before, but I love singing and acting now! It's given me more confidence in myself. I'm even thinking of running for university ambassador!

The only thing I hate – apart from maths class – is the rules. Like, you're not allowed to leave campus before twelve o'clock. Sometimes I have an early class and I'm finished by ten, but even if your father or your brother comes to collect you, security won't let you out; not unless you get a permission paper at the beginning of the semester.

I don't know what it is they're trying to stop us from doing. Anyway, I don't think there's much point; if the girls want to do something, they'll do it, rules or no rules.

Our families are closer

I've known my best friend for twelve years; we're always on the phone. I've only seen her maybe five times since junior school though. She lives nearby, but her mother doesn't like me to visit. I don't know why; maybe she feels I'm a bad person; maybe she thinks girls who go out together get into trouble. Normally, if your parents won't let you see someone, at least you can meet up at university, but she doesn't even go to university – so we're stuck.

If I want to go for lunch with a friend or something, my mum will say yes most of the time; she just likes to know who it is. She's happier if it's someone she's met, or at least someone I've talked about a lot. And, well, we all use the same driver, so of course I have to ask before I go.

I don't mind it though. Even if I could live with my friends, I'd prefer to stay with my family. Whenever I'm not with them, I miss them – even if I sleep too long! If I have to travel for a couple of days, I go crazy missing my father. I know people in other countries love their families, but I don't think they stay as close or spend as much time together as we do.

I don't call guys; I don't get in anyone's car

I would like to get married one day. Not now – I'm too young, but after I've finished my studies.

But I don't want to meet him first. Here in Saudi Arabia, if he sees you before, he won't respect you. He'll think, 'Well, she calls me' or 'She sees me, so she'll see someone else.' It doesn't matter if you love him, if you spent forty years talking. Once he's spent time with you, you can forget about him marrying you. And even if he does, he'll never respect you.

Once you've signed the engagement papers, you can take your time; you can meet him with your family, and if you don't like him, that's it, there's no marriage. But it's better to do it like that, officially.

You know, it's not like your country. If a girl meets a guy for coffee, they don't really go to drink coffee. I don't want to say it but, I mean, most of the time they go to bed. It's not a good way to get to know him. And most boys, if they meet a girl, they don't meet them alone; they come with a group, and then the girl ends up going somewhere she doesn't know, somewhere she doesn't want to go.

It happened when I was at high school. One of the girls was talking to a guy a lot. He was calling her for more than three years, telling her he loved her, that he wanted to see her. Finally she agreed to meet him with one of her friends. When they came to his car, there were four other men inside. They found the girls' half-naked bodies in the desert a week later.

So I don't call guys; I don't get in anyone's car. Not just because it's dangerous; it's also really disrespectful to your family. My father would be so upset if he thought I did that kind of thing. Some fathers kill their daughters for things like that. Mine wouldn't; but some do. Even if they love her – *really* love her – it happens.

If it's a brother or an uncle, he'll go to prison. But if the father does it, no, there's no punishment. As a father, your money and your children, they belong to you. And anyway, she's the one who chose to do wrong, isn't she? I'm not saying it's okay to kill your daughter, but it's also not okay to earn your family's trust and then abuse it.

If it were immoral, men wouldn't be allowed to do it either

I don't know where the concept of male guardians comes from. They didn't take it from Islam because Islam says you only need a *mahram* for one thing – to get married.

There's nothing else you need a *mahram* for. Except maybe when you go from one city to another, but that's just for protection; if you went on a long journey without a man, maybe someone would try to do something bad to you.

But Islam doesn't say women can't drive, or a woman can't do anything without getting the green light from her father or her brother, no. I already know how to drive; my father taught me on our farm in the south. It's normal in the countryside anyway; women drive outside the cities. I have six sisters and he taught us all. He said, 'Why not? Driving is not something bad or immoral. If it were, men wouldn't be allowed to do it either!' He's a clever man, my father.

It's not easy, needing a guardian

It's not easy for me, needing a guardian. My father's not well; he's been very sick for years. And my big brother's in prison. He's been inside for three years and four months. He has another eight months to go. It's hard. My mother doesn't sleep much.

My brother used to be a soldier, but one day he did something really stupid. He held a knife to this driver's throat. He wanted money, or, rather, he wanted to help a friend who needed money. He's a good person, he is, but in a stupid way. He'd kill himself to help you live.

I guess that's why my father prefers girls!

Nuns cover their heads for God. Why is it different for us?

When my grandmother was young, there was no technology, no cars and no schools for girls. Women wore their clothes without an *abaya*, without *hijab*, without anything. A lot of the country, they didn't really understand Islam yet. Men and women sat together; the women had a million friends, both men and women, and it was okay. Even my mother, she didn't cover her face until she was about twenty; her generation didn't know you were supposed to.

We cover our faces because it's written in the holy *Qur'an*. The *Qur'an* says we should follow the example of Prophet Mohammed, peace be upon him, and Mohammed once said his wives covered their faces whenever a strange man came to the house, then they would take it off again. But nowadays, in the city, there are men everywhere! You can't keep pulling your veil on and off. That's why we wear *niqab*; it's just more convenient. It's really not a problem for me.

It's not just a Saudi thing; women wear this in Pakistan, India, Turkey . . . My sister lives in America and she still wears *niqab*. Sometimes people shout at her; they say they don't want her in their neighbourhood, but she doesn't care. If I travel, I'm keeping mine on too.

I don't really understand why it's such a big issue. In your country, you have Christian women – nuns – who cover their heads for God. Why is it different for Muslim women? In France I heard they make women pay a fine for it, just for covering their heads.

I didn't used to like people from the West

People think we're like birds in cages. I don't know why. I guess because we don't drive. But not driving doesn't mean you're not free; I feel free. Or they say that we're dangerous. I don't know how they can say that when they've never met us.

But then, honestly, I didn't used to like people from the West. My father said it was dangerous to travel there, and my mother has always been afraid of Westerners. You see all these stories on social media about how they hate Muslims. I was afraid of them too.

I remember there was a big story here about a Saudi girl who had gone to study in England; she was murdered on the street. The man who did it said, 'She scared me; with her *niqab*, she scared me!', but he was the one who looked scary! I also thought, if an English girl was murdered like that on the street over here, it would probably start a war . . .

But then at university, I met these teachers from England, from America, and they were really good people. They helped me so much, I just loved them! Even my mum likes them. They changed my mind. Also one of my sisters told me that not all people in a country are the same.

But I don't want to leave Saudi Arabia. When I see the way women live in some other countries, I feel sad for them. I read about places like Japan and Russia where a lot of women make money from, you know, selling their bodies. And they say, 'This is freedom!' They say, 'Women live better in our countries.' I don't think so! Do you?

In some countries, when their daughters turn eighteen, they say, 'That's it, goodbye', and push her out! Can you imagine? You must feel like you're nothing. Here, even if a girl gets married and has a million children, her family home is always her home.

I hope we don't change everything

We keep changing, and most of it is good, *alhamduLillah*, but I hope we don't change everything. I don't want everything to be like the West. I don't think everything they do is healthy. I always think, if you are doing something that would be dangerous for a baby, you know it's not really right.

For myself, I want to be a lawyer, I want to be a mummy and I want to travel! When I started university, I was completely certain I would never leave Saudi in my life. I never thought my parents would allow it, for me to travel. But now I have my own passport, and last month one of my brothers took me to Dubai for the weekend. Suddenly, everything seems possible!

THE ENGINEER

SAMIRA

Engineer, aged twenty-four, Riyadh

Samira became the first Saudi woman to graduate in her chosen engineering field inside the country. Initially doubted and dissuaded, she is now proudly held up as the 'engineer of the family', and has inspired many other young women to follow in her footsteps. Samira works for a major multinational innovation and manufacturing firm and lives with her parents and siblings in the family home in Riyadh.

My parents assumed it was a phase

When I was fifteen, I went parasailing abroad. It was an amazing feeling, gliding through the air like a bird! I immediately told my parents I wanted to be a pilot. They said no; they told me it would be hard for a girl and that I couldn't have a family. It's true, it would be difficult if you want to get pregnant or you have young children at home.

But I didn't let go of that dream; I still haven't. And in the meantime, I couldn't shake my fascination with flying itself; like, how can 100-ton objects just glide so peacefully through the air? I started reading a lot, looking at diagrams. I found a one-hour documentary online called 'How to Build a Jumbo Jet Engine', like a recipe tutorial – by the end I was hooked. I told myself, *Okay, this is it, this is what you want to do with your life.*

My parents assumed it was a phase. I have a cousin who's in

the same field, so at the next family gathering my dad brought me to him and said, 'Listen, my daughter wants to go into engineering. Tell her about what you do, maybe she'll change her mind.'

His plan backfired. At the end of our conversation, my cousin told me to go for it. I was triumphant. 'You see, *Baba*! I'm going to go for it!'

'Engineering is a guys' thing'

I told everyone outside the family I wanted to be an interior designer. It just seemed easier that way; I didn't want to have to debate my decision until I'd actually submitted my application.

But then it started: 'Engineering is a guy's thing!', 'What are you going to do? Fix cars?', 'How are you going to have a family?' But I'm stubborn I guess, and I started my course, the first and only girl in a full class of boys.

The university has a balcony system, so the guys would attend their classes on the first floor, and I would watch from behind a glass barrier on the second. I took every class by myself. When we had group projects, the work would be separated into stages: the boys would take part one, I would take part two, they would take part three . . . so we never had to work in the same room.

But it never put me off. Not having anyone sitting next to you to ask questions or swap notes with means you have to really focus on the professor. And even though we couldn't meet, the guys on my course were always helpful: if I had a question or we had a shared assignment, I would contact them; first it was by email, then WhatsApp and so on.

No one knew what to do with me

When I went for my first internship at a research centre, no one knew what to do with me. They sat me in front of a computer, because they assumed I was IT, 'like the other girls'. I eventually convinced them I was in the engineering group, but I was kept in a separate building from the male interns and wasn't allowed any direct contact with my supervisor.

My second experience was far more positive. We were working at an electrical mechanical company and we had direct access to the production line. I never imagined I would work in a factory, but it was so cool! But even there, a female friend who was training to be an electrical engineer had her own supervisor ask what she was doing there: 'Don't you want to get married?'

At my graduation ceremony, nobody mentioned that I was the first girl to complete the course. Honestly, I've never really thought of myself as a pioneer. I've always said if it hadn't been me, it would have been someone else; it was only a matter of time.

So it's been amazing to see how it has affected other girls. I used to volunteer at open days at the university, talking to high-school students. They would ask me what I studied, and then I would have girls stay to talk with me for half an hour or more, and when they left they would thank me and tell me I inspired them. I never thought I could have that effect on people, just by doing what I wanted to do.

I understand very well how the engine works, but I've never driven a car

A couple of years ago I took part in this big international contest. They sent a team of us Saudis, and we had ten days to design and manufacture a prototype car from scratch. It was such an amazing experience, to have all this hands-on practice. But of course that's where you feel the difference with the guys.

I've done a course on automotive design – I understand very well how the engine works and all the different systems – but I've never driven a car. I've always had to rely on my brother or my dad to relay the practical experience to me; I'm always asking them, 'What's the problem? How does it feel?' But, honestly, you don't know that much until you have to do it.

I think everyone understands that the reason women don't drive here is cultural, not religious, and culture takes time to change; we can't just switch things overnight. The whole system here was built on the needs of men. Repair shops, driving schools, traffic police – they've never had to interact with women.

I'd love to learn to drive; women should have that right. But, I also feel I'm just now realising what a luxury it is to have a driver. I always have my laptop with me, and it's actually really nice to be able to use the time to work instead of navigating traffic. So, in the future, if I still have the means to keep a driver, I don't know that I'll change.

It's not fair to blame boys

I always say minorities work harder; they want to prove everyone wrong. And women are a minority, maybe not in the population, but still in workplaces and universities in so many fields.

I've never had this mentality that there are some things for guys and some things for girls. I've always felt that whatever you enjoy, you should go ahead and do.

There are some jobs that are going to be harder for women. We aren't equal to men when it comes to physical ability, and having kids does limit you – I think any mother would say that. But if a woman is determined to do something, I think she can do anything – so long as she's willing to accept the realities. A bit like me going into engineering: I knew I could do it, but I also knew my opportunities at the end might be limited.

But I don't think it's fair just to say it's easier to be a boy or to blame them. They have their burdens too: in our society, a boy is expected to graduate, get a good job and then provide for his family. A girl has a bit more freedom in what she wants to do because she doesn't have anyone to support, basically.

The rights of a woman are simply the rights of a human; sometimes, recently, it seems like 'feminism' is guiding us toward a hatred of men. Why? We're all human, and we should all be fighting for justice as a whole, for all people, not working against one another.

People can love each other, even if they're not soulmates

Oh, it happened to me probably a month ago. I come home and my parents say, 'Tada! There's a gentleman here to meet you!' It's such a weird experience, because the guy and girl are sitting together but the parents are there too and they're trying to brag about their kids at the same time: 'He does this and this . . . ', 'She's an engineer,' – wait, maybe not that; he'll say I'm too independent!

But often arranged marriages like that do work. People can love each other, even if they're not soulmates. They can care for each other and they can build a connection through the family that they raise. Maybe there was a better person for him or her out there somewhere, but that doesn't mean they're miserable.

Nobody forced me to wear it

I don't really understand how wearing an extra piece of cloth on your head or your face became such a big deal. Nobody forced me to wear it; I chose it, and it's the same for almost all of my friends. They just prefer not to show their beauty to men they don't know – because women are beautiful. And if a woman feels more comfortable that way, what is it we're all judging her for? *Hijab* is just a form of protection, a way of covering your assets! But it doesn't cover your mind from thinking. It doesn't prevent you from flourishing and discovering.

I think, all over the world, we can be quick to judge people; maybe someone has too many piercings, too many tattoos. I've worked hard to teach myself to look past that, and actually meet people before I form an opinion. After all, I don't want others to see me as just 'a scarf'.

I don't feel owned; I feel cared for

Some people see guardianship as a form of ownership, but I never felt owned by my 'guardians'; I felt cared for. I consider myself lucky in this regard. I grew up believing that my *mahram*'s main role is a protective one; if you're travelling alone or you're going to a place that might be dangerous, your guardian will want to accompany you.

To me it's like a friend wanting to walk you home, or a mother accompanying her child somewhere out of worry. We all know that there's safety in numbers, right?

Of course, I'm only one case, and there are many others to consider. Having regulations that give guardians such authority, it is possible for them to abuse that power. I think people will abuse power everywhere. There's definitely room for change and improvement, and hopefully that's not too far away.

Women in science in the West still face discrimination

'You're oppressed.' 'You don't have any rights.' 'Did they force you to wear that?' 'Did they beat you?' It's always like that.

People think we're hiding away, that we don't know how to ask for our rights, or that we need someone else to come and fight for them for us. People don't understand that you can't come into an environment that works in a certain way, and just force it to work your way. You have to understand the society to know how to fix it. We are fighting, in our own way.

We do have problems and I think we should be honest about them. If you try to hide everything away and refuse to talk about it, how can you ever improve? I talk about the negatives, not because I am unhappy here, but because I love my country, and I want to make it better.

It's like designing a plane: you have to study previous planes; you have to point out the flaws and the weaknesses if you're going to understand how to improve it.

But it's not like all women are living wonderful lives in the West either. There's still discrimination when it comes to women working in science and engineering and so on; they're still not taken as seriously.

I remember watching that EU educational ad, 'Science: It's a girl thing!'[55] The girls are all wearing stilettos and mini-skirts under their lab coats, there's a lot of posing and playing with test tubes – it's really some remarkable directing – and in the end, what are these 'scientists' making? Make-up!

It was hilarious. Really? This is how you want to inspire women? Aren't we interested in aeroplanes and cars too? I think that women in the West have to deal with a lot more objectification.

It's just a matter of time

I think we're going to see a lot of changes in the education system here. Even governmental sectors will eventually start hiring female engineers – like everything else here, it's just a matter of time. Having universities teach women these subjects is the first step.

There needs to be a loosening of certain cultural barriers too; it's still not easy for a woman to train in a workshop or to learn more about cars.

For myself, there are so many things I want to do; my dreams

---

55 'Science: It's a girl thing!' was a 2012 video clip from the European Commission created to encourage young women into careers in the sciences.

are all over the place. Some days I want to get a Masters in Aerospace; I want to do heaps of research in aeronautical engineering. Other times I just want to ditch everything and become a skydiving instructor, teaching other people how to do it and spending my days jumping out of planes. I still haven't given up on getting my pilot's licence.

I want to fly.

THE BUSINESSWOMAN

A BEER

Businesswoman, aged forty-seven, Jeddah

Abeer Al Fouti broke convention in her teens by moving to the capital alone to pursue her education. In the decades that followed, she managed hospitals, launched a pioneering comedy and entertainment company and assisted Princess Reema bint Bandar in establishing Alf Khair, an all-female organisation that works to train Saudi women for the workforce. Abeer has since moved on to work in another major philanthopic organisation. She lives in Riyadh with her British husband.

Women give to their families first

I think the same thing happens everywhere: women give to their children and families to the extent they often feel their own lives have passed them by. The difference is that, here, you have rules and laws that support that. It's built into the culture; a woman's role is giving and caring.

If someone falls sick, the women in the family take turns to care for them; no one here ends up in a hospice or an old people's home. But it also means that women rarely follow their own passions or dreams. When we ask women on our program about their priorities, they usually talk about their families, their husbands – even men in general.

We work a lot on values and on self-branding. At the beginning, we often just ask the question, 'Who are you?' And then, you should see how the tears fall. A lot of them just don't know how to answer that question. It's the same when you ask, 'What do you want to do?', 'What do you want to be remembered for?' No one's ever asked them before. They've never had to ask themselves.

But they are capable of everything. The only work I think a woman shouldn't do is the work that she herself doesn't think suits her. The limits you impose on yourself should come from you alone. And even then, we can work on it and help you change your mind!

It gave me the drive to prove myself

My father grew up in Medina, surrounded by pilgrims from all over the world, and long before we became so closed and conservative in the 1980s. He was naturally open, and respect and tolerance were his greatest teachings.

He also believed in education, for both sons and daughters. 'Education is the key!' he'd say. He himself hadn't had the means to study past fourth grade; all his children are graduates.

Of course, not everyone was so forward-thinking. When I opened my first business ten years ago, a lot of men didn't take me seriously; a lot of people around me tried to dissuade me: 'Are you sure you want to do that? Oh, but that's a lot of headache.'

Maybe that's what gave me the drive to prove myself. You have to find the resources within yourself; if you don't take yourself seriously, you pretend that you do, with the way you dress, the way you speak.

There were other challenges. In our culture, most of the deals happen while people are socialising. It's all about your circle. We women didn't have access to the men's networks.

Until five years ago, things were segregated even when you went to conferences. It was very, very challenging to link in. You had to have the initiative to organise your own dinners in private homes so you could invite people to meet with them.

Since we started *Alf Khair*, I've always run networking events; women need to stand by women and network with each other first. Nowadays we run sessions where we invite both men and women. We've come a long way!

It was shocking when women started working in public places

I mentored a girl who worked as a cashier. She told me, 'Every day when I leave for work, my parents say, '*Allah lay uwaf kik*' or, 'May Allah not bless you.' Can you imagine the psychological strain? That every single day, your parents wish you ill? That they claim not to care what happens to you?

But it was shocking to many people when women started working in public places, retail especially. It was resisted by the religious authorities and by certain socio-economic sectors of society.

There is a feeling that women should always be protected, that they shouldn't be left exposed, especially in a place where they have to interact with men; men who could be good, could be bad, could be crazy. My feeling has always been that that assumption is as insulting to men as it is to women.

Now, *masha'Allah*, that girl is a very successful woman. She's a supervisor in my company and her family respect her achievements. Suddenly opportunities are opening up to women left, right and centre. But we still have a lot of catching up to do.

Women entering the workforce tend to lack skills in critical thinking, teamwork and, crucially, work ethics. Work is still very new to women here, and for most, family remains their central priority. If someone's sick or something's wrong at home, she's late or she skips work altogether.

It's the nature of our culture, but it's often very difficult for international firms here to understand. So we work with all of that; plan, prioritise, and don't give all of yourself to others.

I'd rather my driver was a woman

Studies show that the main reason women aren't staying in their jobs here is poor transportation. Imagine you work in a shop and your salary is 5,000 or 6,000 *riyals* per month. You spend 2,000 on the driver, and then you have to buy the car as well. In the end, you'll find a lot of women would rather sit at home and register for social support.

Driving is part of a woman's ability to be self-sufficient and independent; to have autonomy over where she wants to go and when she wants to be there. Personally, though, I'll be keeping a driver. That's nothing to do with being a woman; that's just my own phobia. I've been involved in too many car accidents. But, you know, I'd rather that driver was a woman. I think we're safer drivers. If we had a total switch and there were only women on the road, perhaps that's when I would get behind the wheel!

Guardianship is supposed to be about consensus, not control

When I started my business, I needed a man to help me do it. I had to have a *mahram* to sign for me, to do certain things. I was ripped off because of that law. You don't always get to choose someone you truly trust as a partner; sometimes you just take the guy who's there willing to do it. You'd be surprised by the number of people who'll cheat you.

In Islam, having a *mahram* is supposed to be about ensuring consensus between husband and wife. They have to agree on what they want to do in life. So if you want to leave the country, you have to reach an agreement; you don't just do things separately. I believe successful relationships are built on mutual agreement, so I support that.

But the way it's been interpreted, that you can't travel, you can't get this or do that without this person's approval; it's basically saying that someone else has to take my decisions for me.

When it becomes control rather than cooperation, I'm completely against it. I'm all for letting those laws go. I can sign my name all by myself, you know.

You shouldn't dress for male approval

I don't wear *niqab* or *hijab*, but I respect women who do. If that's her own choice, I think everyone should. Personally, though, I don't like covering my face; I think it takes away from who you are. I also don't believe it's part of our religion. According to Islam, a woman should dress conservatively, in a way that's not provocative — that's as far as it goes.

And that I respect; I think it's important. You don't want to be branded as a product that needs to look pretty all the time to appeal to men. If you're dressing that way because you yourself feel that you are gaining something from it, then again, that's your choice. But you should never feel pressured to dress in a certain way just for male approval.

Men are afraid of what will happen if they talk to Saudi women

I believe that in order for any marriage to succeed, you need both families' approval — especially here in Saudi where we have such close family ties. Luckily, I'm very good at convincing people. And it's just as well, because the man I chose to marry was a work colleague, a foreigner and a Christian.

The way he tells it, it was love at first sight — but we worked together for a year before he plucked up the courage to approach me. You know, when Westerners come to Saudi, their companies give them all these rules and scare them half to death telling them what will happen if they talk to Saudi women.

When we met, he was a conservative Catholic, which was

fine by me; I understand conservative very well! But for us to get married, he had to convert to Islam. It wasn't something I encouraged; I was raised to respect other people's faiths.

But he started talking to friends of mine, to moderate people, and they shared their vision of Islam. I guess he was convinced, because one day I came back from a business trip and he said, 'I've converted. And I really want to marry you!' It's been twelve years since our wedding.

I think it's important for couples to meet and approve of each other before they marry – marriage is hard enough as it is. At least when you make the choice yourself, you take the responsibility that comes with that, and try and make it a success.

We all find it more interesting to focus on our differences

Suppressed and miserable or shopaholic airheads – I think that's what the world thinks of us. I would like people to know that we're strong, intelligent women. We haven't stood down from all the challenges that face us.

This country is being developed by strong women. Even the founder of the Kingdom, King Abdulaziz, would introduce himself as 'Ukhu Noura', brother of Noura. He defined himself by the strongest woman in his life.

I see the way women live in the West and I see how hard they've worked for their rights. I look at what they have achieved with a great deal of admiration; I want us to learn from their successes. I wish they'd look at us with the same respect.

I know they still have their struggles too, though. My European friends tell me they're still pushed to be more masculine – in their behaviour, in their clothing – to be taken seriously, especially in business.

I'm married to a Westerner, so I really see it from both sides. I'll sit with my husband's family and hear how they perceive

Islam and the Arab world. Then my friends and family here will talk about the West. They'll have completely different opinions, and they all hold them very strongly, even though they don't understand each other at all. I guess we all find it more interesting to focus on our differences, rather than all the things we have in common.

We can only continue to move up from here

Right now, we're facing a challenging economy, and honestly, I think it's the best thing that could happen to us. It's pushing people to change. Societies change after problems, after wars, after struggles; periods of chaos are usually succeeded by progress and better order.

We've been spared these misfortunes, *alhamduLillah*. But when you're comfortable, when life is ticking by and everything is taken care of for you, you don't push for change. We need this pressure now, for society to mature and for more things to be accepted.

It's already starting to happen. Entertainment is accepted, theatre and cinema are growing; it's incredible what's happened just in the past two years. And at the heart of all this change is 'Saudi women'. Right now it's women first, and if you establish anything or you do anything and you're the first, there is this flurry of publicity and celebration. It's a time of real optimism.

I think we can only continue to move up from here. I dream that one day I'll get to see my nephews and nieces hanging out on the street, together, without being segregated from one another. In business I want to see women as CEOs of their companies, free to take their own decisions without being dictated to.

I want to see women reaching the highest level of government. I dream of seeing a woman minister. I don't think it's such a leap any more. Give it a couple of years, I think they'll be there.

THE SHOPGIRL

Aasma

Shop assistant, aged twenty-four, Riyadh

Aasma is a shop assistant for a well-known make-up brand. When she started five years ago, she was one of the first group of women to work in retail, after a royal decree opened lingerie and cosmetic stores to female employees. Aasma defied her father to take the job and secure her independence. Several of her sisters and cousins have now followed her lead. She lives in Riyadh with her mother and siblings.

A girl is judged for everything

I thank my God for the way he made me. But still, I wish I had been born a man. Not for the freedom – for the responsibility. If I were a man I could look out for my sisters, I could take care of my mother so she wouldn't have to work at the bazaars any more.

A man is allowed to make mistakes; nobody judges him. A girl is judged for everything. They watch us just like exhibits in a museum, *w'Allah*! If I don't cover my face or I put some lipstick on, they'll call me a bitch. If I want to smoke, I have to hide in the car.

Okay, I know I shouldn't smoke; I'm Muslim and it's forbidden. But if it's *haram* for women, it's *haram* for men too, right? Shame is shame, whether you're a woman or a man. So why are only women made to feel it?

Perhaps that's why we keep more inside, why women are

more patient. When a man doesn't like something, he'll scream, he'll raise his voice in your face. But we hold our tongues; we keep it in our hearts and we cry later, amongst ourselves.

Sometimes I think men are like monsters. When they find a girl, they just want to consume her, to break her, take what they want from her and throw her away. Most of them are like that anyway, from what I've seen.

People think we don't have any fashion

Outside, people think we wear *niqab* because we don't know what else to do with ourselves. They think we don't have any make-up, any fashion. But make-up is a big deal here – you should see how the girls turn up at university! If their parents won't allow it, they'll make themselves up in the car on the way. Sometimes it's just to keep up with the crowd; sometimes it's for a girlfriend – she wants to keep her eyes on her!

When I was a kid, I was always amazed by the way my big sisters would transform themselves – and me. When I was twelve, I started to teach myself, from YouTube. When I got my first job as a secretary at a hospital, my boss was always asking me, 'Do my nails.' 'How are my eyelashes?' 'Fix my eyeliner.'

I found the job in the store by accident. My friend and I were bored at the mall; there was nowhere else to go. We walked round and round until the shops started to close. I started chatting with the store manager. She saw I had a little talent, and she offered me a position.

They said we should be at home

Before, when you wanted to buy underwear, you had to buy it from a man. When you went to a make-up shop, the man would take your hand to test the colours, or even test it on himself! It was really embarrassing for a lot of women.

My mum was super happy when I got the job. My father was

not. He told me I had to stay at home. I asked him if he'd give me the same money the store would pay me. He refused, so I told him I'd be starting work on Sunday. I didn't even ask my brothers; it's none of their business.

A lot of people didn't like it at the beginning, women working in shops. They said we should be at home. But I didn't listen; if people said bad things to us, I didn't hear them. I have something to protect me, you see, like a balloon I blow up around me – it only allows positive words in.

Anyway, my customers are all women. In the shop where I work, there are two sections: one for women and one for men. And that's not a stupid rule; some women really shouldn't work with men.

Like one of my cousins. I helped her get a job in my store but then I found her taking phone numbers – from the customers, from anyone. The manager complained to me and I had to let her go. She should work, but someplace closed, where there are only women around.

For me, it's okay; I'm not like that. I'm like a man – a woman with a man's mind. I'm there to do my work and I won't be distracted. And I'm proud that I was one of the first. Now all my sisters and friends, they're going to work in stores. I opened the way for them.

If it was really for God, I would wear it

Whether I cover my face or not really depends on who I'm with. If I'm with my family, of course I'll wear *niqab*. If I'm alone or at work . . . well, they don't need to know.

Whenever I take it off, my mum yells, '*Haram*! What will people think of you?' If it was really for God, surely she wouldn't care what other people thought? If it was really for God, I would wear it. But it's not – it's a custom; we wear it for others. As a Muslim, I should just wear *hijab* – that's how I see it.

She gets upset when I uncover in the car – it's a big car with blacked-out windows: 'Why aren't you wearing *niqab*? Allah will see you!' I tell her, 'Allah always sees me! You want me to wear it in the shower too?'

Even at home, I can't wear jeans or tight clothes; she says people can see everything. I asked her when I'm supposed to wear them then. She said, 'When you're married.' Everything is 'When you're married.'

Recently, my older sister came to visit wearing leggings and no *niqab*. My mum asked, 'Why is she wearing that? It's shameful!' I told her, it's because she's married. You told her she could do whatever she wanted once she was married. That's it, she's doing it, and I will too.

Drivers take half your salary

Women should drive – but not here in Riyadh; there's too much traffic. Even without women, the streets are packed. What will it be like if they're allowed to drive too? The cars will stop, I'm sure of it!

Look at my house – there are three girls. Right now, we have one driver. If we were all driving, there would be three cars coming and going from this house. If all the houses do the same it would be chaos. I think there'd be more accidents too.

I'm more excited about the metro they're building. Even my mum says she'll use it when it's finished. We need more transport like this. A driver takes half your salary, and then what are you left with? I know a lot of women who stopped working at the shop because they just couldn't get there.

For me it's okay; I don't live so far. If I can't use the driver, I take a taxi. If I can't afford a taxi, I'll get there on my feet!

A woman is fragile; she needs a man to protect her

My mother says, a girl should always have a man around her, because she's like a candy. If there's no one there to protect her, somebody will open her up and then she won't be sweet any more.

In Islam, we women are compared to *kawarir* – it means a bottle. Anything can break us, even the heat. The Prophet said you must be good with these bottles because we're fragile.

We're like men in our hearts sometimes; we're strong! But you can't be like a man all the time. A woman is glass; she needs some metal to protect her. This is the *mahram*, the metal.

Whenever I see a successful woman, like these make-up artists on Instagram with more than a million followers, I know she has a good man who supports her. Whether it's her husband, her father or her brother – he has her back. He's lifting her, not thinking about how to box her in.

That's what your *mahram* is supposed to do – help you, not stop you from doing things that aren't wrong. Not like my father.

You know, I was offered a promotion to be a trainer. I would have travelled all around the Gulf, but he refused. He doesn't want me to be independent. He wants everyone to beg him for money, so he can ask what it's for, and control us that way.

Having a *mahram* is part of our religion, but these laws and restrictions are not. My father doesn't even live with us most of the time. No one should have to ask permission to live their life from a man living 500 miles away. Would that work for you?

I will do everything I can to be his only wife

A lot of men came to our family and asked to marry me. They saw me, they sat with my parents and they liked me. But I refused. I could see in their eyes, by the way that they talk, what kind of men they are, and I didn't like them.

I want to marry a man with an open mind, who will love me for me, who will lead for me, who will support me. We should support each other. And I will do everything I can to be his only wife. I won't let him see anyone else; I will be his world. But in the end, you don't get to make that decision; he does. My mum didn't choose for our father to take a second wife two years older than me. You see now why I want to be a man?

My mum says she'll help me find a wealthy man who lets me live my own life. If I marry someone rich, I could send my sisters and my daughters to international schools; I could finish my studies abroad. Then again, my father is a rich man, and he's never given us anything. Everything depends, you see, on whether you find a good husband.

People do date before marriage too, but it's not easy. That's why we have so many tomboys. If a girl goes out with a boy, she's worried all the time about *muttawah*, about her reputation. With a girl it's easier; she can kiss her, she can do whatever she wants with her, no one will care. She can call her in front of her mum, she can even have her stay in her room. She says, 'Mama, I will go to Noura's house,' and Mama thinks, 'It's okay, she's a girl. It's safe.'

I don't know how I feel about it. When you love, you don't choose. Your heart chooses, right? Even if it's wrong.

People have the wrong idea about us

You know Heidi? That's the image I used to have of women in the West. Long blonde hair, living in the fields and the mountains.

Now of course I know that's not true. Women in the West are not at all like Heidi; they're like men! They're more equal there. I think it's better like that.

People there still have the wrong idea about us though. They think we're living out in the desert, without anything, like poor people in Africa. They don't realise we have jobs and malls and parties and friends and we chat on Snapchat, just like they do.

Everything starts with the will to try

The minds of women here have changed in the past ten years. Now we're thinking about life more; we have our own opinions on the way things should be; we're educated.

Nowadays we're out of the house, we're working in shops, in markets. In my mother's time, there was nothing; now we have everything. Now all I want is for the minds of men to change too. Because it doesn't matter what year it is, or how much technology you have, the way you live depends on the mentalities of the men around you.

Insh'Allah things will get better. We love our country, and when you love something you will try. Think of a baby; a baby didn't know how to walk, but now she's running; she didn't know how to stand, now she's jumping. You only get there by trying. I tell my clients this when they're struggling with eyeliner! But it applies to life too. Just like the baby, it's okay, we will fall down, but we will try again. Everything starts with the will to try.

WHAT WOULD YOU DO IF YOU WERE A MAN FOR THE DAY?

I would get married. We women can't choose our partners, but as a man, I could. I would marry a girl I loved — just one, not more, because I only have one heart. I would not cause the pain my father did.

And I would be a good husband — I wouldn't ask her to do everything, like I see men doing; I'd let her do anything she wants.

That, and I'd smoke on the street. Every day, everywhere!

WOMEN'S WORK

طلب العلم فريضة على كل مسلم

'Seeking knowledge is an obligation upon every Muslim'

—Hadith

'Look, no one is going to just give a woman her rights,' one women's rights advocate in the capital explains to me. 'The only way she can relieve herself from the dominance of male authority is if she is economically independent – and she will only reach that point through education, and through work.'

Before the unification of the Kingdom in 1932, education – if basic and often informal – was open to both sexes. At *katatib*, small gatherings often held near the local mosque, girls were taught to read and memorise *Qur'an*, as well as the rituals of prayer. As the new nation became more firmly established, however, these groups were gradually replaced by more organised forms of schooling, incorporating arithmetic and basic sciences – but their doors were only open to boys.

According to the newly empowered Wahhabi religious authorities of the time, the formal education of women was not only unnecessary, but potentially harmful in its capacity to lead women away from their God-given roles as mothers and caregivers at the heart of the home.

More cynical observers have argued that the abandonment of girls' education may even have served a strategic purpose. 'It weakened half of society, which helped the new political regime to establish its forces inside the country,' claims activist Hussah. 'It was a very smart move, if you look at it from the political point of view.' Whether for piety or for power, the education of girls was neglected for decades.

It was a single, determined woman who took on the clergy to bring girls into the classroom. Princess Iffat, the wife of King Faisal, had been raised and educated in Turkey. On arriving in the Kingdom, it is reported that one of her first questions to her new husband was, 'Where are the schools? Where is the education?'

She challenged the religious establishment using verses from Islamic scripture that clearly endorse learning as a virtue regardless of gender, and argued that educated mothers could only be of benefit to their children, and therefore society as a whole. Her position was supported by a number of male reformers, in part because they saw educating women at home as a positive solution to the growing 'problem' of Saudi men taking foreign wives abroad.

Iffat opened her first school in 1956 in the relatively permissive coastal city of Jeddah, taking care of every detail, down to the sewing of the classroom curtains. But not everyone shared her enthusiasm. Secular education was viewed by many as a gateway to Westernisation and all its ills, and more practically, classes would take girls out of the sheltered domestic realm and into the outside world on a daily basis.

Such was the resistance in the Wahhabi heartland of Buraida that when the first girls' school opened there in 1963, King Faisal was forced to send armed troops from the capital to keep the angry mobs from the students and staff within – some of whom, given the shortage of qualified women, were little more than children themselves.

But as the furore subsided, mothers began to seize the opportunity to give their daughters what they themselves had been deprived of. 'I'm *umiya*,[56] but every year I won the Perfect Mother Award at my girls' school, because they were always on time, always clean and braided and always top of the class,' recounts settled Bedouin Mona, 64. 'One year, after the ceremony, they shut me in a classroom, the teachers and the other mothers, and demanded to know how I did it – "You don't even read or write!" I told them how I did it; I was going to make sure they learned what I missed.'

> 'Whenever I caught them [my daughters] napping, I
> would slap them awake and send them to their books.
> I was too hard on them. It makes me cry to think of
> it now, but I was frightened; I thought every second
> they slept, their opportunity was slipping away.'

> —MASHAEL, housewife

Since those early days, state education has transformed from cautious experiment to national priority. In 2017, Saudi Arabia committed a full 25 per cent of national expenditure to education, more than double the rate of most developed nations (the UK allocated 11 per cent over the same period). The benefits of this investment, including free public education from primary through tertiary levels and universal university stipends, are now enjoyed by girls and boys alike.

Correspondingly, female literacy has rocketed from a

---

56 Illiterate woman.

barely-there 2 per cent in 1970 to 91 per cent today. A whole generation of women, deprived of the opportunity to learn even the most rudimentary reading and writing skills, are now attending their own daughter's university graduation ceremonies.

In fact, female undergraduate students now outnumber the males. Following a global trend, they are getting higher grades than the boys too. 'Girls work harder at school. I think that's the same everywhere in the world, isn't it?' says nutritionist Ashwaq. 'And here they feel like they have something to prove.'

～

In keeping with the unique status of the country in the Islamic world, religious instruction still forms the backbone of state education. A review of a typical ten-year-old girl's report card shows that more than a third of classes are dedicated directly to Islamic studies. 'The other classes too, maybe they're not religion exactly, but they use religious examples,' says translator Hala. 'It influences everything.' A similar emphasis is placed on national history and Arabic language.

With such a strong educational bias, some more secular content inevitably loses out. 'When I was offered a scholarship for my Masters degree in Australia I was initially hesitant,' confessed one university teacher. 'I knew that it was in the southern hemisphere and I was afraid that, well . . . gravity might not be the same there.'

Like schools and public media, universities must stay within certain parameters with regard to the content they teach and discuss. Libraries are frequently censored and subjects like sexuality, different religious affiliations and national politics are strictly off-limits. The list of forbidden topics distributed to international female teachers on their first day in class (this author included) comprises items such as birthdays, Christmas, adopted children, magic, sculpture and, inexplicably, the number twelve.

Saudi Arabia's strong oral tradition – with history, stories and poetry transmitted more by word of mouth than through written literature – also maintains an influence on teaching styles. There is a strong preference for rote learning over problem-solving, even in higher education, which has in turn often been blamed for a lack of initiative and critical-thinking skills in graduates entering the workforce.

> 'They're used to memorising everything, like
> Qur'an . . . They have a lot of knowledge,
> but they're missing a lot of skills.'

—NADEEN, university lecturer

As with all elements of public life, schooling is gendered. Until 2002, girls' education, unlike boys', remained under the control of religious authorities, whose primary objective was to prepare young women to be successful wives and mothers. Consequently, while boys take a weekly physical education class, girls will often undertake a course in family or feminine studies. In addition to cooking and sewing skills, class textbooks at some schools are illustrated with diagrams explaining how to dress for your body shape and how to give a relaxing foot massage.

The perception of women as naturally more patient and nurturing has also affected the courses open to them in higher education. Viewed as more suited to roles in nursing, education and care, and with a view to limiting their access to male-dominated working environments, courses in fields such as engineering, petroleum studies and international relations have never been taught on the female campuses of public universities.

It's a bias that appears again at postgraduate level, where the female student majority falls away. 'They [parents] sometimes don't always encourage it because they're afraid,' says Masters student Sara. 'When a girl is young, she can marry any good man. But if she's older, she's educated, she has higher expectations and she wants a man to equal all of that; she doesn't have so many options.'

It is a perspective that is gradually changing. In recent years, female programmes for law and architecture have been added to public universities, and are now heavily subscribed. In addition, private universities have shown increased flexibility in allowing female students to study alongside – if screened from – the boys on traditionally 'male' courses (see The Engineer, p. 207). According to one such student, 'It's not just about "girls aren't allowed to do this"; not many girls even wanted to take those courses. But everything is changing, you know – supply and demand.'

~

University life has done more for women than improve their employment prospects. On campus, students experience a freedom of expression rarely enjoyed in public. 'It's all women here; we don't have to wear *hijab* or *abaya*,' says student Hanan. 'We don't feel different.' For some young women it is the only place they go without their relatives, and the only place they meet other women from outside their immediate family circles.

Left to their own devices, young women organise health and environmental campaigns, student elections and theatre performances; they even drove before the ban was lifted, albeit on electric golf carts.

Nonetheless, in many ways their experience differs widely from their counterparts in the West. The periphery of Qamar's flagship university campus (see p. 199) is delimited by a

3-metre-high concrete wall, and uniformed security guards are posted at every gate.

Once inside, *abaya*s and *niqab*s, obligatory on the street, are discarded; the concealing garments have been prohibited within the academic campus in an effort to combat attempts by young men – the curious, the predatory and the lovelorn – to enter this sanctum of young women.

Security measures are in place not only to keep interlopers out, but also to keep the students in. Free from the surveillance of guardians and family, some take the opportunity to seek ownership of their own time by sneaking out to shop, have lunch or even meet an admirer.

Comings and goings during class hours are restricted to hamper such dalliances. 'You know, they are small,' explained one motherly security guard, 'and we see them getting into cars with boys. We tell them not to, but we know it happens. We are afraid for them, that's all.'

For a small subset of female students, the university's stringent duty of care continues after the campus gates are locked at 6 p.m. It is unusual for unmarried women to live outside the family home, but for those who have travelled across the country to pursue their education, life in halls is an option.

Students are allocated modern studio apartments, and enjoy access to a well-equipped gym, complete with swimming pool – still a rarity in women's facilities – as well as a corner shop for groceries; it's a life well contained.

For around this small residential area runs another wall; a compound within a compound. The gates to this are manned by uniformed male guards, twenty-four hours a day. With the exception of a monthly organised trip to a local shopping mall, those who live inside may not venture beyond this area, even for a few hours, without the presence of a close male relative – who himself must be in possession of the appropriate paperwork. A student may not visit a friend's home; a mother cannot take her daughter out for lunch.

> 'It gets lonely sometimes; it feels like a prison . . . We
> cannot leave without a brother, father or husband. Most
> of the girls here don't have any family in the city.'

—SHAHAD, student

'Sometimes I do feel trapped,' says law student Hanan, twenty. 'If I want to go out, my dad has to say yes, and maybe my dad doesn't want me to go out.' In such confined quarters, young women do of course succeed in small acts of rebellion.

There are tales of midnight parties after lights out, barbecues on the roof, cigarettes smoked out of bedroom windows and hidden love affairs sustained through text messages and snatched glimpses at the campus gates.

Some even make it out on their own for a while, catching a private driver from the main academic campus when the day students go home for the evening. Student Shahad makes do with smaller bids for freedom: 'There's a secret door at the back of the gym that nobody watches. Sometimes I run out there, see what's there and come back. It's dark so no one can see me. I just stand there a little, outside the wall.'

> 'We have a huge campus here. I wish they would
> let us out, just far enough to ride a bicycle.'

—HANAN, student

However high the walls that surround them, they are no match for the modern powers of the internet and television. Women living here have watched enough American series and high-school movies to know that students in other countries experience far more independent lifestyles; nonetheless, there is little opposition to the current system. 'It's better this way; it's better for us,' says Shahad. 'They are tough on us, but we deserve it. If they weren't, we'd have boyfriends, everything. They're right not to trust us.'

But such rigid boundaries can only be enforced within the Kingdom. In 2005, women were granted the right to take up government-funded international scholarships. Since then, tens of thousands have travelled abroad, mostly to the US. It is an experience that impacts more than just their formal education. 'It's where I learned to be independent,' says Malak, twenty-four. 'Just planning your day for yourself, going out, getting on with things. When I came back, I wasn't the same.'

~

Despite forming a majority of the country's expensively educated youth, Saudi women make up just 16 per cent of the Kingdom's workforce. Such figures have often been used as evidence of women's oppression. But it isn't that simple.

According to Saudi tradition, a woman is not expected to work. Both Islam and local culture dictate that all financial responsibility entailed in supporting a wife, children and household falls firmly on the shoulders of the man of the house. For men, this ability to provide is often a matter of pride, but for women, too, it remains a common expectation.

Women, on the other hand, take sole responsibility for the domestic sphere. In Saudi Arabia, being a housewife is not a role that is looked down upon. 'We are queens,' says artist Lama. 'We are powerful and influential in this society because we take care of our children; we raise the nation.'

'Girls are privileged. You can have a career if you want one,
but you don't have to work – it's completely up to you.'

——RAZAN, art agent

The country's strict segregation rules have also played a role in shaping women's professional prospects. For several decades the only form of employment considered respectable for those who needed or wanted to work was as a teacher in an all-female school; a conviction which left the profession massively oversubscribed and made the process of education a somewhat circular exercise.

Another doorway opened when women were granted access to certain retail positions in 2011. Princess Reema bint Bandar, who manages the Riyadh branch of Harvey Nichols, seized the opportunity by filling her store with female sales assistants. But almost immediately she faced an unexpected setback: 80 per cent of her new recruits dropped out within the first three months.

Women cited childcare issues, a lack of transport and family objections to working in a mixed-gender environment as reasons for their rapid departures. Often the first women in their families to work outside the home, with no role models to look to, the transition to professional life has been challenging. 'Why is she playing on her phone? Why is she leaving early?' asks shop assistant Aasma. 'Perhaps she has a problem in her family, perhaps someone is sick, perhaps there's no one to take care of her child – this is her first responsibility.'

There is a less-spoken-about issue that also saps women's motivation. 'There was one study by a doctoral student in the 1980s,' one academic tells me. 'She found that 70 per cent of working women gave their entire monthly salaries directly to their guardians.'

Things have changed enormously in the Kingdom since then,

and the study was never repeated, but a wealth of anecdotal evidence suggests that the practice never fully died out. 'I know a couple of ladies who have to give half their salary to the man or he won't approve,' says primary school teacher Maysa. 'In Islam he's not supposed to let her work anyway, so he thinks, *Why not make a profit out of it?*'

It is a complex range of issues, and unfortunately it has had an impact on women's employability. The government's attempts to force the issue by introducing quotas on the number of Saudi women a company must employ have been repeatedly under-mined by international firms who employ the women on paper, pay them a nominal salary and then send them home, while more reliable imported workers put in the (wo)manpower.

This has been especially true for less prestigious positions. After decades of being able to rely on cheap imported labour, accepting employment in the service sector can be a source of shame. 'All you want is your parents to be proud of you,' says businesswoman Abeer, 'for your mom to be able to say, "Oh, my son is a doctor." She doesn't want to say, "My daughter is a cashier girl at the supermarket"; they still believe these jobs are for "someone else".'

~

Hurdles like these cannot reverse the steadily growing tide of women flowing into the country's boardrooms, workshops and offices, however. Female employment may seem low in comparison to other nations, but it is already 50 per cent higher than it was in the 1990s. A steady combination of increasing educational opportunity and economic necessity is pushing more and more women out into the world. Although a small minority, women have worked their way into positions as doc-tors, journalists, engineers and lawyers. The head of the Saudi Stock Exchange is currently a woman.

'When you're educated and you graduate and you just sit
at home, it's so frustrating – it just eats through you.'

—RUBA, ministry worker

With more roles to aspire to, today's generation of young female graduates has a far greater expectation that they will put their studies into practice. 'The majority want to work!' says university lecturer Sara. 'Now everybody wants to be an entrepreneur, everyone wants to be the next Steve Jobs; even just informally, you see their Instagram businesses popping up everywhere!'

Such informal markets, not recorded in official statistics, have proven especially valuable to Saudi women in establishing economic independence; Instagram businesses like Moudi's (see p. 289) have sprung up like mushrooms across the Kingdom, the internet providing women of all backgrounds with direct access to the market without the need to leave the house, secure childcare, mingle with men or secure permission from their guardians.

Finally, state and society appear to be firmly behind them in their efforts to succeed. Economically, Saudi Arabia can no longer afford to import millions of foreign workers while half their educated citizens sit at home. Women's participation in the labour market is a key aspiration of the country's development strategy, Vision 2030.

'Because there's this women's movement now, and companies are required to hire women, you'll find that even if me and a guy have the same bachelor's degrees, for me as a woman, it's going to be easier to find a job,' says academic Nadeen. 'I have brothers, I have cousins; I see it.'

*'The government is actually supporting women
like there's no tomorrow. Now is really the best
time there's ever been to be a Saudi woman.'*

—ABEER, businesswoman

All this is not to say that Saudi women are looking to renounce their primary roles as mothers or the support of men that is still guaranteed to them. 'I don't favour that kind of lifestyle at all because it's very harsh,' says HR director Huda, comparing her own lifestyle to that of Western women. 'A woman is left to pay for everything, and you want her to take care of the kids!'

But with education and increasing economic independence, whether in the office or the home, women's roles as leaders and decision-makers are clearly on the rise; and in a country experiencing such a remarkable rate of change, it seems impossible that this growing influence will not have a significant impact on the shape of the Kingdom to come.

THE ADVOCATE

A ISHA

Women's rights advocate, aged seventy-six, Al Khobar

Affectionately known as the Mother of Saudi Feminism, and regularly featuring in Forbes Most Powerful Arab Women list, Dr Aisha Almana has been at the forefront of the women's rights movement in the country for more than thirty years. She first gained notoriety for her participation in the now-legendary women's driving protest of 6 November 1990.

'I want something different for you'

It was my father who made me a feminist. He was educated in India, so he had seen the world outside, he had seen women educated, and somehow he saw potential in me. When I was seven, he decided I should go to school, but there were just no schools here in Saudi Arabia at that time. He wanted to send me abroad. Of course the family all refused it; they said I was too young.

So he kidnapped me. Literally, he kidnapped me. He made me believe he was going on a business trip and that I was just coming to the airport to say my goodbyes. But it was my clothes he had packed in his suitcase. Once I realised what was happening, I burst into tears; I begged to be allowed home to my mother and my grandmother.

But he just knelt down in front of me and he said, 'I don't want you to be like your mother or your grandmother. I want something different for you.' And that was it; I was boarded on a plane for Egypt.

'What did you do today, for the women of Saudi Arabia?'

He didn't stop even when I finished my studies and came back to Saudi Arabia. When schools for girls opened, he nominated me as principal, so that there wouldn't be stigma for women to work in schools. Can you imagine? With just an elementary school certificate.

He would drop me off at the gates and check my work when I came home in the afternoon.

He was the one who decided the girls should have a uniform. He went to the market and just bought up whatever there was most of – it happened to be blue and grey tunics. People said it was an act of communism, making the girls dress the same! But, you know, those tunics are still the uniform for most girls' schools to this day.

He was always asking me, right until he died, 'What did you do today for the women of Saudi Arabia?' So I carried on his dream. I didn't stop.

Unless a woman is economically independent, no one will listen to her

It's definitely easier to be male here. But this is not something particular to Saudi Arabia; this is the case worldwide. We have this philosophy of, 'Might is right' – the physically strongest take power. You see it through history.

The feminine is always seen as soft or weak. A woman can give birth, she has a higher pain threshold than the man, but her physique always gives the impression that a man is stronger.

The fact is that unless a woman is economically independent, no one will listen to her and she will never be able to get her rights in society. So how do we get economic independence? Through education and professions. Once you have a profession, nobody can take it away from you. You can lose your money, you can lose your beauty, your health, whatever it is; but if you have a profession or a trade, it's yours for life. And this is what our women need.

A lot of people don't know it, but our religion itself dictates that women must have complete financial independence; she must be free in business and so forth. All these regulations and restrictions we are facing now, they're new. This is a misinterpretation of Islam.

I believe that a woman is capable of doing anything she wants. I don't think there is anything she couldn't do, or shouldn't do.

I stopped the car and told the driver to get out

It was the Gulf War that first pushed me to drive in Saudi. I worked in Riyadh, and as other means of transportation were suspended, the only way from Dammam to the capital was by car. One day we drove past an American Army convoy; there were all these big trucks, and some were being driven by female soldiers, by women.

I looked at one and I said, 'This lady, she's coming here. She's driving a car and having her freedom and I'm sitting in the back seat with my driver.' I felt awful; I can't explain it. I just stopped the car and said to the driver, 'You go back, I'm taking over,' and I drove, all the way from Dammam to Riyadh. Nobody stopped me.

When I got to Riyadh, I told everyone I had driven, and a big group of us came together. That's how the 6 November protest came about. I remember on the day, my car was second in the procession. We had the roads to ourselves for about half an hour. And then of course we were stopped by the religious police.

These were all very courageous women who took part. We

knew they would stop us, that they would react. All these women – mostly doctors, professors, teachers – they were stopped from working, banned from travelling. They published our names everywhere. It was a horrendous period.

If you are not mobile, you cannot develop

Mobility, whether it's physical or mental – this is a necessity. Women, or men for that matter – if they are not mobile, they cannot develop. If you want to go the library, you want to learn, you want to go to school, you want to work, you want any kind of independence, you need the ability to get there.

This is not a luxury. You know something, I don't even like driving! I drove in the US, and it meant nothing to me. But there are women in this country who cannot get their basic human necessities, you know, getting help, medication, getting to the hospital, taking their children to school.

For me, I am a practical person; you have to practise what you preach. You can write a hundred, a thousand articles and people will say, 'Oh, beautiful, fantastic!' and they'll retain something from it, but not all. Nothing will really change. But if you have something concrete, if you have built something or done something, it remains for ever. That's how I see it.

The Bedouin would cover their faces for protection

I don't cover my face. It's not part of the culture in all Saudi Arabia's regions; neither is it part of Islam. The *niqab* may have been traditional to certain tribes; the Bedouin would cover their faces for protection, from the sun, wind and heat and so on, but it certainly never applied to all of Saudi Arabia. This has all been manufactured and imposed by a minority who have interpreted the texts in their own way.

If you look at old photographs of women from the south or the east of Saudi Arabia, they wore straw hats, a blouse and a skirt and that's it. There is no place in the *Qur'an* that mentions covering the hair at any point.

The Prophet Mohammed did not talk about it. His wife, Aisha, led a war! I certainly don't believe she did so from behind a veil.

How are you supposed to raise a child who is also your master?

Of course a woman doesn't need a guardian. There's a confusion between the idea of a *mahram*, which in Islam is just any kin you cannot marry, and a guardian, which is entirely a legal creation. It's based on the assumption that a woman is less mentally able than a man, and therefore needs someone to protect her and help her make decisions.

I even commissioned a sheikh – he's an ex-judge – to do a research paper on the subject. What came out of it is that it has nothing to do with *Sharia*, now or in the past. Even pre-Islam, it just didn't exist.

But now, if a woman wants to get legal papers or a passport or a national ID, travel, whatever it is, she needs a man. And if she isn't married, but she has a son who's fifteen years old, then he becomes her guardian. How are you supposed to raise a child who is also your master?

I always say, the only women who give birth to their own guardians are the women in Saudi Arabia.

A woman rarely chooses to share a husband

We have big families here in Saudi Arabia. It's not so much that there's pressure on women to have a lot of children, but for uneducated and unemployed women who stay at home, well, what does she have to do? Give birth and eat – that's it. You won't find a teacher or a school principal who has twelve or fifteen children.

I don't think an educated women would accept sharing a husband either. I think women in general refuse this; it's rarely what a woman chooses for herself unless she's been indoctrinated to accept it or her financial situation makes it necessary.

They've also developed these kinds of marriages, not only in Saudi Arabia, that they call temporary marriages, *misyaar*. A man marries a woman so he can legally spend the weekend with her, then he has it annulled. It's just a form of prostitution, that's how I see it. And, even worse, it's the man's choice, not hers.

They have shown that they're far more courageous than the men

I think many people have misconceptions about Saudi women. Yes, there are restrictions and she doesn't yet have her full rights. But there is a certain percentage of Saudi women who have broken the barriers, and we are proud of them.

And we *should* be proud of them – those who did not submit. They have proven that they are far more courageous than the men. The renowned scientists who have come out of Saudi, the Saudis climbing Mount Everest, they are women. More Saudi women have held UN posts than Saudi men.

They are very strong, and this strength came out of the restrictions placed on them. It builds in them a power to resist. The way they are being treated here, it gives them more determination to excel, to do something out of the ordinary.

We must develop in our own way

Communication has revolutionised everything. It's incredible; I can't keep up with it! It's made not just Saudi Arabia, but the whole world, one village.

I hope that we will keep changing and opening up to the world. But we must develop in our own way, not just to please the East or the West! We will learn from the Americans, the

Japanese, the Germans, everyone. But we only need take what works for us.

As for women, I hope for my great-granddaughters that they have all their rights, that they don't feel discriminated against culturally. That they don't live under guardianship, that they are completely financially autonomous. I wish for them that they are free.

WHAT WOULD HAPPEN IF WOMEN RULED THE WORLD?

I believe that women are more humanist than men. Because we bring life to the world perhaps, we tend to be more concerned with protecting it than destroying it. So women have it in their genes to be more loving, kinder. But that doesn't mean they are not strong enough to be leaders.

I'm sure they would still have their fights, their disagreements, but I cannot believe they would be as territorial, as vicious as men. A woman will not point a weapon until one has been aimed at her.

THE PRISONER

LOUJAIN

Activist, aged twenty-nine, Riyadh

Arguably the most prominent activist of her generation, Loujain Al Hathloul gained international attention in 2014 when she attempted to cross the UAE–Saudi border behind the wheel of her own car. She was incarcerated for seventy-four days on terrorism charges. She was arrested again in May 2018, along with a number of other human rights activists. At the time of publishing, she remains in prison. Her location and the specific charges against her have never been disclosed.

I don't think men and women are so different

I've always wanted to be a man – always, since I was a child. My male guardians have been angels to me, and as a child I was educated in France, so I know I've had it much easier than most Saudi women. But still, I could not help but immediately notice the difference between me and my siblings. The way my relatives whispered about my trousers when we returned to Saudi, how my hair and my voice caused a scandal in public places, or the fact that when my parents started sending my brothers abroad for summer schools – to London, to the US – I was left behind.

You can say it's great to be looked after financially, that it's cool to be driven around, but those benefits come at the cost of your independence. It's only cool if your family is extremely kind, balanced and supportive. I have been exceedingly lucky.

When it comes down to it, I don't think men and women are so different. What you achieve really depends on how you're educated, how you're raised and what your society expects from you.

I couldn't just wait to be given my rights

My father was in the navy, and he had this fear of his children being surrounded by water but not knowing how to swim. The only public swimming pool was for men, so when I was three years old, he put me in a pair of my brother's swimming trunks and took me along. The men were scandalised: 'How dare you bring a half-naked girl in here!'

But my dad just looked at them and said, 'If you're aroused by a little kid, then you really need to get yourselves checked. That's a pretty serious problem,' and threw me in.

After a few weeks, other fathers started bringing their own little girls. That was my first experience of a feminist movement. I guess I learnt pretty early on that I couldn't just sit there and wait to be given my rights!

I started vlogging when I was studying in Canada. I was a woman from the central region, from a well-known family, uncovered, speaking boldly about social and political issues. It was quite a phenomena I guess; people were interested.

Of course I've received a lot of abuse; most of it is cyberbullying. I would get threats; a lot of pictures of guns, all sorts of sexual content – videos of guys masturbating over my picture. They want to break you from the inside; it made me think of the way soldiers use rape during conflict.

At one point I was afraid; it was when I was in Canada and I was scared about how people would react to me when I got back to Saudi. But as soon as I landed, I realised that people only dared talk from behind anonymous accounts; they weren't courageous enough to confront me in real life. So I thought, *Okay, I'm stronger. Obviously I'm stronger. I'm the only one among all these men who is prepared to speak publicly.*

I didn't tell anyone what I was going to do until I reached the border

When I first started supporting the driving campaign, people said I was a hypocrite. I was studying in Canada at the time and they said it was wrong to push women to participate in such a dangerous activity while I was being protected by a Western country. I had to agree with them.

So three days before the 2013 protest, I landed in Saudi, and I drove myself home from the airport. My dad filmed the whole thing; he presented me as his daughter, gave my full name and laughed about how insane this would all look in ten years' time, that women were ever banned from driving.

But the next year we still weren't any closer, and that's when I came up with a plan to cross the border. While I was working in the UAE, I got a driver's licence. When I looked at it carefully, it dawned on me that it had the GCC[57] stamp on it. Any document that has this stamp is valid in all six countries of the GCC. I had found my loophole.

I didn't tell anyone what I was going to do until I reached the border. (It was only a week after I got married by the way; my poor husband.) But I didn't want anyone to be charged with being an accomplice. I made sure I had my own car for the same reason.

When I arrived at the border . . . well, the poor guys had no idea what to do. I had my licence, I was a Saudi citizen. The Minister of the Interior was abroad; there was no protocol.

---

57 Gulf Cooperation Council; member states include Bahrain, Kuwait, Oman, Qatar, Saudi Arabia and the United Arab Emirates.

It took them twenty-six hours to arrest me. I was expecting to be arrested. I was expecting to receive the same punishment as previous women, which was basically to be under arrest for a couple of hours, a maximum of twenty-four. I wasn't expecting terrorism charges.

But I have no regrets.

I decided to face jail with a positive attitude

I really enjoyed my time in jail. I got to spend time with women from a different social circle, a different region, a different sect (most of the inmates were *Shia* and I was *Sunni*). I decided to take as much as possible from it, to face it with a positive attitude. Since I had nothing else to do, I thought I might as well look on the bright side!

Honestly, the conditions are great; all the women are treated fine. We spent our days mostly playing games, watching TV. But the problem isn't the place, it's the legal system.

The majority of the women inside were there for 'prostitution', which I found quite shocking, especially considering a lot of them were under the age of twenty; not even real adults at this point.

I asked one of the employees one evening, as she was locking us in for the night, how old the youngest inmate to have stayed there was. She said ten years old. Of course I was surprised. I asked her what she had done, and she just gave me that look, the look of shame that says, 'I can't say, but you understand.' I don't think any ten-year-old belongs in jail. She's a victim, not a criminal.

It doesn't matter if you live in Paradise in jail, not as long as the legal system is broken.

Today, a guardian can't protect you

At the time of the Prophet, a *mahram* was required because of the intensity of life, the hardship, how vulnerable women might be if they left their towns alone. It's understandable. But today, if you're confronted by a criminal waving a gun at you, a *mahram* wouldn't do much. It's obsolete.

My dad tried to protect us from the reality of it as much as he could. I didn't have to confront my parents for the right to education, travel or work; my documents were prepared without me asking. But it didn't make me any less aware that I could have everything faster, more directly, if only I were a man.

As my dad got older, I would fill out the papers myself and he would just sign. And I would cry every time because I felt humiliated every time. To be an adult and still be seen as incapable in your own country . . .

You're not even capable of committing your own crimes. The first time I was arrested for driving, it was my father who was called into the Ministry of Interior. He was the one who had to sign the pledges and apologise for my actions. It infuriated me; it's an indirect way of disregarding women's existence and their movement.

Romance is a pleasure to be enjoyed in secret

Do people date in Riyadh? Who *doesn't* date in Riyadh? It's always existed – all those old Arabic love poems came from somewhere – it's just not accepted in public. Romance is a pleasure to be enjoyed in secret.

My marriage was very rebellious; I met Fahad on Twitter! It certainly wasn't the traditional way, but for our generation, it's becoming more common. The internet has made things a lot easier, for men as well as women; remember, if we can't meet them, they can't meet us! And they fear for their reputations just like we do.

And there are other changes. Polygamy is much rarer now; it's less socially acceptable and I think fewer people can afford it! I know a lot of women from my mother's generation who actually sought out second wives for their husbands. Perhaps she didn't want a divorce, perhaps she couldn't bear children, so she found another wife to save the marriage.

The most negative caricatures attract the most attention

Last year I agreed to participate in a documentary that promised to show the world the 'real' Saudi Arabia. It was a disaster; the final documentary was shameful. They sensationalised it to the point that they endangered me.

Unfortunately, the journalists who attract the most attention are the ones who produce the most negative caricatures of Saudi Arabia. Which is unfortunate, because the country is changing and we are changing as people.

I don't think the West has reached Utopia either. They still have a lot of issues to work on; they still have the wage gap, they still have domestic violence – like everywhere in the world.

The great advantage women in the West have is access to established and well-equipped NGOs that know how to participate in the public arena. That is not the case in Saudi yet. Here, activists are viewed as dangerous, as criminals; we certainly aren't seen as reformers.

I want to see deeper change

If I have a daughter, I would hate for her to reach an age where she could clearly understand her reality, her surroundings, without there being a clear change in the system itself.

I'm not talking about visual change – that's already happening; you see women covering less, men and women mixing in public more, more cultural events, but it's all still quite superficial. If you go deeper into the system itself, it hasn't improved enough yet; women are still inferior to men.

So I'm hoping for a more in-depth change, a change that would actually permit women – and men – to empower themselves in this country: in education, in the workforce, in political participation.

IF YOU COULD CHANGE ONE MISCONCEPTION ABOUT SAUDI ARABIA, WHAT WOULD IT BE?

That we are barbaric! We're not. We're actually very nice people! The outside world tends to view us all as brutal terrorists or masochists.

But there is a really beautiful side to the Arab world; you see it in our social life. We are a warm people, we are welcoming, we help each other. I lived for a time in Vancouver and I had the most wonderful experience, but I couldn't stay any longer because, to me, the people are too closed. I feel I belong more to the East than the West.

THE POLITICIAN

HODA

Shura Council member, aged fifty-seven, Riyadh

Hoda Al-Helaissi was one of the first cohort of thirty women to be admitted to the Kingdom's Shura Council, the highest consultative assembly in Saudi Arabia's absolutist monarchy. She spent part of her childhood in the UK due to her father's diplomatic posting, but returned to her homeland as a young adult. A former university lecturer, she is now serving her second term on the Council as a member of the Committee for Foreign Affairs.

The same tired clichés

'My name is Hoda Al-Helaissi, and I am not a terrorist.' That's how I sometimes open my talks. I was at Cambridge University a year or so ago, addressing all these bright young students, but unfortunately, because of what they read in the papers, because of the way our country is portrayed, this is how they perceive Arabs, and more specifically Saudis, and therefore, this is how we have to speak.

The West views us through the same old stereotypical lenses created by the media. It's difficult to deal with because you hear it all the time – the *abaya*, the driving, women; it's the same tired clichés over and over again.

I do believe, though, that we are partly to blame, because we as a country have a role to play too. We're not representing ourselves as well as we should be. At the end of the day, all newspapers take their information from the Saudi Press Agency, and where there is ignorance, a lack of knowledge and understanding, journalists will fill the gap with whatever suits them.

But even then, I don't think we'll ever stop the sensationalist news outlets doing what they do. They will always look for the wild factor or the humiliating line of approach; it makes money for them and it is easier to paint us with the same brush they always have. I suppose that's part of our make-up now.

The bottom line is that I shouldn't have to defend the way I live. I don't have to justify my choices, the way I dress, the way I eat, what I eat, how I raise my children. I don't go to the UK or the US and say, 'You're doing it all wrong!' It's none of my business.

I'm more than willing to explain, but I do object to being bombarded with accusations and insults; or the assumption that the system that works well in one country can be imposed neatly in Saudi Arabia, without taking any of our differences — religious, cultural, traditional — into consideration.

It's like going into your house and saying, 'Change the colour of the walls, change the curtains, pull up the carpets. You're so out of fashion. You're living in the Middle Ages. We need to bring you into the twenty-first century because the way you live your life is all wrong!' To that I would like to respond, 'Well, this is the way we're doing it, and we'll reach our goals by ourselves, from within society, in the time it takes us to get there, and without external interference.'

There is no one society in the world that is so exemplary and trouble-free that its model and value system should be universally imposed on other societies.

Everything is possible for women, given sufficient time

Growing up in London, I was like any other teenager: into movies, friends, fashion, travel; everything I think all young girls were into and very little to do with politics. I did have aspirations to carry on with my studies, of going as far as I could in that regard. But to end up where I am today was never in my head.

The fact that women would join the Shura Council was never implausible to me though. I think anything is possible in this country given sufficient time. And I do believe it is just a question of time. The development, the way things change inside Saudi Arabia – it happens at the pace it takes for Saudi women and society to accept that change. It is part of the evolutionary process of Saudi Arabia, just like any other country has its own evolutionary mechanism to continually reach a modernity that is specific to that particular country.

Ultimately, I believe there is nothing a woman is incapable of doing. Whatever profession she chooses as a career, it's her choice. I really don't believe there's anything a woman isn't capable of, given the proper opportunities and environment.

We're not there just for show

The first year on the Shura Council was very, very difficult. King Abdullah wisely introduced the idea of women joining the Shura a full year before we came in, so society had time to understand and assimilate the idea. But that didn't stop people from making negative comments or from insulting these thirty women. Social media was very tough on us.

But with time, our skins thickened; we managed to understand the ins and outs of the system and to really move forward with our ideas, the way we talk, the way we present issues.

I know that the international media has presented our

inclusion as some kind of token gesture for women's rights, but believe me, we're not there just for show; we're not a vase with flowers in it. We enjoy exactly the same level of influence, rights and respect as our male counterparts. And we're not just dealing with 'women's issues' either, if there is such a thing. You have women bringing expertise from so many different sectors; we work in every area of Council, and we work extremely hard.

By the second year, I believe, the president of the Council actually said on public television that ever since women were appointed, they've raised standards to the point that even the men are absent less often; they've become more animated.

Some of our male colleagues have jokingly told us, 'You know, we were pretty relaxed before you came. Now we have to work harder,' so we keep them on their toes!

Young women want to lead

To all the young Saudi women who want to join the Shura Council, or run for local council or head their own companies, my advice is: 'Don't stop dreaming! Get out there and do it!' But work hard, give back to society and remove the feeling of entitlement from the equation.

And we are definitely seeing more women in leadership roles because more women are prepared to fill them. We're seeing more leadership initiatives in our schools and universities – anybody who's ever taught knows there's always a leader in the classroom.

Then there's the fact that young women today understand what's going on in the world much more than previous generations; they want to be involved, they want to make a success of themselves. There's a motivation to become stronger, better people, better leaders.

And it is important that we have more women in these positions; they bring a human touch which is an important factor in leadership, and one that I think sometimes men tend to leave out of the equation. Plus they understand that they have to doubly prove themselves; firstly as a woman and secondly as a leader.

A woman in a veil has the same ambitions as any other

I think that more and more women are now showing the outside world that, yes, there might be an *abaya*, there might be a scarf, but there is also a face behind that. And there is a brain, and a competent woman capable of going about her day-to-day life. It's foolish to believe that just because a woman is wearing an *abaya*, she doesn't have a voice or she doesn't have the same ambitions as any other woman. She definitely does! And I think it's very important to always emphasise that.

Covering my hair does not limit my participation in the Shura Council. We are not separated from the men during the sessions and when we meet in our committees, we sit down face to face with our male colleagues. If a woman prefers not to meet in the same room as the men for a meeting, she has the option to be in a separate room and participate in the meetings through a voice or video link – it's entirely her choice, a choice that is to be respected and also one that does not hinder her or our work.

People often claim that the wearing of *hijab*, or indeed the separation of men and women, is a form of discrimination against women. But if you really think about what the word 'discrimination' means, you're talking about people who don't have their rights. We can take the example of African Americans in the US during the 1950s and '60s; people who were completely discriminated against, who didn't have a voice. Women do have a voice here, especially today. We have flaws in our system, no doubt about that, but we are not powerless. Gender segregation is not apartheid, and it's something that's evolving all the time.

Guardianship was intended as a form of protection, not prohibition

I would like to change the way the concept of male guardianship has been interpreted by the law. It can be extremely problematic, especially for women who are widowed, single, or are just of a certain age.

The system is too easily abused. Whereas, when it was part of daily life centuries ago, it was really to protect women. In the days of the Prophet, women had to travel from A to B on camels, and in the desert and the heat and the unknown, it was preferable for them to travel with a man for protection.

But now, we are no longer in the desert per se. We are capable of protecting ourselves; we raise and protect our children and, in one way or another, we protect our husbands too!

In Islam, guardianship is a form of protection and not prohibition, and all we need to do is see how the Prophet Mohammed's wives, peace be upon him and them, lived their lives. Yet today's interpretations and abuses have changed it to mean women are forbidden from doing certain things.

It's as if there was never a ban

In September 2017, it was announced that the driving ban would be lifted. The move has been made swiftly; driving schools for women were established, tests taken and licences given, and it's a fait accompli. It's as if there was never a ban. People talk very little about it here and the foreign media have stopped annoying us about it!

Family is at our core

Family is crucial to Saudi Arabia and I hope it's something we don't lose. Sadly, I believe we are losing it already, slowly, because we're having children later in life, getting married later.

Career comes first, out of necessity more than anything else. Nevertheless, the importance of the family is still at our core. I can't imagine life without my family. This feeling of belonging, of unity, it is part of our roots. I don't want to lose this and I know many people here feel the same. It's something very particular and very special in our society.

Development doesn't mean abandoning our culture

In some ways, in the past three decades we've actually gone backwards with regard to women's freedoms. There was a time when Saudi Arabia was more open socially, in terms of women's clothing, in terms of being out on the street.

Women were 'freer'. It wasn't until the 1970s, until after the Iranian Revolution in 1979 and the realisation that the same thing could happen here, that things started to change and become as we see them today.

In some areas we've come back stronger than before; women's education is a great example, where gender roles are reversed, and today we have more girls in university than boys!

And I believe that the changes in this country are going to be brought about through a younger leadership. Seventy per cent of the population is under the age of thirty, so it makes sense that they are going to change things, and it's going to happen quickly – faster than we think!

Development doesn't mean abandoning our culture. My children studied abroad, they travel a lot, and even though they accept what is outside and have adopted values they have learned and appreciated abroad, they always come back, bringing these values with them. This is because there is something that is extremely important to them here, and that is their own identity, which comes from them being Saudi and Muslim and understanding their background and their roots. There is no one template for modernity.

As for our relationship with the rest of the world, I want dialogue to be constantly open between us and the West. I want to see more tolerance and understanding on both sides. I would like to see – and I'm going to sound like a beauty pageant contestant – but I want to see peace in the world.

VOICES UNSILENCED

إن كنت ذا رأي فكن ذا عزيمة

'If you have an opinion, you'd better be determined'

—Arabic proverb

There is an oft-told anecdote regarding the late Saudi King Abdullah and Queen Elizabeth II. The story goes that the pair were finishing lunch at Balmoral when the Queen suggested a tour of the grounds.

What the then-Crown Prince did not expect was that the Queen herself would be their chauffeur. He spent the best part of the next hour swinging around in the passenger seat, hoping the car would slow down, as Elizabeth, who had served as a military truck driver during the Second World War, navigated the bumps and turns of the country estate.

His dismay was perhaps unsurprising. Back in his own country, not even his sisters or daughters were permitted behind the wheel. For decades, Saudi Arabia maintained the dubious honour of being the only nation on earth to prohibit women from driving.

The de-facto ban, which was implemented under King Saud in 1957, as the arrival of oil revenue was making vehicle ownership attainable to ordinary citizens, was maintained largely through the simple refusal of local government to issue drivers' licences to women.

Punishments for those who flouted the ruling varied from verbal warnings to both the woman and her guardian, accompanied by the signing of a written pledge not to repeat the offence, to jail terms, when the act of driving was deemed a public display of civil disobedience.

In a country with no inner-city public transport infrastructure, the ban left women entirely dependent on men to get around. Officially, the legal driving age in the Kingdom is eighteen; in practice, custom has it that the oldest male in the household is responsible for transporting his female relatives. The sight of a thirteen-year-old boy peering over the steering wheel while his mother and aunts huddle in the back remains a common, if disconcerting, sight.

When male relatives are otherwise engaged, women have relied on the services of private drivers to get them from A to B, be these privately employed chauffeurs or, more recently, Uber drivers. The irony of having to spend hours each day in a confined space with an unknown man, when their culture deems it immoral to spend more than a few minutes in the company of their future husbands, is not lost on all women.

Within the country, the ban has often been explained not as a constraint, but as a means of ensuring women's safety. Saudi Arabia, it is argued, is a huge and largely barren country. A woman driving alone would be left vulnerable if her vehicle broke down; the possibility of sexual assault is a recurrent concern.

'I prefer to have somebody drive me. I like
sitting in the back; I feel like a queen.'

HUDA, teacher

In addition to physical security, abstaining from driving has also been linked to a woman's moral standing. A woman who can come and go as she pleases without informing anyone of her whereabouts could find herself in any number of morally questionable situations. Even in the back seat, women are customarily shielded from public view by smoked glass, and sometimes even curtained from their drivers in front.

Finally, there remains a widespread belief that allowing women to drive will compound already dire traffic conditions in cities. The fact that women have already long been on the roads, albeit not in the driver's seat, has not been accepted as a valid counter-argument.

However, the ban has not stopped everyone. Outside the cities, the ban was always less strictly enforced; Bedouin families in particular take pride in teaching their daughters. 'They drive the water truck,' explained one Bedouin father. 'It's more practical in the desert; they drive to the lakes to fetch the water, or if anyone is sick they need to be able to contact neighbours or get to the doctor.' Even among city girls, many have been taught the basics when out in the desert with fathers and brothers.

The opinions of women themselves on the ban have ranged from those who found it to be dehumanising and a major obstacle to women's development; to those who considered driving as a token issue, of more interest to the Western media than themselves; and finally to those who viewed driving as a burden they were relieved to be free of.

Where they have stood on this spectrum is often linked to socio-economic status. While affluent families may enjoy the privilege of a private chauffeur, for low-income families and those without husbands or brothers willing to ferry them around, the world can become very small indeed. 'If they don't have a husband or a driver, they don't get out of their houses at all,' says student Hanan, 'they are always at home. Just once a week maybe they take a taxi. It's wrong, it's *haram*.'

'It's more than mobility, it's also an economic issue.
When a girl has to pay her driver every month,
you're essentially placing a mandatory tax on her
salary. She doesn't have any way around it.'

THORAYA, researcher

The driving ban was not the only government-backed regulation to affect women's lives, nor, some would argue, was it
the most restrictive. Nonetheless, for many years it served as
the most tangible symbol of the state's perceived oppression of
its female populace, both for the international media, and for
a small but determined number of women's rights advocates
within the country.

~

At 2.35 p.m. on 6 November 1990, forty-seven women gathered in a Safeway car park in Riyadh – but they weren't there
to discuss the weekly groceries. As the afternoon *asr*[58] call
to prayer rang out across the capital, the group piled into the
thirteen cars owned by those women holding international
driver's licences. Then, leaving their drivers to retrieve their
jaws from the supermarket forecourt, they pulled away into
the city traffic.

Participants recall mixed reactions from those who witnessed this modest but unprecedented act of defiance. Some
stared, some cheered them on, some cursed them; another
woman spat at them from the back seat of her own car. The
police reacted as expected, and the group was arrested.

They were not imprisoned; instead it was their male guardians who were summoned to the residence of the regional Emir

---

58 The third of five daily calls to prayer in Islam.

to explain the actions of their women. But the public backlash that followed was perhaps even more harrowing.

Branded whores, deviants, secularists and communists, the women were denounced by name from mosque pulpits and in widely distributed flyers – some received death threats. Socially and professionally ostracised, it was twenty-one years before women dared to protest again.

In 2011, information security consultant Manal al Sharif filmed herself behind the wheel of her car. She was arrested, and imprisoned for a week on the charge of 'driving while female', but a handful of other women uploaded their own videos in solidarity – a group that grew in the subsequent campaigns of 2013 and 2015 – although they never drove in unison again.

In September 2017, the years of struggle finally bore fruit. With the government's announcement that women's driving licences would be issued within the year, large swathes of the female populace rejoiced. Many of my interviewees who had previously justified the ban soon confessed that they were already applying for lessons.

On the stroke of midnight, 24 June 2018, female drivers poured onto the roads in all the Kingdom's major cities; many were greeted by police officers distributing roses. In the end, the transition was a peaceful one; it will also be gradual. The only women able to make immediate use of their new-found freedom were foreigners and well-travelled women with international licences.

'Once women start driving, they will have opened a door that can never be closed. Activism and demands for social change will boom, and they'll never be able to control it.'

—HUSSAH, activist

The majority of Saudi women will have to wait a little longer to take the wheel. 'I called them this morning,' secretary Tania told me breathlessly on the morning the ban was lifted, referring to one of the country's six female driving schools. 'They say the minimum wait for a class is seven months.'

Whatever the bumps in the road, with the promise of autonomous freedom of movement, at least within the nation's borders, other restrictions seem sure to crumble. At least that is what activists are hoping for.

~

Despite rapid progress in the fields of women's rights and freedom of information, any form of activism remains a risky pursuit. In the autocratic state, any manifestation of civil society or public demonstration, however peaceful, can result in harsh reprisals. As one activist put it to me, 'In this country, you're supposed to say thank you, you're not supposed to say please.'

> *'I'm happy. I'm living my life; I'm being supported; I'm*
> *doing what I like. Is that enough for me to be selfish, to tell*
> *you, "No, it's okay, all women are okay."? Absolutely not.'*
>
> —HAYA, photographer

The women who do say please, publicly at least, benefit in their majority from higher-status backgrounds, international education and, perhaps most importantly, understanding families. 'A lot of our activists have had to stop halfway because their families threaten them,' explained Hussah. 'They say, "If you don't stop we won't get your passport, we won't let you work, we won't get you a driver or whatever"; they're still not independent.'

Women are reluctant to label themselves as activists due

to the word's political connotations. Likewise, the term feminist is exercised with caution, given its popular associations with illegitimate children and other Western social 'ills'. 'I consider myself a feminist,' says researcher Thoraya, 'which is not an easy statement to make in this society; people think if you're a "feminist" you must be lobbying for homosexuality and promiscuity."

Those who campaign openly for women's freedoms are keen to stress their patriotism and desire to work *for* their country, not against it. The first step in any demand is usually a petition to the King or regional Emir.

It is worth noting that most of these women have the opportunity and the resources to pursue rewarding careers in countries where there would be no need to campaign for their basic liberties. When I asked one such advocate why she stayed, her answer was one of puzzlement: 'I'm part of the fabric of this society, and I'm a humanist; I work in humanities. My role is to try to make life better for people in my country.'

Nevertheless, their efforts are not always appreciated by the women they claim to be fighting for. 'Support for women's rights, it's not a matter of sex,' explains researcher Thoraya, 'it's people's backgrounds, their education, the way they were raised. We're dealing here with a mixture of culture, tribal community, religious influence, extremism; and it's all been accumulated in the subconcious minds of both men and women.'

In a patriarchal society with no history of activism or political opposition, and a deep, quasi-familial loyalty to the house of Saud, women who rock the boat are often labelled agitators, attention-seekers, or even agents of foreign powers.

'I don't like the way some of these "activists" are going about it, people like Loujain Al Hathloul, the one they put

in prison. She just took her car and drove. If you were a
mum and your child came to you and asked to go out and
you said, "No," and she went out anyway, how would you
feel? How can you trust me when I'm behaving recklessly?'

—WEJDAN, legal student

Neither has the state softened its stance on those who cross the line into perceived political activity, as was made clear in May 2018, when at least fourteen peaceful human rights advocates were arrested in a coordinated operation and accused of threatening social peace and order; many remain imprisoned at the time of publishing. Around the same time, pro-government publications started circulating images of those incarcerated with the word 'traitors' stamped across their faces.

To international observers it has been an unexpected and disheartening turn of events, not least because women's rights are the only area where an active civil society seemed to have gained a definite foothold; the movement has thus been broadly associated with a drive to strengthen human rights in general. But with arrests and incarcerations, some female activists have been able to shine a light on a largely invisible area of national life: women's experiences in the criminal justice system.

~

When Loujain Al Hathloul (see p. 255) attempted to cross the Emirates–Saudi border in her own car in 2014, she was not arrested alone. Her friend and supporter, the journalist Maysaa Alamoudi, was caught in the fray when she stopped to bring the activist food and sanitary supplies after she had been held in her car by border police for twenty-four hours.

Despite having no intention of joining the protest or crossing the international boundary in her own car, she was taken into custody together with Loujain and held on the same charges, citing a newly introduced counter-terrorism decree. 'I think she was the unluckiest person I've seen in my entire life,' says Loujain.

The pair faced identical charges and each served seventy-four days behind bars – albeit in quite different surroundings. Maysaa, aged thirty-three, was sent into the general prison population, but Loujain, aged twenty-five at the time, was confined to a juvenile detention centre. Men are tried as adults from the age of eighteen; women, usually from the age of thirty. 'I was treated as a teenager; she was treated as an adult.'

But Loujain is now too old to be considered a minor, even by a Saudi court. Following her 2018 arrest, she is reportedly being held at an adult prison in the nation's capital. Unconfirmed allegations of mistreatment and even torture of the female activists being held there suggest she may now be facing a considerably harsher environment.

Differing ages of adulthood are not the only discrepancy that she and others have noticed regarding the application of the legal system. 'There was one woman I was inside with whose case was about *zena*,'[59] says Amani, 23, who spent some time in juvenile detention following a family dispute. 'Her sentence was one full year with a hundred lashes. This is the Islamic punishment – it comes from the *Qur'an* – but it's supposed to be equal between men and women. She got the full sentence, with an extra fifty lashes not to repeat her crime; the man only got six months and the lashes were dropped.'

Perhaps the most infamous aspect of this gendering of the judicial system occurs once a woman has already served her

59 Unlawful sexual intercourse; may encompass adultery, sex outside of marriage and prostitution.

sentence. 'When they do in fact lock you up, you're not allowed to leave prison without your father or legal guardian to pick you up,' explains blogger Nouf. 'If they don't want to take responsibility for you, you can be in there for years.'

Conversely, some women reject their own guardians. Given the choice between remaining in prison or being released into the custody of a violent husband, some choose to outstay their terms. 'So they'll keep them in jail,' says social worker Lamees. 'Obviously they'll be treated as criminals because they wouldn't leave the prison – because they're in there.'

It is no coincidence that renowned activists maintain contact with international journalists and publications, and that they do so in English. It is much harder to disappear without trace when a hundred human rights organisations are chanting, and Tweeting, your name.

~

Before the arrival of the internet, all channels of communication within the Kingdom – television, radio, sermons broadcast from mosque minarets and sold on audio cassettes – were controlled by a highly conservative Wahhabi male minority.

The 1990s in particular have been referred to as 'the decade of silence'. 'The only access we had to the outside world was through long-wave international radio stations that broadcast in Arabic,' academic Hatoon Al Fassi has explained. In short, no alternative world views or interpretation of women's roles were available.

> 'When my mother was still at a village elementary school,
> she found a magazine in the top of a garbage bag. The cover
> shot was of a European blonde woman wearing a red dress.
> My mother thought she was an alien. She thought, Who

is this, and how can she dare wear this in public?'

—DINA, housewife

With access to a new world of ideas and information, women increasingly started to question the traditional religious justification for certain practices, including male guardianship, the wearing of the *abaya* and the driving ban. Many now hold their own opinions on what 'true *Sharia*' means to them. Crucially, through social media, they have also gained the means to share their conclusions.

While men have long had their own forums and associations to discuss personal philosophies and current events, women had been kept remarkably isolated – even from one another. But with the advent of online communications, they began to make contact.

'If we can succeed in bringing true Sharia *– yanee,
really – and put it into effect, this will be more
than even the women in the West have.'*

—AISHA, women's rights advocate

This increased awareness and opening to new possibilities coincided with the explosion of the Arab Spring in 2010. Saudi Arabia remained politically stable throughout this period, but its citizens were watching from the sidelines, and observed how social media, Twitter in particular, was used to impressive effect.

Today, Saudi Arabia has the highest proportion of internet users active on Twitter in the world. More than 40 per cent of all Twitter accounts across the MENA region are Saudi. A quarter of these are used on a daily basis, and publish an average of

five Tweets per day. 'If they had had Twitter in 1990,' says one
activist, 'can you imagine how that protest might have looked?'

In social media, women discovered a far-reaching and, crucially, anonymous platform to debate, organise and lobby for
change. Topics that were previously taboo have been brought
into the public sphere for discussion – and ordinary working-
and middle-class women have been invited to the table.

> *'Activists in Saudi only function through social media;*
> *that's how we connect, how we organise. It's not easy*
> *and it's not safe; we often have to change groups, change*
> *names; we only have trustworthy people among us. And*
> *when I say "we", I would like to point out that we are*
> *not just women! There are a lot of men involved too.'*

>   —HUSSAH, women's rights advocate

Of course, social conservatives know how to use social media
too, and their presence is just as visible. Not everyone is ready
for the reforms the country is facing; there are many conservative elements, male and female, who view the strengthening
of women's liberties as a dilution of the faith. 'And they may
continue with that,' says one women's rights advocate, 'but,
eventually, I always say, "You can't stop the wheel of change."
No way. The change is bound to come.'

For some, the route to that change is not via protest, but
through the system itself.

~

In 2013, thirty women filed into the ornate chamber of the
Majlis Al Shura, or Shura Council, the highest consultative body
of Saudi Arabia's theocratic monarchy, tasked with advising the
royal leader and drafting proposals for new laws. They were

appointed by the late King Abdullah himself, who also decreed that, from this point forward, women must always account for one-fifth of the 150-member assembly.

Since then, through hard work and professionalism, and in the face of considerable domestic resistance and international scepticism, these women have proven themselves and earned widespread respect in their society – even if, as a minority presence, they have been unable to substantially challenge the patriarchal status quo.

Two years later, in December 2015, Saudi Arabia became the last country on earth – with the important exception of the Vatican City – to invite women to the ballot box, permitting female citizens over the age of eighteen both to vote and run for office in the country's four-yearly elections for municipal councils.

But while news providers around the world dedicated headlines to this milestone in global women's history, at the scene of the story, the day passed with little commotion. There were no celebrations on the streets, no public ceremony. 'I didn't vote,' says student Maha. 'I don't think any of my friends did. Maybe I would if I could vote for a woman' – apparently unaware of the 979 female candidates who ran across the country.

The lack of excitement around the event may be attributed to Saudi Arabia's political culture, or lack thereof. Politics is still something of a taboo subject, rarely discussed at universities or in polite conversation. Saudi men had only gained the right to vote in municipal elections ten years previously and, to date, fewer than 15 per cent of all adults have registered to participate.

In the historic election of 2015, fewer than 15 per cent of those registered voters were women. When I asked a class of female university students why not one of them was registered to vote, the laconic reply was, 'Why, teacher? Even the men don't vote.'

For the first group of women brave enough to put themselves forward for office, working the campaign trail wasn't easy. 'I had to work day and night to pay for my campaign,' says researcher Thoraya, who ran, unsuccessfully, for a seat in her province. 'I did social media, posters, interviews, everything. The men who were running did nothing to campaign at all.'

Female candidates had to convince an often apathetic electorate not only of their policies, but also of their capacity to hold down such positions as women. The world of leadership and politics is considered an exclusively male domain – and not only by men.

However positive their evaluation of women's status and professional capabilities in general, when asked how a world might look under female leadership, the vast majority of my interviewees responded with almost the same phrase: 'Women are too emotional.' Men, I was repeatedly informed, are clearer-headed when it comes to making key decisions.

At the other end of the process, female voters grappled with a different set of teething problems. As part of its ruling on women's participation, the government had specified that they be permitted to register to vote without the consent of their guardians. But independent registration required the submission of a personal ID card and proof of home address; in a country where lease agreements and home bills are almost exclusively signed under the name of an adult male, it was no easy task. 'It was a nightmare,' said the sister of one candidate. 'I helped fight for this right – I had to vote – but my house was purchased by my father; everything's in his name. Nobody would give me anything.'

Despite the hurdles, it was with great pride and a sense of victory that almost 100,000 women succeeded in casting their ballots; and with even greater joy that female candidates were announced among the winners. 'Usually, across the world, women don't tend to win a lot of elections,' said one member of the Shura Council, 'so we are pleasantly surprised that we had twenty-one winners, and some from very conservative areas.'

But the battle didn't end at the polling booth. Successful female candidates entered councils as a very small minority in a highly conservative male environment. Some initially refused to sit at the same table with their new female colleagues, forcing them instead to participate via conference call from a neighbouring room. 'They wanted me to sit behind a glass screen,' sighed one councillor, 'it's so silly, I'm just there to work.' Another woman in a conservative province recounts receiving death threats. 'The worst of it is, I discovered it was a male colleague within the Council who had been giving out my phone number.'

While they are still working to hold their ground, their hard work and perseverance has already proven that the introduction of female candidates is not a token gesture. 'That's what people said when women joined the Shura Council,' says Council member Hoda, 'but believe me, the women and the municipalities, they're not for show; they're businesswomen and they're tough.'

~

Whatever the challenges faced, the visibility of women, even as a small minority, in positions of leadership and influence is an important step. To some extent, we all become what the world around us shows us we are capable of, and with half the country's population under the age of twenty-five, for a large section of female society, today's breakthroughs are their normality.

*'These young women, I call them the women of
hope — they are our hope for the future.'*

—AISHA, women's rights advocate

And as battle-hardened activists begin to witness that change is indeed possible, some vow to push for more changes, for both women and men. 'I'd like to see a lot more civic engagement, a real civil society,' says one young female activist. 'I'm not out to get rid of the Royal Family; keep the Kingdom. You want your name, you want your palaces; keep them. Let us steal the rest!'

THE INSTAGRAM QUEEN

MOUDI

Entrepreneur, aged twenty-six, Riyadh

Moudi is one of a new generation of women making their living and their reputations on social media. Through her Instagram business she has amassed almost 100,000 followers, making her a minor celebrity in the Kingdom's capital, although her true identity remains a closely guarded secret. Moudi is divorced and lives with her family in Riyadh.

When you're a girl, you're always under a spotlight

I think it's better to be a girl. It's better to be a girl, but it's easier to be a boy.

If you're a boy you can do whatever you want, go wherever you want; you don't even have to think about it. Just chill out, play video games, drive around with your friends.

When you're a girl, you're always under a spotlight. Everyone's watching what you're doing, what you're planning, what you've done in the past. Everyone is waiting to judge you.

But the truth is, women are smarter. They're better with money, they're better at planning for the future, and when they work, they don't just work for themselves. A woman works hard for her family, for her sisters. I think we're less selfish.

We can do anything a man can do; we only need the chance to prove it. I tell my friends, if they ever allow it, I want to train to become a soldier.[60] If it's my choice and I want to help my country, why not? I'm strong and I'm ready for anything!

We want to be gorgeous, we want to be confident

We women take care of ourselves; appearances are very important. We want to be gorgeous, we want to be confident, we want to feel like models. We feel more powerful when we know we've made an effort; it lifts us.

People wonder why we bother, I mean, we're always wearing a veil, right? But we don't show off on the street, we show off amongst ourselves – just us girls. It's like a challenge to see who can be the most beautiful.

And, well, even in a *niqab*, your eyes are still on show, so eyebrows, lids, lashes – it's all important. Perhaps that's why my business with the false lashes and coloured contact lenses has been so successful. Whether you're in a *burqa* or a mini-skirt, everyone uses what they have, right?

Hijab doesn't mean *niqab* and *abaya*

I started wearing a *niqab* when I was twelve. I took it off when I was twenty-one; I haven't put it on again since. I just decided I was old enough to take charge of myself. Anyway, I never believed in it; that you need a piece of fabric over your face to be a good person. You can't breathe in that thing. The first day I went out without it I felt great; I felt normal, like anyone.

My family, though, was furious. Well, my sisters didn't care, but my parents and my brothers didn't accept it. I don't know, they thought I was up to something. Now they don't talk about it any more, but my sisters haven't dared take off theirs.

Of course I still wear my *abaya* and *tarha*. If I don't, people are

---

60 In February 2018, the Saudi government announced that the army would accept female applications for non-combat roles.

gonna shout, they're gonna follow me. They'll think I'm crazy or an attention-seeker or both.

But I wouldn't wear them abroad. I think outside people would just look at me the same as anyone else. They're not gonna see my face or my body and say, 'Wow!' I'm not special; I'm just a woman like any other.

In Islam, *hijab* is important, but *hijab* doesn't mean *niqab* and *abaya*. There are other ways to dress decently and present yourself positively. I mean, I'm not going to go out in a bikini! But whether I wear an *abaya* or not, whether I cover my hair or not, I think that should be up to me.

She told me it was time to get married

My family married me off when I was twenty-one. I was so disappointed. I felt that my family didn't want me any more, that they were forcing me to leave.

They had tried a couple of times before, but I fought them and I always got away. But this time my mum came to talk with me and she played on my heartstrings. She told me that she wasn't able to take care of me any more, that it was time for me to get married. It was a pretty emotional conversation and I had a moment of weakness. I agreed.

My family thought he was a catch, you see. He was quite a well-known businessman in Saudi Arabia, and very, very rich.

Everything happened so quickly. I had the whole wedding prepared in a week, a huge Cinderella dress and everything. If you have the money, anything is possible. I could have done it in two days. I didn't feel any kind of excitement though; it was just something that had to be done.

I'll be honest, he treated me very well. I only had to text and he would bring me money or whatever it was I wanted. But he was so much older than me and he was never around. It wasn't a balanced relationship. And we couldn't have a baby.

We were only married for four months in the end. But that's not so unusual; I was wife number four. The fourth one, you know, they always swap that one in and out. And she's always the youngest. It's like we girls – we don't want just one handbag, right? We want two, three, four. Men are like this with women. And they have the option.

But, listen, I believe every time something bad happens to you, it opens another door. It's easy to feel sorry for me – it's easy to feel sorry for myself! – but now I look back on it as a success. It opened my eyes in a lot of ways. It made me realise that I have to be financially independent, that I have to make my family hear my point of view. I won't let anyone control me any more. I wouldn't have found that strength if I hadn't been so badly hurt.

I hope I will get married again. But this time I don't want a husband; I want a partner. And I want to choose him myself. If I allow him to share my life, he has to really share it, not just my bed. I won't share him with anyone else either!

Some women don't mind sharing a husband; she gets more time to herself that way. I didn't mind the first time; why should I? I didn't love him. But if I did, then no, I wouldn't allow it. You have to be a smart woman if you're not going to allow your husband to take another wife or two. But I know how to say no now; I know how to fight.

Not everyone has a good relationship with their guardian

Not everyone has a good relationship with their *mahram*. Maybe I don't get on with my brother; maybe I don't live with my dad. Maybe they don't want to spend time with me. But I'm still expected to take them everywhere I go?

I love Jeddah. I love going to the coast. I'm always dreaming of renting a small house there so my sisters and my girlfriends can take a little holiday. But I can't because I don't have a *mahram* around; I don't have that relationship with my dad. It doesn't matter that my mum and my auntie are with us.

A woman should be free to make her own choices, and to take responsibility for them. She knows right from wrong as clearly as she knows black from white. Isn't that enough?

If nowadays a woman can be a manager, can run a company, can sit on the Shura Council, why does she still need a *mahram* to rent an apartment?

Every time I see a woman driving, I feel proud

I've never driven a car, not yet, but I'll learn the first chance I get. Right now, all our money is spent on drivers – poof! – and a lot of women can't afford one at all.

People think we want this as some kind of luxury; that we just want to drive around with our friends like the boys do, playing music and showing off. But, *w'Allah*, I just want to take care of my stuff, get to work on time, that's it.

Every time I see a demonstration or a video of a woman driving, I feel proud. I think, *Yes! Go on and do it! Show them you can!*

They think we're fundamentalists, that we're violent

I know how people look at us. They think we're bad, we're fundamentalists, we're violent and all these things. They only see these negative stories in the news and on TV. They don't see a husband buying his wife a house and a car, a woman being taken care of.

They don't see that we're having fun and throwing parties. They don't see that we're living our lives, that we're doing whatever we want, even when it's not allowed. Nothing stops us!

Honestly, I think women here are treated a lot better than in the West. Over there I see how women are treated like anything; like a chair, like an object. I'm sorry, but that's what we see, that they're cheap for men. Not like us. Here a man knows that a woman is tough; even if he gets a phone number, he knows he's going to have to call her for three or four months before she agrees to meet – *if* she agrees to meet.

I think women here are viewed as more special in that way. You know how men are: when they can't get something, they want it even more.

I believe the Prince will deliver on his promises

My grandmother's world was very small; she stayed at home, she cooked, she visited family members. She certainly didn't have pink hair and make her own money like I do.

Life is getting easier. We travel more; people are becoming more open, even in my family. Women are educated now; they work, they shop, they study abroad. So many things. I think my daughters will have even more options, and I doubt they'll have a driver or a *mahram* to worry about.

It's only the older generation slowing us down, people in their fifties, sixties, seventies, eighties. These old men with influence. They don't respect our rights. They want everything to stay as it is; they're afraid of any kind of change.

But I believe that our King is very open. I believe that his son, Prince Mohammed, is very strong; he's going to make a lot of changes, too. He promised us driving, and it's come. I believe he will deliver on his other promises too.

WHAT IS THE MOST REBELLIOUS
THING YOU HAVE EVER DONE?

Once I went out dressed as a man. It was about five years ago; I put on a hoodie and covered my hair and walked down a street in the centre of Riyadh, just like a boy. Nobody noticed. I just wanted the challenge, to prove to myself I could do it.

THE MODEL

NOOR

Model, aged twenty-four, Dammam

Noor is one of Saudi Arabia's first female models. Passionate about fashion and photography, she has also found success as a blogger and stylist. She is currently completing her graduate studies in the field of fashion and design.

Fashion comes hand in hand with religion in this country

I know the Western world views us as totally non-fashionable – they only show the rednecks of Saudi Arabia, right? – but we're pretty into fashion. Women here, they're very proud of their Gucci, their Prada, their Isabel Marant. Seriously, sometimes it's something I've just seen yesterday on a Vogue runway edition. And they're wearing it today. It's pretty cool.

Really, I feel like fashion comes hand in hand with religion in this country. Just like people are super serious about their faith, it's the same kind of focus with their fashion – we're kind of fashion fundamentalists!

We deal with less pressure than European models

Modelling is a seriously grey area. It's not illegal per se, but it really depends on the situation you're in. If your photographer's a man, then it's illegal; if there are no men around but you've made yourself visible in public, it's illegal. I remember once I took my *abaya* off outside when we did a shoot in the desert by the main highway; I was terrified the whole time.

I think people don't know how to handle it because it's just so new here. For me, my mum was also very into photography, so I just grew up as her model. The process really intrigued me; I liked that I could express myself through emotions, not words. It's very empowering.

I was amateur modelling by the age of fifteen. At that time there weren't any studios. As a career, it just didn't exist. My first real job was with this European photographer; he lived on a Western-style compound, so we'd go there and shoot in secret.

It also meant there was really no competition at the beginning either, which I'll admit made it easier to establish myself. To uncover yourself, not just in public, but to have that image reproduced, was just totally unthinkable back then.

On the plus side, I do think we deal with less pressure here than American or European models, just in terms of staying skinny. Here they're focusing more on the fact that I'm exposing my face than what my body looks like. I had a photographer tell me to suck my belly in once; I never worked with him again. No, here it's all about the hair; I've never been pushed to lose weight, but I'm always being asked to get extensions. They want it long, thick and lustrous, baby!

In any case, I wouldn't want to express myself through nudity. Not only because of my religion, but just personally, I don't think it's necessary to go there to be successful.

But even without the bikini shots, yeah, there's been a reaction. I've had a lot of beautiful feedback from politicians, writers, photographers; mostly people in the arts. But a lot of criticism too.

My family has been harassed; they've been attacked on social media. My mother had to close all of her accounts; they would slut-shame me through her. They basically said I was a whore.

I wish they hadn't got to my family. If it was just me they were threatening, I would be a lot more excited to explore new things; acting for instance, or some more international modelling contracts. But the negativity that would bring my family, it's just not worth being in the spotlight that way.

But I'm happy that I was able to push societal norms. I like to think I opened the door to other girls. I think it's a way to open people's eyes to Saudi women in general because we are so rarely exposed. But when I model, I get to say, 'Hey, I'm a Saudi girl, look at me, this is what I can do! And I look just like everyone else – I *am* like everyone else.'

It's hard to be yourself behind a veil

Once you put the *niqab* on, I feel you kind of disappear; you just blend into the wall; it's hard to be yourself. Plus, I don't find the material breathable; I mean, you can smell your own breath in there – that's not something that anybody wants.

But there are certain places, like *souqs*, where you really do have to cover your face, just to stop men gawking. People here might be educated, but that doesn't always mean they're open; it doesn't mean they've been exposed to other cultures.

I wouldn't want to put myself in a situation where I'm exposed, standing in front of a man who's never seen a woman outside his immediate family and his television set. At the end of the day, men are usually stronger than us, and you never know what could happen.

But hey, on the plus side, sometimes I like the fact it's kind of a mask. If you're just not feeling it today, skip the make-up, throw on the *niqab* and check out.

Why do they think we'll be safer in a car with a stranger?

Dammam is a big city, and the traffic is crazy – I mean, it takes you at least forty minutes to get anywhere. I'm not going to lie to you and say I wish I could drive myself through all that and then spend another half-hour searching for a parking space. Honestly, I'm in no hurry to get my licence.

But for me that's just a question of convenience, not safety. I'm very lucky in that we've had the same driver since I was a kid; he's like an uncle, *w'Allah*. But a lot of women here have to rely on Ubers or unlicensed drivers.

They say if women drive, we'll be more exposed to rape or kidnapping. Why do they think we'll be safer alone in a car with a stranger? I knew a girl whose taxi driver said he was taking her home, but drove her into the desert instead. Luckily she was smart and he was stupid and she managed to diffuse the situation, but hers isn't the only case.

It's nothing to do with safety; it should be a woman's choice. It's insane. We've ended up in a situation where society is more accepting of seeing teenage boys driving than their mothers.

I'm a grown woman; I should be able to do as I please

Getting a permit to travel is a pain. It's a long process, and, you know, sometimes my dad is just not in the mood. I'm a grown woman, I'm twenty-four, I make my own money; I should be able to travel, drive and do what I please, without his consent.

And I'm one of the lucky ones; I consider myself very blessed that my dad is so open when it comes to me doing what I want to do. Within his terms of course.

But I know a couple of girls who've been raised by single mothers; they're very strong and very independent, but when they want to travel, their fathers refuse to sign, just to spite their mums.

Imagine this situation: I'm a mother, I'm very well established, I earn good money. I have three kids, and I get a divorce. I can't even get my own place to live. I need a male guardian to sponsor me, and if my ex-husband won't do it, maybe I have to ask my son, like, 'Hey, you came out of me, and now I need your permission to live my life!'

Of course not every situation is horrible; there are plenty of good people. But it's so easy to abuse. I mean, you wouldn't want any vindictive or angry person having power over you, right? But you don't get to choose.

Men tend to think they're kings

'You have to know how to please him! Cook for him, clean for him, he's going to love you for ever!' That's how a lot of women do think here, because of tradition, because of gender segregation.

And then Saudi men tend to believe they're the king of the household, a dictator in a sense. I mean, why wouldn't they? If you're a man, you can drive, you can smoke in the street – whatever you want; you're pretty much your own caretaker.

We need permission from our fathers to travel, handwritten approval from a guardian to work, a contract signed to rent an apartment; if you don't have a guardian in your life, you're pretty much screwed.

Maybe a woman is better at cooking, at running the household, but that's obviously not all she's capable of. In terms of what we can contribute, really, I think we're all equal. When you go to the doctor, you don't care if they're male or female, as long as they can help you fix your problem. It doesn't matter if your teacher is a man or a woman, you just want someone who gets the point across, right?

If you'll date a guy, you're not fit to be a wife

You can't even get a coffee in Starbucks unless you're in the female line. Segregation is everywhere, and I feel like it's caused a lot of trouble in terms of men and women understanding each other, or even knowing how to interact.

It's why you get so many girls dating girls. They're not exposed to men (in more conservative households they're not allowed out of the house except to go to university), so in the end they're just more interested in what's in front of them. I really don't blame them for trying to fill that void; they're just looking for intimacy.

Of course girls and boys do meet. I mean, I know a lot of girls who have boyfriends and hang out with them all the time. But never in public. Everything has to be underground and discreet. And you're still taking a risk – with your reputation and with your heart. There are plenty of men here who feel that, if you'll date a guy, you're probably not fit to be a wife.

I would like to get married at some point in my life. Honestly, I wouldn't mind if my family arranged it, so long as I had the opportunity to get to know him, to explore this person before I married him. I would be totally open to something like that.

Unless of course he had a problem with me modelling and wanted to keep me hidden at home. Then he can go f*** himself.

They think we're terrorists

I think people look at Saudi women as . . . savages. Is that a good word? It's entirely negative; they just see us as these black, ghostly figures – grim reapers even. There's no sense of identity there whatsoever.

They think we're terrorists. To me that's the saddest part. Just at the airport – the way you're searched, the way they root through your personal stuff. You see it's not the same with other travellers.

It's probably true we're very hot-headed – I put that down to the climate! – but I wish people saw the warmth and hospitality here too. It doesn't matter if a family has never met you before; by the time you leave they'll have fed you so much you won't be able to stand.

In the end, we're really not so different from anyone else. We're all human; we all eat, sleep, drink and try to enjoy ourselves a little. I wish people could hold onto that idea a bit more, rather than what they see on the television.

We're not afraid like we were before

Once upon a time, it was okay for Saudi women to talk to men, for women to host men at home without *abaya*s on; there were no *abaya*s. Women wore bright colours, eyeliner was a must, and they rode their camels wherever they wanted – no driver required.

I come from a Bedouin family, and that's the kind of life my grandmother lived, perhaps fifty years ago. There was a belief that a Bedouin woman was strong; she could handle herself in a difficult situation. Women were more independent then. There was a saying: 'A good woman is worth a thousand men!' Not exactly the way we're seen now.

But the interesting thing about Saudi is that, when change happens, it happens fast. Ten years ago, women didn't really have a voice. Now we can express ourselves freely on social platforms; we're not afraid like we were before. I hope by the time I have daughters the guardianship will have been abolished and there'll be no need for an *abaya*. All these basic things you just don't even think about in other countries.

For myself, my dream is to be a fashion editor, to collaborate with designers, and to be a Saudi fashion icon – one of many,

I hope! And why not? I think as we grow up, we start to let go of our dreams; we're convinced that they're not 'realistic'. But if you translate your dreams into goals, step by step, you can get there. In the end, other people have made it. Why shouldn't you?

THE FILMMAKER

AMANI

Filmmaker, aged thirty-one, Jeddah

Amani is one of a growing number of Saudi women working in media. She trained in film and scriptwriting in the US, and since then has maintained a popular presence on YouTube and at regional film festivals with her documentaries and short films on local life.

The man walks in front and the woman walks behind

When I was a child, my mother would cut my hair short so I could go out with my cousin and play football, or rent videos, or just play out on the street without anyone harassing me. At that age I was very active; I didn't want to be stuck at home. I hated dolls and make-up made me feel like a clown.

I felt very conflicted; I seemed to like the same things that boys liked, so did that make me a boy? We have such specific gender roles, I didn't know where I belonged. It took me a long time to understand that a man can love to cook and still be a man, that a woman could love comfortable clothes and playing sports and still be a woman.

Now my hair has grown back, but some things haven't changed. Even back then, I immediately recognised that it was better to be born a boy than a girl, that much was clear. Boys are favoured from the minute they're born; they enjoy freedom of movement, they can work, they are supported by the law. Simply put, they have all their rights.

I think it's very unhealthy for society. The man walks in front and the woman walks behind, physically and figuratively. You're immediately rewarded just for having male genitalia; you don't have to work for your goals, you don't have to compete. It's not good for either gender; it's not even good for the economy.

But we women do have one advantage. While men are still being pushed by their families and peers towards careers in engineering or law (things that make money), they shy away from creative arts. When it comes to women, society is much more comfortable with us working in 'soft' industries. People are always telling me it's so unusual to hear of a female Saudi filmmaker, but I was inspired by the women before me; Haifa Mansour is a woman. Women are breaking into the industry much faster than men, and they're finding their voice here. I definitely have.

It's not common to find anyone with a camera on the street

It was very weird for people to find a woman with a camera on the street; you get harassed. Actually it's not so common to find anyone with a camera. Filming on the streets is illegal in Saudi Arabia. If you want to film in public, anywhere, you need a licence from the Commission for Audio Visual Media; you have to present your project, your scripts and then it takes around two months to be approved. After that you'll need maybe three weeks to confirm your shooting location.

You also don't have any actors. This can work in your favour; often when you work with people who have never acted before, they perform very well, very naturally for the first time. But finding women who want to act specific characters, finding men who are willing to work with you – that's not easy.

And then, if you want to make films that touch on social or political issues, you have to work with a great deal of sensitivity. The idea is communicated very subtly. But that's something I love about film: you can fuse it with your intention, and people understand, even if you don't say a word.

That beating heart we're missing – it's just covered with fear

We're a conservative society by mistake, you could say. There was a political miscalculation in the past, whereby education was handed to a group of people who were highly conservative; who were extremist.

That's why we don't have cinemas.[61] In the past, even photographs were considered *haram*. When you add to that the fact it's a mixed environment – men and women sitting together in the dark – it all became very taboo.

I think this extremist thinking is really the core of why women's rights haven't moved forward. Women, culture, art – all of that. That beating heart we're missing, it's just covered over with extremism. With fear. We have to shed the fear.

So the film industry is still extremely young for us; I couldn't say we have our own identity yet. But, you know, if we had one, it would be comedy. *W'Allah*, every time I share a new idea, the response is always, 'Great, but, that topic's really taboo. You should make it a comedy!' It makes difficult subjects easier for people to digest. Everyone in Saudi Arabia is a comedian.

As a guardian, your woman belongs to you

When I went to study in the US, my brother was sent with me. I was told I couldn't travel alone because I needed to be protected. This didn't seem irrational to me, so while I was

---

61 The first-ever public Saudi cinemas opened in spring 2018.

out there, I signed up for self-defence classes. I loved it; I felt powerful, I felt strong. So I went back to my father and asked him again for permission to travel, but still he refused. That's when I started to question what this *mahram* thing was all about.

If you imagine leaving a camp in the middle of the night with hundreds of men on camels, you would want to be protected in some sense, physically. But that just doesn't apply now. Look where we're sitting now – there's a security camera right there.

This idea of a legal guardian, it's part of that extremist culture. From an Islamic standpoint, your *mahram* was never intended to control you, to work against you.

But that's how it is; as a guardian your woman belongs to you, like a thing you can move around. So if you're a man and you're angry, you blame the woman for how you're feeling. If you're angry with her, you hit her. If you resent her, you cover her. There are no clear boundaries between you as human beings; he is you and you are him. It shouldn't work like that.

I respect my country, so I cover my body, I cover my hair

Hijab is meant to protect me. Did I need protection in the US? Were people going to gawk at me if I was uncovered? No. So I didn't put it on. It's as simple as that. I don't do things unless I understand the reason; I'm aware that certain customs have been integrated culturally into our faith that weren't originally demanded by the religion.

When I'm in Saudi, I do cover. I want to be comfortable; I want to feel safe. I know in some countries you could walk around naked and no one would look at you. But in Saudi, this is our societal norm, and I want to respect my country, so I will cover my body, I'll cover my hair. But does anyone force me? No.

But I swear, there are signs in our country – in certain

areas – that tell a man to 'Cover your women!' Because you're not a man if you don't. This is a culture, it's as blunt as that. If you were really to have an honest conversation with a regular Saudi man, he would tell you to your face, 'How would I be a man, if she is not covered?'

I don't want a surprise for a life partner

Boys and girls don't need to be segregated, they don't. Boys and girls are, by nature, innocent. When you separate them, you're telling them that there's something wrong with the other sex. They become emotionally detached from one another; they don't know how to behave around each other, how to interact.

And so you end up with a situation where men are aroused by the shadow of a woman, and women lose all sense of identity and self-esteem at the glimpse of a man.

I always say – only half joking – that in the end, Saudis learn their ideals of love from Egyptian movies. All that slapping, that drama, that, 'I love you!', 'I hate you!', 'I own you!' – all of that objectification is there in their psyches. Romantic love becomes very warped; it becomes demonised.

But I think it's very important to get to know your husband before you get married. I don't want an arranged marriage; I don't want a surprise for a life partner! What if we're not compatible? What if he's crazy? I know people who have been together miserably, for twenty, thirty, thirty-five years in arranged marriages, and it's just tragic because they had no idea what they were doing.

They can't separate; they're too comfortable. Or more often the woman simply doesn't have the means to finance herself.

They think we're lying if we say we're strong

When I was studying in the US, I got the same questions all the time: 'Are you a terrorist?', 'Do you have oil in your house?',

'Do you ride camels?', 'How did you leave your house without a man?' All the time. People found it hard to relate to me; they couldn't imagine we might have something in common.

People outside, they really have no idea about what's going on here. It's enough for them that we don't drive. They think we're lying if we say that we're strong. They probably think, *Poor things, they don't know what they're talking about.*

But if I could change one idea about Saudi women, it would be that. I'd like to tell people that they are strong, that they're human; that they are extremely introspective, intellectual, patient and tolerant. They have tolerated a lot.

But we all have our battles. You know, when I was in the US, I noticed that women are sexually objectified there, infinitely more than in Saudi. In the media, in advertising, in the clothes they are encouraged to wear – they are treated like objects, like sex objects. In Saudi Arabia, you are dehumanised, but you are not sexualised.

That is something I find hopeful for the era we're living in. If we can get our voices heard, I think we can skip the sexualisation; we'll just be humans. Humans who have been working to improve themselves and prove themselves for a long time. Then I think you'll see us rise higher than the men.

We can't be seen in such a negative light for ever

I'm so grateful to my grandmother. She protected me; she gave me room to be myself. She respected me as a human being and she gave me the space to blossom. She educated me.

At the same time, our lives are absolutely incomparable. I was exposed to the world. If I hadn't been, I wouldn't have understood my rights as a human being; I would still be in her shoes.

It would never have entered her or my mother's head that they could make movies. Honestly, five years ago it wouldn't have occurred to me. But history is unfolding all around us. I was just reading about Saudi jazz musicians playing in public! I couldn't believe they were talking about Riyadh. I would be harassed just for walking the streets a year ago. How has all this happened in six months? It's incredibly inspiring.

So I'm looking to the future of film in Saudi Arabia with great optimism. It has to boom; it's our soft power. We can't be seen in such a negative light for ever. It doesn't help us economically, politically, socially – even in a military sense. We have to make our own local media, we have to produce our own cinema. It's about more than entertainment.

POPULAR CULTURE 2.0

'*Music is* haram . . . *but I like it*'

—GHAIDA, student

It is the intermission at one of Saudi Arabia's first-ever public entertainment events – a stand-up comedy show by an international artist held in a makeshift venue on the outskirts of the capital. Inside the canvas auditorium, the audience is divided: white *thobe*s to the left, black *abaya*s to the right, neatly separated by a waist-high partition.

But outside, the refreshments area has become a joyfully grey area. Young men and women apprehensively approach one another during this rare opportunity to mingle in public; some young men even show off their breakdancing moves – in full national dress – to the pop tunes emanating from the DJ booth.

Except it's not a DJ booth – at least, it's trying not to be. The decks, speakers and surrounding barriers are carefully adorned with stacked boxes of a popular breakfast cereal, for which staff distribute coupons, insisting it's nothing more than a promotions stall.

The Kingdom's complicated relationship with the public expression of arts and culture links back to its roots in the

Wahhabi interpretation of Islam, whose teaching, in the words of activist Manal Al Sharif, 'was based on the principle of forbidding not only that which is explicitly sinful, but anything that might eventually lead one to commit a sin'.

There is a *hadith* that condemns the players of stringed instruments – and so it came to be understood that the playing of any music, beyond voice and percussion, was *haram*. Consequently, restaurants and gyms operate largely in silence; radio stations fill their airtime with debates and talk shows interspersed with melodic *Qur'an* recitations.

> *'I was going to Zumba classes at the uni gym, but*
> *they got cancelled . . . Some of the security ladies*
> *came in with a big pair of scissors while we were*
> *dancing and cut the cable to the loudspeakers.'*

DALAL, student

Visual arts are also problematic. Certain interpretations of scripture prohibit the graphic reproduction of human or animal forms, as the artist is deemed to be imitating the work of the Creator; school art classes rely heavily on crafts and still life. The permissibility of photography continues to be debated.

Informal cinemas that had started to proliferate, at least for male patrons, in the 1970s were permanently shuttered in the early 1980s with the revival of strict Wahhabi-Salafi ideology, on the basis that they promoted foreign behaviours and ideologies and could encourage gender mixing.

In the public sphere at least, Saudi Arabia can appear creatively barren. The country's capital is culturally exceptional in its total absence of theatres, opera houses, established art galleries and statues. But statistics drawn from the private sphere tell a different story.

Saudis are the most prolific users of YouTube in the world; in 2018, billionaire Prince Alwaleed signed a $250 million deal with music streaming service Deezer; young women are avid Instagram users and home cinema systems are commonplace.

At the root of this sometimes bewildering duality between declared conservatism and lived modernity is the country's rapid opening to the world through modern media and, especially, the belated arrival of the World Wide Web.

~

When telephones were first introduced to the Kingdom in the early 1930s, rural inhabitants were convinced that such an astonishing invention could only be the work of the devil. King Abdulaziz was forced to arrange for a clerk in Mecca to read verses from the *Qur'an* down the line to his Bedouin subjects before they would agree to use it; the logic being that any creation of Satan would not be capable of carrying the holy text.

The impulse towards suspicion of innovation was repeated with the arrival of the radio and then television; when satellite dishes started appearing on the Riyadh skyline, a good number were shot down by overzealous youths with rifles. Later, when personal computers started to become available, women specifically were prohibited from being trained in the use of these strange Western machines.

So it was with predictable wariness that the Kingdom opened its gates to the virtual world at the turn of the millennium. Pornographic sites, as well as those critical of Islam or the government, were censored. Bandwidth to video messaging platforms like Skype, where political or romantic liaisons might conveniently be convened, was severely constricted.

But despite these precautions, after decades of global isolation, the arrival of the internet was revolutionary. Close to 75 per cent of the population are now active internet users; even in rural areas young people now follow pop culture and Tweet daily; Bedouins seek out areas of good coverage to communicate via WhatsApp. But perhaps most profound of all has been the impact on women.

> *'If I laugh in public or I talk too loud, they say,*
> *"Look, she wants attention, she's not a good girl."'*
>
> —SHAHAD, student

Cultural mores dictate that women in public should neither be seen nor heard. Even when veiled, raised voices and raucous laughter are considered indecent – a woman's voice being commonly perceived in the region as part of her *awrah* or nakedness.[62] In malls and restaurants, mothers can be seen reprimanding children through strained whispers and private family sign languages. But in the anonymous, unregulated spaces of the virtual world, a second identity is possible; women can be provocative, they can be risqué, they can be witty, they can be loud.

Heavily veiled in public, in private, Saudi women are queens of the selfie, sharing a steady stream of carefully edited pictures and videos on private networks of friends and acquaintances. Such is their love affair with online sharing that small portable Wi-Fi routers have become a handbag staple, meaning they need never disconnect. Snapchat especially is favoured by women, allowing them to document their day-to-day lives without leaving a trace, including what they're wearing under their *abaya*s.

~

---

62 Islamic opinion varies enormously on this issue.

To stand at the entrance of a female university campus is to witness a daily morning metamorphosis. Sweeping black cloaks and swirling veils are discarded to reveal a rainbow of hairstyles, piercings, false lashes and designer handbags. Even tattoos have gained popularity in recent years. (Tattoo parlours remain prohibited, but there are domestic workers from the Philippines with smuggled-in tattoo guns who will ink you for a fee.)

In public, conformity is key – the colour black is worn for anonymity, not by religious requirement – but in private, individuality is celebrated, and fashion is a key means of expression.

While women have been raised to believe they should appear and behave in a certain way, the international pop culture they now consume tells them a different story. Its influence is evident in the sea of mirrored sunglasses and the various interpretations of Miley Cyrus's latest haircut on display. When Lady Gaga went washed-out green, so did the girls of Riyadh, never mind the quantity of bleach it took them to get there.

It's a passion supported by an influential cohort of fashion bloggers and influencers. In a culture where it is taboo, and potentially dangerous, to talk dating, sex, politics or even horoscopes, fashion and beauty provide a comparatively safe outlet for women who yearn to have some form of public voice.

> 'Because of the way men and women are segregated here, women don't get to show off what they're wearing on the street. It's for her, not for anyone else. Women dress for themselves, so they dress up like peacocks.'
>
> —NOUF, blogger

For those who can afford it, fashion is a very serious business. The Saudi luxury market experiences gains of up to 10 per cent per year; in spring 2018, the country opened its first Fashion

Week, a star-studded all-female event. To outsiders, the penchant for haute couture can seem incongruous. After all, why spend $1,000 on a dress only to cover it with a black *abaya*? But Saudi women aren't dressing for public display; they dress for themselves, and for each other.

The desire to look and feel good doesn't stop at clothes. Under the *niqab*, liquid eyeliner, contouring products, lip tints and other cosmetics set the average Saudi woman back $3,000 a year. Eyebrows are a particular focus, if an unexpectedly controversial area.

One of the Prophet Mohammed's companions reportedly declared eyebrow-plucking a sin worthy of damnation due to its perceived interference with divine creation. 'I didn't really understand why,' says kindergarten teacher Reem, 'so I asked the *imam* and he told me it's because there's a nerve at the end of the hair that connects to your brain. I don't know if that's true; I'm not a doctor, but if there's a rule, there's always a reason behind it.'

Whatever the true reason is, the need to respect religious edict combined with the desire for a well-defined brow line inspires may women to undergo the arduous process of bleaching the entire brow before dyeing the preferred form back on.

As in many non-Western cultures, Saudi women also tend to subscribe to a paler ideal of beauty. It's hard to find a moisturiser that isn't whitening, and every major supermarket houses at least one entire aisle dedicated to whitening beauty products, with creams designed to 'brighten' every conceivable part of the female anatomy.

> *'We all want what we're not, I guess. The same way that in*
> *the US everyone wants to get a tan or remove their freckles.*
> *Here they all want to be white. They're pretty obsessed with*

whitening their elbows and knees for some reason. A girl
with black elbows is like an insult here. It's a cultural thing.'

—MAHA, student

The only body part to almost uniformly evade beautification
are the fingernails. Nail polish is generally a no-no as it inter-
feres with *wudu*, the ritual washing conducted before daily
prayers. But colours often make an appearance for at least one
week of the month when a woman's period exempts her from
daily worship.

Whatever their personal preferences, thanks to women's
increasing financial independence and disposable income,
they now have the services of thousands of women-only salons
to choose from, as well as sprawling shopping malls stocked
with an impressive array of international brands to complete
their looks.

~

In the absence of other forms of public entertainment, shopping
has become something of a national pastime; consumer spending has more than doubled over the past decade. On Thursday
evenings, the start of the Saudi weekend, long queues of cars
with blacked-out rear windows driven by Indian and Pakistani
drivers snake around city malls, waiting to deposit or collect
their female employers.

While booming consumerism and religious piety may not
seem like obvious bedfellows, they have found ways to accom-
modate one another. During the holy month of *Ramadan*, when
all Muslims in good health fast from food and water from
sunrise to sunset, malls simply invert their opening hours and
remain open all night so that their clients are not forced to shop
on an empty stomach.

As everywhere in public life, segregation of the sexes is maintained. Over the entry to women's clothing and lingerie stores hang signs that read 'Families Only', indicating that unaccompanied men may not enter. Women's faces on fashion posters, and sometimes even shampoo bottles, are covered or pixelated.

Muttawah, or 'religious police', with their long beards and distinctive shorter robes, still patrol the walkways in search of uncovered female heads and unmarried couples; although since their numbers were streamlined in 2016, they have become a far less common sight.

At prayer times, shops are shuttered and adult men are ushered away to worship in the mall's own dedicated prayer halls. Women on the other hand will generally stop and pray where they are – not infrequently in the doorways of designer stores.

Sensitive to the needs of their biggest clients, a handful of malls now house 'women-only' zones. At Kingdom Mall in Riyadh, glass elevators guarded by male security staff transport female shoppers to a floor of their own. Here, the shops are staffed exclusively by women and clients can unveil and enjoy a coffee between boutiques.

Malls are one area where men enjoy no such privileges. Not only are single men excluded from certain stores, they are often denied access to shopping centres altogether. 'I've had guys offer me money at the entrance,' says medical student, Malak, 'so I'll pretend to be their wife or their sister, just so they can get in.' The concern of course is that, in an unregulated public space, men and women may interact in ways not acceptable to traditional society.

In any case, as elsewhere in the world, it is typically women who exhibit the greater enthusiasm for retail therapy; waiting husbands can often be spotted snoozing on plastic benches outside Zara and H&M.

Western fashion brands have a significant presence in most

malls. Fully veiled young women peruse racks of sequinned tops, mini-skirts and bodycon dresses. These garments will be worn, but not in the public domain. Bars and nightclubs may be prohibited, but there's nothing to stop girls from creating their own nightlife.

~

I met Maysa (see p. 121) at a birthday party. Her cropped hair was dyed in stripes of pink, blue, green and purple; her cut-off T-shirt revealed an ornate tattoo circling a belly piercing. She was dancing with her sisters and friends as they sang along to the explicit lyrics of American R'n'B tracks. 'It's okay,' she laughed, 'they don't really understand what it means.'

Birthday parties are a recent phenomenon; according to Saudi Islamic practice, birthdays are *bid'ah* – an imported innovation – and their celebration is *haram*. The result is a lax attitude toward dates of birth and ages in general. 'My brother says I'm nineteen,' translation student Ghada tells me, 'but I'm not; I'm sure I'm twenty.'

But birthdays are not the only cause for celebration. Held to incredibly high public standards of modesty and morality, young women find plenty of other reasons to let their hair down in private. Securing a venue, however, can be a trickier matter. With houses full of siblings, and parents from a more conservative generation, entertaining at home is not always an option.

On the outskirts of cities, small estates of *istrahah*, bungalows for hire, often with swimming pools, have appeared, where families can spend a weekend away – and young people can enjoy an evening of independence. Like all properties in Saudi Arabia, they may usually only be rented under the name of an adult male, but a good-natured uncle or obliging brother can often be co-opted into signing the lease.

At weekends, a mixture of Arabic and Western pop tunes

can be heard pulsing from within these mini compounds;
inside, girls laugh, shimmy, grind and twerk like teenagers
anywhere else in the world. Behind high walls in the country's
conservative central region, girls perform RuPaul-style drag
races – wigs, sequins and all.

There may not be boys around, but girls still dress to impress.
From under black *abaya*s, platform heels and low-cut dresses
emerge – as do packs of Marlboro and tall, flavoured water
pipes. Often *boyat* – tomboys – provide a focus for flirtatious
attentions.

But, however strict the rules of segregation, teenage rebellion remains a universal constant, and some young men and
women do slip through the cultural barriers. Underground
mixed-sex parties are hosted in *istrahah*s, private homes, and
occasionally in basements converted into makeshift nightclubs.
Unsurprisingly, girls rarely attend with parental consent.

'The day before, she'll get an invite made up for a wedding –
there's this person getting married to this person at blablabla
time, we'd love for you to come,' explains Reem. 'So she'd get
this card printed out for five *riyals*, then say, "Mum, look, I'm
invited to a wedding and I'm gonna be back super late because
it's so far; I need a new dress, I need to go to the salon . . . " and
Mum says, "Okay," because it's a wedding and maybe someone
will see her there and even want her to marry their son; she'll
probably even pay for all of it.'

But in a society where girls and boys rarely interact platon-
ically, the atmosphere at such events can be pressured. 'To be
honest, the boys . . . when you go to a party with them, they
think you're just coming for drinking and having sex – that's
it,' says medical student Aya. 'It's not like when you go to a
nightclub outside.'

Mixed parties are also avoided by many due to their association with other vices. While an occasional plastic bottle of

home-brew or a half flask from a father's secret liquor cabinet might make its way into an all-girl's party, after-dark deliveries of black-market whiskey bottles are more often orchestrated by the boys.

And not everyone stops at alcohol. The abuse of *hashish* and prescription drugs is more widespread than anyone would like to admit – and amongst young women, more than anyone really knows. The concept of female drug addiction is socially taboo; women have been excluded both from official studies on addiction and from the primary inpatient rehabilitation facilities.

> *'When you do bad things, you mustn't tell people. Of course God knows, but with God, when you tell him, "I'm sorry for what I've done," he will always forgive you because he's so merciful. But imagine if people here figure out you're drinking, or the government – you would be in jail.'*

—AYA, medical student

'Although they approach it recreationally, I believe what's really happening is that they're self-medicating,' says doctor Afnan. 'You don't have recreational alcohol and the only thing that calms you down is this medication where you become addicted. And someone behind that gets rich.'

But while alcohol and drug abuse certainly exist, even in a dry country, their use is not mainstream. Most young women continue to respect the demands of their faith that they not indulge in alcohol or other illicit substances. 'If there's a restriction in our religion, there's always a reason,' says legal student Wejdan. 'A lot of bad things happen when you're drinking. You might go home with another man, even when you're married.'

Nonetheless, with the world now at their fingertips, a perfectly understandable curiosity for the forbidden does sometimes arise. 'I would never, ever touch alcohol,' vows student Ghaida. 'It's forbidden by God. But if I did, I mean, if it wasn't . . . I would only drink flaming sambucas!'

~

Today, half of Saudis are under the age of twenty-five. The rural customs of their grandparents are alien to them and decades of Wahhabi-Salafi suppression of cultural expression has left them with little to fill the void; simultaneous exposure to the outside world has resulted in a certain level of cognitive dissonance between practice and belief. Household cassette players went from playing Friday sermons to Justin Bieber, with no transition to soften the blow.

> 'Culturally, we're living in this kind of chaos right now,
> where everything makes sense and nothing makes sense.'

—SARA, university lecturer

In recent years, the government has attempted to address the widening breach between dogma and reality by making important concessions. Concerts and performances from international artists have been sanctioned; in 2018, cinemas started to open – at all these events, women have been welcomed.

In this way, the consumption of different forms of culture is being legitimised, but its creation remains problematic. Given religious attitudes, culture and the arts have not been highly prioritised or invested in; neither have creative careers been encouraged. 'Let's say you love to sing,' says businesswoman Abeer. 'It's not something society accepts as a wonderful profession, culturally. Maybe you're a natural-born artist, but you never get to enjoy that talent.'

But Saudi Arabia is working to strengthen its own unique

artistic identity, and women are proving to be equal partners in its construction. The lack of financial responsibilities assumed by most Saudi women here works in their favour. While men are pushed into careers that will guarantee their ability to provide, women are freer to pursue creative interests.

> *'Men are thinking about money.*
> *They're not thinking about art.'*

—LAMA, artist

There is a new trend for local cultural fairs in the country's cities, and they are undeniably dominated by women in the form of classical artists, fashion designers and home-craft entrepreneurs. In this framework, creative expression is increasingly seen as a blessing, not a blight. 'Sometimes I'll tutor a student and they'll say, "I cannot draw a face, it's *haram*,"' says artist Lama, 'but I tell them, this is a skill; it's a gift from God. You have to take it, and you have to think of God and his creation when you use it.'

> *'I want to use my art to communicate with a lot of people,*
> *to tell them about us — about women here; about how we*
> *think, what we dream; to show them we have lives here.*
> *We have a lot to share — we have a lot inside, too.'*

—HAYA, photographer

Perhaps the greatest breakthroughs have been seen in film. The most well-known Saudi filmmaker and the director of the country's first-ever feature film is a woman; Haifa Mansour's 2014 film *Wejda* follows the story of a young girl in the capital.

As Saudi women strive to produce engaging and original

content, they have found that the stories in most need of telling are their own. Almost all Haifa Mansour's films have focused on the experiences of women in her homeland, and she is far from the only one to adopt this approach.

For now, though, they remain the storytellers, not the protagonists. The exposure of Saudi women on screen and on stage as actors and performers is not yet accepted – much was the case in Europe but a few hundred years ago. But the stories are being told, in their own words – if the world is prepared to listen.

THE HENNA ARTIST

MARAM

Market vendor, aged thirty-four, Riyadh

Maram is the daughter of Somali refugees who to fled Saudi Arabia to escape the violence of the Somali Rebellion in the early 1980s. She has always lived in the Kingdom, but has never been able to secure citizenship for herself or her son. Her situation is precarious, and fear of the authorities combined with illiteracy have prevented her from seeking necessary education or healthcare for her child. Maram lives in Al Batha, one of the poorest areas of Riyadh.

I'm always terrified of making a mistake

If you asked me where I'm from, I would say I am Somali. I've never been there; Saudi Arabia is the only place I know. I use their words, I eat their food, but I couldn't say I'm Saudi, because I'm not. People would never treat me like a Saudi; they treat me like a Somali.

We came because of the conflict at home. My dad came over first and found work as a driver. My mum followed later; I was born once they were already here. But I was never accepted here; I've always felt different.

It's hard. I never really know if I can stay put or one day we'll be sent back to Somalia. I'm always terrified of making some kind of mistake. What would I do in Somalia? I don't know anyone at all. I would just like to live peacefully, like everyone else. My child was born here, his mother was born here – why can't he have a passport?

We're not refugees any more, but we're still foreigners.

The rich are above and the poor go below

I've never known a Saudi that I could . . . call a friend. Saudis are higher in society, you understand? In any case, Saudis don't mix very much. You don't know who your neighbours are, you don't know if they're sick; people don't even greet each other in the same building. Everyone is kind of anonymous. It's not like Somali culture.

Saudis are rich, *masha'Allah*, and Somalis are poor. The rich are above and the poor go below – it's always like that, isn't it? We are treated well, *alhamduLillah*, but no, we don't get too close. We're afraid of them. What if they found out something they didn't like about our lives? They could report us and have us sent back to our country.

We're not the same. School isn't free for us like it is for them; my family couldn't afford it. My sisters and I have never spent a day in school – not one; we stayed at home with Mama.

I wanted to go; I want to go even more now! I know exactly what I would have studied: *Qur'an*, English Language and Medicine. If I'd had the chance, I would have been a doctor, so I could help my family and treat my little boy. As it is, I know how to write my name, I know all the numbers, but that's about it.

But I have a family; I still have to work. When I was about sixteen, I started looking at pictures of Henna designs. I thought, *You don't need a school certificate or a passport to do that*. So my sister and I taught ourselves. Now we do parties, weddings, we go to fairs and markets, we visit ladies' homes. A lot of Somali girls do the same thing.

I don't do it for the joy of the art, you know, and I know

people look down on us. If I had enough money I would stay at home; maybe I'd just do it for girls who live around me. But it's the only work I know.

Everything in the home, this is our role

I thank God for making me a woman. But it's harder than being a man.

For one thing, men don't get periods, they don't get pregnant, they don't give birth – none of this pain. They don't have to bother about the kids at all really; that's a woman's work.

Caring for children, cooking, washing, cleaning, everything in the home, this is our role, and why not? We do it much better than the men – Somali women especially; we are very good homemakers.

If I had the choice, as a woman, I would stay at home. If your husband has a good job and can pay the bills, isn't that more comfortable than trying to do it all? I can take care of the house, look after my little boy, get the cooking done; I could even take him to school.

Of course a woman can work; I work. I think she can do anything she puts her mind to. She can be a doctor, a teacher, w'Allah, even a policewoman; she is capable. It's all good work.

Anything – except going to work in another woman's house, washing her clothes and cleaning her dishes and all that. Anything is good except being someone else's maid. A lot of African women here do that; that's what they think we're good for. But not me; I won't. I think a woman should take care of her own home.

I don't have to love him

I don't love my husband; I never have. We've been married for seven years.

He's Somali too. He came to see my father when he was

almost eighty years old. He had heard I was twenty-seven and still without a husband so he asked for permission to take me. Of course that wasn't my dream; who would choose that? But I was afraid if I said no there would be problems at home. I'm scared of my dad sometimes; maybe he wouldn't let me out after that, maybe he'd hit me.

So we had a small wedding at home. We had a baby after our first year together, but mostly he just needed a wife to take care of him. He's old, he's sick, he can't walk so far. But it's okay. I don't have to love him. We eat together, I put him to bed, turn out the lights and that's that!

If he wanted a second wife, I don't think I'd mind. If you don't love them, what difference does it make? I think he's too old now, though, to look for another.

My younger sister has a different dad to me; he's not so strict and he let her choose her own husband. I don't know how she did it. You can't have boyfriends here; it's completely forbidden. Maybe on the phone or online, but never in person; in Somalia, sure, but not here. But, *masha'Allah*, they love each other so, so much. I hope they will always be happy.

I'm not mad about the way it happened with me though. In our culture it's more respectful for a man to come and speak to your father than to come to you straight away; I still believe that. My dad just did what he thought was best. I think for most Somalis it's the same.

And of course I could never have married a Saudi man. They would say, 'No! You can't marry a Somali; she's black, she's a slave!' There's not actually any law against it, but that's what people would say.

Even if a guy here really fell in love with a Somali girl, his family would completely forbid it. And a Saudi man would never turn away from his family.

I mean, it does happen occasionally, that they'll marry a

Somali girl. But a few months later she has a baby, and then he leaves.

Insha'Allah I will still have a daughter of my own. I want so badly for her to go to school and learn something. I just need to get the money together. My boy, too, he's six already and I've never been able to send him.

I dream of one day getting married again, you know, to a man I really love, and who really loves me. A younger man, strong, who would treat me like a princess and make sure I have everything I need. Even better if he's British!

It's not part of my religion, this face thing

I cover my face, just because I have to. The religious police yell at you otherwise; I'm afraid of them, these *muttawah*s. If they locked me up, who would come to get me out? We don't have any papers.

It's not part of the religion, not part of *my* religion, this face thing. In Somalia you can wear short skirts and tops if you want. I mean, I wouldn't, but I think everyone should do as they want.

I can't afford the taxi

Of course I want to drive. We don't have any buses here and I want to go to the market; I want to go to the bazaars to work. A few months ago I met a teacher who offered to teach my sister and I to read for free, maybe even learn English. But I couldn't afford the taxi to her house every week. Some days we don't have food. We don't go out unless it's urgent.

Last year, my son had a seizure; by the time we found a neighbour whose husband was at home and had a car, he had turned blue. Thanks be to God, we got him to the hospital in time, but I was so afraid. There was nothing I could do, nothing I could do.

If we were refugees in Europe, it would be so much easier

In Somalia, people say that Saudi Arabia is a safe place, and that the people are good. Somalia is a poor country, so of course we live better here; we have air-conditioning, we have super-markets. Although I've heard the weather is better in my country.

It's true we don't have any friends here, but I think racism exists everywhere in the world. If I was in any other country in the world, I would be seen as a foreigner too, right?

But sure, the West is better. You know what? We hear about Somalis who go to Libya, then to Europe by boat. Once they're in Europe, they don't pay rent, they don't pay for the hospital; everything is free. They even give them money – imagine!

If we were refugees in Europe, or even America or Australia, we would get all of these things ... That would be so much easier than here.

My little boy has a problem with his heart. He needs an operation. Here I'm struggling because no one will support us; it's frightening. But in Europe they would, I know they would. Everyone has rights there.

I want to go to America, or Switzerland, or Europe. All us Somalis do, either to live or just to visit. Life is outside.

WHAT WOULD HAPPEN IF
WOMEN RULED THE WORLD?

A woman in charge would be more like a mum than a boss. Masha'Allah, mothers see everything. She would know everything. It's a different kind of wisdom, yanee.

She would care more about people. She would know what women need and she would take good care of the kids. I think it would be more peaceful too.

THE CLEANER

ROSAMIE

Cleaner, aged twenty-nine, Manila

Rosamie moved to Saudi Arabia from the Philippines five years ago on the advice of an employment agency in Manila. Since then she has seen her husband and young daughter only once. Financial obligations at home mean she does not feel she will be able to leave for a further two years. A former student of business management, she works as a cleaner in a state university.

'You'll love it there – it's hot and sunny'

I wanted to be a nurse. As soon as my baby was old enough to go to nursery, I enrolled at the local college. But when I called my dad to tell him – 'Papa, I've done it, I'm going to start nursing!' – he panicked. He asked me why I'd chosen such an expensive subject; he said he didn't have the finances for me to finish the course.

So I cancelled and transferred to business administration. It wasn't my dream, but never mind – it's still a good subject, and it was cheaper. It's supposed to be a four-year programme, but during my third year my father had a stroke. I had to go back to help look after him, and anyway, there was no more money to pay for my tuition after that; I had to drop out. I didn't get the chance to graduate.

I managed to find work in a mall, but after paying rent, water and electricity each month I only had 3,000 *pesos* left. I couldn't support my child; my husband was still studying. So I resigned. It was scary, but I did it; I packed my things, left my daughter with my parents and went to Manila to look for work.

That's where I saw the agency building, for foreign contracts. I went in and asked what was available. The lady there told me, 'We have jobs in Saudi. You'll love it there – it's hot, it's sunny, you'll have a pool and the pay is great; all the bills are included.' I didn't know anything about Saudi Arabia, really. I don't think I could even point it out on a map. I just asked her, 'Really? Saudi Arabia is a nice place to live?', and I signed my name.

As soon as I arrived at the airport here, the Saudi security guards started yelling at me: 'Where's your *abaya*? Put your *abaya* on!' I didn't have an *abaya*; I didn't know what an *abaya* was.

Then they took me to the apartment building. I think I cried for a whole month. I was so homesick; I missed my husband, I missed my daughter – I was lost. I'd made a mistake; I couldn't live here after all; I just wanted to go home. But what could I do? Now I have no choice; I'm here.

They click their fingers at us

It's not what I imagined I'd do. In the Philippines, if you're a cleaner it means you didn't go to school; you're uneducated. I did study, but here my studies are useless.

We didn't get any training; I'd never worked as a cleaner before. But it's not complicated. In the Philippines we don't have maids; you have to look after your house by yourself, so I know how to clean.

The girls here, though, I don't think anyone teaches them anything. They eat and they just drop their wrappers on the floor while they're walking. Back home the students don't act like that. Even little kids know where the garbage goes.

The Saudis look down on us, like we're lower than them — like we're servants. Not just us, the Indians and the Pakistanis too. They click their fingers at us or shout, 'Clean this!', 'Carry that!', not 'Please do this,' or 'Thank you,' like in other countries. Back home, you might behave that way with a dog, but not with a person. They talk to us like animals. Not all, of course, but most of them.

It's hard for me, but I try to put up a barrier in my mind: *This isn't about you, this is just part of your job, and you have to be brave and deal with it. Because if you don't, that's it, back you go to the Philippines, with nothing.*

We're afraid to talk to the managers. If they don't like you, they'll make problems for you. The Saudis mostly use email; they won't say anything to you. It's *ping* — they send a mail and you're fired. If I could talk to them, I'd ask for a raise. We get 700 *riyals* a month. We work five days a week; it's not enough.

Every morning we take the company bus to work at 5 a.m., and it takes us back to the apartment building at 4 p.m. It's a long day. But once you're back, that's it, you can't go out again.

There are five women in my room; we're in bunk beds. You try to make your corner your own; sometimes the international teachers give us things they don't need — pillows and things for the kitchen — but it's not easy there. The building does have a pool, like we were promised, but there's no water in it.

There aren't any buses and you can't take a taxi; it's not allowed. At the weekends you just have to stay at home. There's one lady with us, one of the older ones; we call her 'the mother'. She's kind of the boss. If you try to leave the building, she reports you, or at least she confiscates your *iqama*, your ID; you can't get very far without that.

We're allowed out once a month; the company bus takes us to the market to buy groceries, if the salary is on time. Then you have just a couple of hours to pick up everything you need for the month – fruits, vegetables, all of it; it's your only chance.

The rest of the time it's home, work, home, work. It's a boring life. Sometimes I think I'm going mad. We try to look after each other; sometimes if there's a birthday we'll throw a small party, and at Christmas some of the foreign teachers snuck us some decorations. We try to find happy moments like that – to be silly, to laugh.

It's not comfortable having this thing around your head

If I could, I'd rip this *abaya* up; I hate wearing it. It's hot, it's uncomfortable, and it's impossible to walk upstairs without two hands free to hold it!

All the other workers here are the same; none of us likes it. Maybe you're wearing nice clothes underneath; maybe you have a new dress on, but what's the point? Nobody can see it.

I don't wear *hijab*. Maybe just on the way into the university, I pull it over my hair, but the rest of the time, I don't do it. It's not comfortable having this thing wrapped around your head and your neck. Sometimes the *muttawah* shout at us, but not often – not like they do with the Saudi women. Maybe they think we're not worth the trouble.

Women work harder than men

In the Philippines, men and women are the same. It's not like here, not like Saudi. What a man can do, a woman can do; we don't have different jobs for each. My husband, for example, is a very good cook. I'm horrible in the kitchen; without him I think we'd all starve!

I think we should be equal. If anything, I think women work harder than men. We're more efficient and we don't just take care of ourselves; we look after our children and our parents too. I come from a noble family in the Philippines, on my father's side, and I take pride in providing for my family. From what I've seen, men can only focus on one thing at a time, but women can handle anything you throw at them.

But in Saudi Arabia there is no freedom for a woman to do anything at all. We can't even wear what we want.

The company is our guardian

Why would a woman need a guardian? We know our own minds, we have brains in our heads; we're not children.

In the Philippines, maybe you tell your parents, 'Ma, Pa, I'm going,' but there's nothing they can do. They'll say, 'Okay, it's up to you.'

But here, every woman needs a man. She has to have one to sign her papers, to allow her to travel. Otherwise she's stuck; there's nothing she can do.

We're all here without our husbands; that makes the company we work for our legal guardian. They're the ones who get to decide what we do, if we can leave the country or if we have to stay.

At home I drive a motorbike

In the Philippines, I drive a motorbike! I miss it; I miss the freedom. You can't go anywhere by yourself here. You have to find a driver, you have to wait for him, you have to pay him. Even the Saudi women, they have to beg their husbands to take them.

I miss my husband, I miss my baby

I haven't seen my husband or my daughter in two years. There are some Indian ladies here who haven't seen their kids in four years. Sometimes I think about making a visit, but then I think about the money. The flights are so expensive, maybe three months' salary, and I think about my sister's college course and my parents looking after my daughter, and in the end I always send the money back home.

I met my husband online. We started chatting and eventually we decided to meet in person. We met in a café and we never stopped talking. Three months later we were married, just like that! We were pretty young, but when you know, you know!

Here they don't let them mix, the girls and the boys, even when they're kids; nothing is open, nothing is innocent. That's why there's so much rape in this country; that's why the boys like boys. You see girls going into the toilet cubicles together here when you're cleaning. I'm bad – I knock on the door to scare them and run away!

And some of the men here have three or four wives. Can you imagine a husband who has to make a schedule to spend time with you each week? I couldn't bear it. Much better to separate, to divorce.

I miss my husband. I miss my baby. I talk to them every single day; we use cell phone, internet, video calls – whatever is not blocked by the government! We have extra-long calls on Fridays and Saturdays.

We are far apart, but we love each other; we make it work. I don't understand the Saudi way, that your mother and father choose your husband for you. A woman should find her own man. If you don't love each other, you're not happy, right? It doesn't matter if you live in a different country or the same house.

Don't come

People in the Philippines think Saudi Arabia is nice, that Saudi is a good place to work, that there are a lot of opportunities there. Just like the agent said to me.

Honestly, when people back home ask me, I tell them, don't come here. Don't come to Saudi; it's not a good place; you can't live with the rules here. This is how I see it.

Just two more years

I've been here for five years. Everything feels the same to me. Maybe some of the girls are wearing coloured *abaya*s now, but there have been no big changes. Only that the price of food has gone up and our salaries have gone down.

I hope in the future they will let boys and girls mix more, and let women drive. But I don't think it will happen. Not for another twenty years!

And I don't want to be here that long; I want to go home. I want to be able to walk outside, go to the beach with my daughter, wear a bikini!

I want to start my own business and work in import/export, and be successful enough that I never have to travel abroad again, and that no one in my family has to either.

I just need to stay here two more years to save enough capital to start it up, and to finish paying my sister's tuition. Just two more years.

WHAT IS THE MOST REBELLIOUS THING YOU'VE EVER DONE?

No, no; we try not to break the rules. But some of us sneak out for part-time work, private cleaning jobs. The company doesn't allow it but sometimes I escape from the building to clean the teacher's villas or help out in hotels. Serving in a hotel you can get 200 riyals in one evening.

THE EXPAT

JINANI

Housewife, aged thirty-three, Manchester

Jinani is a British Muslim of Pakistani heritage. Six years ago, she and her husband decided to leave Manchester to try life in Riyadh so their children would be assured a traditional Islamic upbringing and the family could learn to speak Arabic. Her seven children now attend Saudi state schools and she is a stay-at-home wife and mother.

It's a lot more laid back here

I got the usual reaction from people when I told them we were moving here: 'Are you sure?', 'Saudi Arabia?', 'Women can't go out!', 'Women can't drive!' 'It's just a desert!', 'You'll be stuck at home as a prisoner!', 'Why do you want that sort of lifestyle?' My family were very concerned.

But I chose to come to Saudi Arabia because I wanted to experience a different lifestyle and culture, and I wanted our children to have the opportunity to grow up learning Arabic, the language of the *Qur'an*. I never had the chance.

Life was so hectic back home in the UK. Before I came here, I had four children under the age of six. I was running back and forth between home and school, sometimes four times a day because one child was full-time and one part-time, all the while dragging two little ones in a buggy. In between I was taking care of the daily household chores, the grocery shopping, doctor's appointments and so on – whatever the weather, come rain or shine.

I was told there was a more relaxed lifestyle in this part of the world, and I wanted to experience that; I definitely wanted more sunshine too! And it's true, life is a lot more laid-back here. The kids are picked up in the morning by the school bus and dropped back home – that alone was like a huge burden lifted off my shoulders.

Even better, now the kids come home at midday, so I have more time to spend with them – playing, talking, creating, having fun. There's definitely more quality family time here; I think that's what I most enjoy.

And the biggest surprise was how developed it all is, how fast it's progressing. You can get everything here that you get back home and more; the supermarkets and shopping centres are enormous. It's amazing; the desert has become an oasis, and it's still growing.

I do miss the aspect of equality, the freedom to get around easily. We don't live on a compound like most expats, so I have to wait for my husband to take us out. It isn't normal to see women walking on the streets either, so in the beginning it did feel a bit lonely. I just tried to adapt and make the most of the situation and look at the positives. I focus on what I *can* do rather than what I can't.

And there is a big expat community here; people have been so helpful and friendly. The locals themselves are amazingly hospitable; they're so generous. I have made very close Saudi friends who are more like family now. I can't imagine they get the same welcome when they go over to the UK.

I don't regret our move here. Not one bit.

I feel liberated from public view

I choose to wear a *niqab* for modesty; it's my personal preference. It's just the norm here; I feel more comfortable wearing it rather than not. And I want to follow and respect the customs of the place where I have chosen to live.

In some countries, wearing a *niqab* might actually attract more attention, but in Saudi Arabia it's the opposite. When I'm wearing the *niqab* I feel freer; I feel liberated from public view.

There is definitely a religious basis for a *niqab*, as our dear wives of the Prophet wore it. People like to follow that tradition. Though some people wear it, and some people don't. Personally, I feel it's not a hard-and-fast rule. It depends a lot on the circumstance and place. My religion gives me flexibility like that.

My life as a woman is defined by my religion

The position of women in Islam begins with the elevating of no woman on earth to the status of Mary, the mother of Jesus. She is the most revered woman in Islam; the *Qur'an* talks about her more than the Bible does.

I believe that we women have a very high status as it is – as mothers, daughters and wives. Just looking through the texts, from the *Qur'an* and the Prophetic statements, you can see how important our role is. Unfortunately, though, many sociocultural elements have found their way into the religion over time; that's what sometimes gives a negative image of Islam, which isn't really fair.

Women's roles are different, that's for sure. My life as a woman is defined by my religion, my culture and my social upbringing – and I'm happy about that. Since I know exactly what's expected from me, it's easy for me to set boundaries and not to get carried away down the wrong path.

Of course, the differences between men and women are even

more pronounced here. We're completely different: different jobs, different roles, different responsibilities. I do believe in equality, but let's face it, egalitarianism isn't the perfect jigsaw piece for every job.

I feel women-related subjects, like gynaecology, should be studied by women. I would definitely encourage my daughter into something like that if she's interested in medicine. I would always prefer to see a female doctor anyway, so encouraging our young women to aspire to these roles is very important.

Education in general is really important; Islam encourages women to educate themselves. After all, women play a vital role in society; we are just as responsible for the well-being of our communities as the men. Most of the Prophet's authentic sayings were taught to the rest of the world through his wives, so it makes sense that our girls and women should have access to education.

Driving is such a trivial thing

I have a British driving licence and I do drive in England. But driving here, ha! I would only consider it if I see a bit more discipline and people start respecting the laws of the road. Really, in my opinion, driving is such a trivial thing. Yes, of course it would be wonderful to have that 'get-up-and-go feeling', but I've never felt that it affects my rights or my freedoms. It's not the 'Suffragettes' issue people make it out to be.

Honestly, I've found that depending more on my husband has just brought the family closer together. We've had a lot more family outings than we ever did in the UK; I'm so enjoying that!

I enjoy the grocery shopping better together; I've discovered my husband picks out much better fruit and veg than I do. We go out for picnics more often here than in the UK too. I guess not driving does have its benefits.

We both wanted our parents to make the match

I found my partner in my own sphere of family and friends, like I think most people do. Me being quite shy and private, and he being a busy, out-and-about kind of man, we were brought together by some of our elders who thought we might balance each other out very well. My husband and I both agreed that our parents should do the research and make enquiries about our compatibility on our behalf. It's like community Google! They do all the digging for you. But the decision on whether to accept or not, to marry or not, was always left to me.

Islam, by the way, has no issue with the sexes mixing so long as it's within the boundaries of Islamic laws. Right now my male cousin is staying with us while he gets himself settled here. It's not an issue – actually, he's a lifesaver with the kids; I just keep my *hijab* on in the house.

Every society has its own boundaries on how the sexes interact with one another. I don't think we need to say that one is right and others are wrong.

Guardianship has a long history

To understand the idea of male guardians, you really have to look back at history, well before Islam. Even prior to the Judo-Christian era, women have always been guarded by men. I remember growing up in the UK, I always enjoyed having a 'guardian' – someone to drop me off to school or friend's houses or the shopping centre. Being under guardianship of a male relative has never felt like a drawback or a constraint to me. It has its benefits; I actually really like the protected feeling.

'Beauty is in the eye of the beholder'

The rest of the world sees Saudi Arabia as very conservative and very socially closed. I think most people imagine a difficult way of life, full of constraints. I don't know how I could change people's perceptions about that. I guess I'd just ask them to try it!

The focus has always been on the fact that women can't drive, that they can't travel abroad without permission. Okay, these are the constraints, but I can't say I feel oppressed in any way; now I have the privilege of being chaperoned and enjoying the ride – like a queen.

From what I've seen, these rules don't prevent women from getting on with their day-to-day lives. The system is different here, but it fully caters to women's needs for travelling. With the driving habits in this country, it's truly a blessing women aren't driving.

As for the way people talk about Islam, of course it's upsetting to have it so misrepresented and so misunderstood. But, well, you know the saying, 'Beauty is in the eye of the beholder.' That's how it is with our perception of faith.

These changes aren't being driven by politics

I've already seen a big change since I first arrived six years ago. Back then there were no female cashiers in the supermarkets, no female shop assistants. I did find it awkward at times. I'm so relieved that there are women working in the lingerie departments now!

It's good to see women working in other places, not just schools any more. Women are becoming a lot stronger; I see a lot more businesswomen, more girls interested in computer sciences and engineering, things that are really male-dominated here – and everywhere to be honest. I really want to encourage them!

These changes aren't being driven by politics; it's just the cultural development of Saudi society, and it seems to be very widely accepted. Saudi Arabia is catching up with the rest of the world in every way.

I envisage a lot more women on the streets in years to come – women using public transport: a working metro, regular buses. This will help us bust some myths about women not being able to go out without a 'male chaperone'. Soon Riyadh will be a hustling, bustling city, more so than it is now, with all the development and progress that comes with that – a place you'd want to visit for sure!

In my daughter's lifetime, if she wishes to continue living here, I would just like for her to have the rights she'd have in a Western country, where she's allowed a sense of belonging, and her contribution to the society as a British Muslim citizen would be recognised. I'm proud that my daughters are being brought up with a British ethos, entwined with Arab culture.

And I hope that we can continue living here. It's getting harder now; the way that life is progressing in Saudi Arabia, lots of expats are leaving because of the taxes and expenses. I might need to think and face the reality.

Maybe universities in the UK would be better for the kids. But honestly, I don't feel as welcome back home as I used to; I've been spat at, people look at you like they're scared of you, because you're wearing a headscarf. I find it so sad, but the truth is, I'm not sure where we belong any more.

IF YOU COULD CHANGE ONE LAW, WHAT WOULD IT BE?

I would like to see all children born to Saudi women to be recognised as Saudi nationals, never mind where their fathers are from. We have to go through all the bureaucracy of living here, but that's our choice. I still have my British passport, but to be born in a place and not really be able to call it home, that must be really hard.

LIFE ON THE EDGE

'I'll call you back, the madam is coming'

—Sudanese housemaid

The women of Saudi Arabia have been the topic of much media rumour and intrigue over recent decades. But what has drawn less attention is that not all women in the Kingdom are Saudi. According to official statistics, more than a third of the country's 33 million inhabitants are non-nationals. Some come to work; others are born and raised in Saudi society. Few will ever truly call it home.

From the early days of the Kingdom, as the young country worked to regularise state machinery and its citizenry, there have been tales of civil servants offering passport appointments to people on the streets. The only conditions being that the applicants, or their fathers, had lived on the peninsula since before 1932. Later, as oil wealth flowed into the country, so did migrants, and as a Saudi passport rapidly became a much more desirable document, the door to citizenship swung firmly shut.

Naturalisation can now only be achieved through a points system, and applications are reviewed on an individual basis by the Ministry of Interior. In order to qualify for consideration, candidates must have spent a minimum of ten years in the country and have converted to Islam. Points are then awarded for level of education, number of years spent in the Kingdom, and heritage. A Saudi father earns you three points; a Saudi mother, only two.

The huge social value attributed to the paternal line means that for one section of society, even being born of a Saudi womb is no guarantee of a homeland. Increased participation in international scholarships and in the workplace has led to a new phenomenon: Saudi women who take foreign husbands. It is reported that the number of women with non-Saudi spouses now sits at close to three quarters of a million.

But before a 'mixed' marriage can be approved, the bride must sign a document acknowledging that the children born of this union will not have an automatic right to Saudi citizenship. This means that should a mother die, her children's right to remain in the land of their birth is no longer guaranteed.

> *'A Saudi woman can't marry a non-Saudi man until she's twenty-five – not without a lot of bureaucracy and going through the courts. I find it so insulting; the idea is, once you're over twenty-five, you've clearly been left on the shelf, so you can't have the privilege of marrying a Saudi man.'*
>
> —MALAK, student

Even as adults, these individuals must maintain a sponsor and a valid residency visa, like any other foreign worker. They will not automatically receive the paid university education, international scholarships or positive employment discrimination afforded to their maternal cousins.

The arguments against recognising these children as Saudi nationals are rarely consistent. Some claim the divided loyalties of such children pose a threat to national security; others that they will create competition in the labour market; it has even been posited that these individuals – and not the millions of foreign workers that the country relies upon – will place an unbearable strain on the Kingdom's water supplies.

Women who have been affected by the legislation have been quick to point out that no such panic seems to ensue when a man chooses a foreign bride. If born in the country, the offspring of these marriages are granted Saudi citizenship at birth.

The root of the objection, then, might more honestly be found in a sense of betrayal that women are choosing partners from outside the fold, and a fear that the time-honoured Saudi custom of tracing one's tribal ancestry through the paternal line may ultimately be laid to rest.

The debate has roared over social media for several years, bringing it into the mainstream consciousness and prompting many sympathisers, both female and male, to push for a more equal system. In 2017, the Shura Council finally agreed to review the issue; current proposals look towards granting nationality to such children, once they turn eighteen.

In addition to easing the struggles faced by those individuals who find themselves foreigners in their own land, such a change would also go a long way to proving what the state insists is already true: that women's citizenship holds just as much weight as a man's.

For other women born in the Kingdom, any form of citizenship is still a distant dream.

~

In every Saudi city, women like Maram (see p. 331) hide in plain sight. They work, without papers, as cooks and cleaners, or set up stalls on the edges of *souqs* selling home-cooked meals and offering ornate henna tattoos. Like undocumented migrants in many countries, these women inhabit an underprivileged sector of society which largely survives hand to mouth.

Their poverty and vulnerability is magnified by their lack of access to basic services. Without passports or residency visas, obtaining medical care, opening a bank account or even purchasing a mobile phone become near-impossible tasks.

In theory, all children between the ages of six and sixteen have guaranteed access to schooling. In reality, illiteracy and fear of the authorities prevent many mothers like Maram from taking the steps necessary to enrol their children, perpetuating the cycle to which they have fallen victim. It is the same fear that prevents such women from integrating socially.

> *'My husband is a lawyer, you know, but he's had clients ask him where his employer is. We're Indian originally, and they just assume he's the driver.'*

> —KHULOUD, housewife

Saudis often express pride in the fact that their culture and their faith do not discriminate against race and nationality. But moving through Saudi society, it is hard not to notice the lines of a caste-like hierarchy, with Saudis at the top, skilled Western workers in the middle, and Asian and African immigrants, like Maram, undeniably at the bottom of the chain.

~

'I'm sorry, it's not much; I haven't had a maid for a month,' says teacher Huda apologetically as she serves lunch at her home. Casual references to domestic workers pepper women's conversations. 'This one's new,' says student Dalal, her maid still in earshot. 'We had to take her; the neighbours didn't want her any more and no one knew what to do with her.'

In the period 2015–17, Saudi Arabia issued more than 3 million visas for foreign 'house help'. A sizeable proportion of these were for men to be employed as private drivers. It is a role that few Saudi men aspire to, and in any case the huge importance attributed to privacy and reputation means most women simply refuse to be driven by a local man who may know her family, or gossip about where she goes and who she's seeing.

As a consequence, Saudi Arabia is currently home to some 800,000 foreign drivers, mostly of Indian or Pakistani origin. With the removal of the female driving ban, this number is set to decline, although some women will certainly opt to retain their services.

But other household workers – maids, cooks, nannies and cleaners – remain in high demand (it is estimated that 89 per cent of Saudi households employ at least one housemaid), and these professions are, almost exclusively, female.

Saudis have a long history of depending on imported domestic labour. Slavery was not formally abolished in the Kingdom until 1962; until then, keeping slaves of African descent was not uncommon in middle- and upper-class households. After the law was changed, all former slaves were offered full Saudi citizenship, and many adopted the tribal names of the families they had served.

'Yes, my grandparents had slaves; it was a different time. But slavery wasn't like what you've seen in Roots! *Some slaves would breastfeed members of the household, just like mothers, and they would live with them like sisters; they were very much a part of the families they lived in.'*

—SUHAILA, philanthropist

But it would appear that the ties between master and servant have never truly been severed. As wealth from the exploitation of oil reserves found its way into household incomes, families were able to replace slaves with paid, imported labour.

For women with broods of ten or more children, and husbands who don't traditionally contribute to household chores, the employment of domestic help came to be understood more as a necessity than a luxury. Today, homes are constructed with 'maid's quarters' as a standard feature.

The majority of housemaids are sourced from Indonesia, Sri Lanka and the Philippines. These women usually come from economically insecure backgrounds and are often the sole breadwinners of their families. 'I came after my husband died,' says one of Rosamie's colleagues. 'I have three kids; they live with my mum now.'

Women are enticed into positions in Saudi Arabia by agencies in their home countries who offer attractive salaries and a range of benefits, some of which invariably fail to materialise. They are often not qualified for the roles in childcare or cooking to which they are assigned, or prepared for life in a culture that is completely alien to them.

On arrival at the airport, they will pass under the custody of their new employer, their sponsor, who, in the absence of their fathers and husbands, will act as their guardian. What kind of sponsor they will be signed to they have no way of knowing until they are already on Saudi soil.

There are those who undoubtedly live very well in their new homes. Each morning, Norah, a young princess in the capital, stretches and yawns in her polka-dot pyjamas before embracing her maid Marisol in a vice-like bear hug and kissing her face. In student Qamar's house, maid Mini twirls around guests in a 'Tequila is my spirit animal' T-shirt as she serves coffee, singing and demanding kisses and selfies from her bemused but amiable employers.

When placements are happy, domestic staff have been known to stay for decades with a single family, joining family holidays and celebrations, even having their education sponsored. When they finally leave, it is with tears on both sides and promises to remain in touch.

But with a lack of clear regulations or follow-up evaluations by agencies, the experiences these women live are as varied in nature as the human beings they work for. The simple absence of windows in the maids' quarters of some modern buildings suggests that not all are treated as members of the family.

There are widespread reports of passports being confiscated and pay being withheld. The contractually guaranteed one free day per week does not always materialise, and if it does, with no public transport and as last in line to make use of the family's driver, many have little way of using it.

Within the home, working hours are long, with women often tasked with taking care of large families with little authority to reprimand unruly children. The sight of a group of Saudi women enjoying a social lunch while the nanny endeavours to keep the children quiet at a neighbouring table, or of a visibly exhausted Filipino maid wrestling with a disgruntled toddler in an airplane seat while the child's parents sit in the row ahead, or even in business class, is depressingly common.

Chances to hold their own children are rare. Workers are entitled to annual leave only after two years of consecutive service, and the high prices of flights relative to monthly salaries means it's seldom a trip made every year.

> '*I haven't seen my children in more than five years.*
> *How can I do it? The pay keeps going down; now*

*I get 700 riyals per month. It's more important
that they eat, that they go to school.'*

—HITA, cleaner, India

But not everyone stays for years. The problem of runaway housemaids is a hot topic in Saudi media, and is estimated to cost the country $235 million per year, with approximately 10,000 maids 'escaping' their sponsors annually.

Saudi women themselves tend to blame such disappearances on black-market labour scouts, who convince women to leave their official sponsor for more lucrative positions in the informal sector; it's a trend which they say leaves them inconvenienced and out of pocket, having spent thousands on flights and visa fees bringing the worker into the country.

This is certainly part of the story, but there are also more worrying flaws in the system. Once behind the walls of private homes, maids have little protection against physical and sexual abuse. When one Saudi woman published a video online of her husband making unwanted advances towards the housemaid, the husband was not punished, neither was the maid compensated. Rather, the wife faced charges for publicly dishonouring her spouse.

Not all women brought to the country through agencies will find themselves working in private homes. In the service sector, too, cooks, waitresses, beauticians and cleaners like Rosamie (see p. 339) are, by and large, sourced from Asia. Saudi women themselves, now a highly educated force, have their sights set on higher professions – roles that, until now, have largely been occupied by qualified female expats from the West and other Arab nations.

~

Saudi Arabia's rapid transition from third to first world permitted the country's infrastructure to develop faster than its citizens. While standards of domestic education and training were still being raised, professionals were needed to staff the new state-of-the-art hospitals and universities already under construction.

Hundreds of thousands of women have come to find work, or, like Jinani (see p. 347), uproot their children and follow their husbands to make a new life in the Kingdom. Jinani is only unusual for the nobility of her motivations. 'Look, no one comes here for the nightlife,' says nurse Karen. 'Everyone's here for the money.'

Unlike the women who clean their homes, most of Saudi Arabia's imported teachers, nurses, doctors and engineers arrive from affluent nations, and in order to tempt them into 'the sandbox', as the country is semi-affectionately known by these temporary residents, the public sector promises generous salaries, paid flights home and often luxurious compound living.

Western-style compounds exist as small islands of immunity from the social and legal codes that govern Saudi life. Protected by high walls, barbed wire and heavily armed guards, only residents and their guests are permitted entry.

Inside, sprinklers and gardeners maintain manicured green lawns and floral displays, even at the peak of a desert summer. Houses and apartments surround shimmering blue pools and music drifts over from restaurant terraces. In short, everything is done for the resident to convince themselves that they're living elsewhere.

Accordingly, all the leisure amenities scarce in Saudi cities are on site: cinemas, gyms, bowling alleys and, of course, bars. Alcohol is illegal in the Kingdom, but is smuggled in via diplomatic vehicles and private cars, or, more frequently, brewed at home by the bar's patrons; major supermarkets, also run by international management, stock an unusually wide selection of natural grape juices.

Of course, such locales are frequented by both male and female residents; gender segregation is abandoned at the compound gates, as is the veil. *Abayas* and *niqabs* are in fact prohibited on most compounds due to security concerns. Mere feet away from the shrouded Saudi women on the street outside, women ride bikes in shorts and dive into pools wearing string bikinis.

These pockets of Western hedonism are tolerated for expats, but strictly forbidden to Saudis. Residents cannot add locals to their guest lists; compound managers fear that Saudis will report on illicit activities and bar managers complain that they can't hold their drink. In years gone by, when the policy was not always so strictly observed, religious police would loiter at the gates of certain compounds on Friday nights, with the intent of catching inebriated Saudi girls red-handed.

Compounds have been so successful in isolating local and international communities from one another that many expats spend years making the journey between office, compound and the occasional embassy soirée without ever stopping in between; never making a Saudi friend or experiencing local cuisine and holidays. Each side has been warned so fervently about the dangers of the other, there's always a fear of getting too closely involved. But for those who do make the effort to cross the divide, a unique cultural experience presents itself.

Foreign women have the peculiar advantage of being permitted access to both male and female spheres. 'It's like you're a third gender almost,' says teacher Laura; they are accepted with men on desert cook-outs and welcomed with women at private gatherings. 'It's crazy,' says ministry worker Ghazi, 'you've seen more Saudi women than I have!'

On both sides of the divide, these interlopers are treated

with typical Saudi hospitality. 'You've seen it; you know how they are,' says blogger Nouf. 'They'd give you the shirts off their backs if you let them.' She's not being entirely figurative. Visitors have to be careful when complimenting objects in a Saudi household, lest their hosts feel obliged to give them away. 'I once came home with a living-room rug,' says Laura. 'I felt awful actually . . .'

> 'With all these new taxes and expenses now, I think I have to accept that my family and I won't be here much longer. It's sad for us, but at the same time, it's amazing to watch it all happening, isn't it? I've seen such a difference just in the past five years; when I first came, you hardly saw women anywhere – now they're involved in everything. Girl power!'
>
> —AMAL, teacher

The golden age of tax-free salaries and generous benefits for skilled international workers is drawing to a close, however. Foreign workers are now facing new taxes and significant pay cuts. With its incredible investment in public education, the government is now pushing for its own citizens to take the reins, including its women.

But that is not to say that those who continue to work in the country have been made to feel unwelcome. More than once, with my face uncovered, I have been approached by a group of teenage girls, eyes beaming from behind niqabs, pushing each other forward to speak before one is brave enough to say, in English, 'Welcome to Saudi Arabia! You are welcome!' Sadly, this is rarely the reaction Saudi women themselves can expect when they are the ones in a foreign land.

~

Saudi women may still need their guardian's permission to travel beyond the Kingdom's borders, but it is no longer an unusual request; the process has now been digitised and permits can be released from a guardian's online account at the touch of a button.

According to representatives from the Shura Council, in 2017, 35,000 female Saudi students were enrolled on international scholarships, pursuing their studies across sixty different countries. Meanwhile, recreational travel with family, and even with other female friends, is increasingly the norm.

It is commonly joked that Saudi women board planes in full *abaya* and *niqab* only to disembark at their destinations in high heels, jeans and lipstick. In reality, transformations are rarely so dramatic, but given the opportunity to follow their own moral compasses and interpretations of faith, dress codes and social mores often gain a new flexibility. 'I don't cover abroad,' says Masters student Sara. 'Why? Because we cover to blend in, to make ourselves safe. If I cover in America, I'm doing the opposite. I want to fit in.'

But their attempts to assimilate are rarely sufficient to protect them from the curiosity of strangers. 'I was asked if there was oil in my tent. In my *tent*,' sighs art agent Nada. Some choose to pre-empt the inevitable assumptions: 'When I was living in London, I took to wearing a leather bag that was moulded in the shape of an oil jug,' says photographer Haya. 'Mind you, it was stylish.'

> 'I'm always telling my mother, "Your generation was the generation of kings and queens; when you said you were Arab, people used to think about Aladdin, the genie, gold — things like this." Today we're scared to say we're Saudi; we're Muslim, because the first thing they see is terrorism.'
>
> —NADEEN, university lecturer

But the stereotypes are wearing thin. 'When I say "Saudi Arabia" and they have no idea where it is – there is no reason for you to be ignorant,' says academic Hanan. 'My mum's, my grandparents' generation, yes, they didn't have the information you have. But today, I know what's going on in South Korea; I know when there's a hurricane in the Philippines – you only have to look.' And most upsetting of all are the allusions to terrorism.

'They're killing Muslims too,' says Princess Amira of so-called 'Islamist' terrorists. 'It's just so crazy; this has nothing to do with Islam. I mean, ISIS – have you seen them praying? Each one faces a different direction!' Some women confess that their real motivation for removing their headscarves when travelling abroad is fear. 'I was attacked at a bus stop,' says academic Rahaf. 'The guy wanted to hit me; it was after 9/11, you know?'

Sadly, fear has often got in the way of finding firm common ground. 'Sometimes I feel they're [in the West] more Muslim than we are,' says municipal councillor Maha, 'being productive, paying back to society, volunteering, dealing well with people – these are all Islamic teachings.'

But with so many Saudi women now scattered around the globe, old assumptions will inevitably be challenged – on both sides. 'You'll find that these students come back and they'll bring something completely different,' says Hoda, 'but they are our ambassadors outside. The way they behave will either make or break those stereotypes.'

In the 1990s, it is said that an esteemed sociologist and researcher wrote a book in which he declared that Saudi women were on the verge of a socio-economic metamorphosis. Rumour has it the Saudi government bought the title en masse from the publishing house and had the copies burned.

> 'We are living in a period of transition, when so many
> things are happening and we have the opportunity to be
> part of those changes . . . Being part of this evolution
> in a country like Saudi Arabia is amazing; you see it
> happening in young women in front of your eyes.'

—HODA AL HELASSI,
Shura Council member

More than two decades on, this prophecy can no longer be destroyed; the transformation is already well underway. Young Saudi women carry the promise of an altogether new Kingdom within them, and a new ideal of womanhood – the effects of which have the potential to make ripples across the Islamic world. Saudi women are living on the cusp of a whole new Arabian dream.

ACKNOWLEDGEMENTS

As it turns out, there is a great deal more to producing a book than simply writing the words on a page. This work would never have made it from personal passion project to your bookshelf without the professionalism, support, generosity and sometimes outright unpaid labour of a large network of marvellous individuals.

I would like to thank first my delightful and ever-positive agent Anna Hogarty at Madeleine Milburn, who saw potential in my proposal and helped me bring it to the attention of those who could help me transform it into something more than a treasured scrapbook.

I am deeply appreciative of the whole team at Simon & Schuster, and especially of Fritha Saunders, who guided me through the many steps of the publishing process, listened attentively to my wishes and concerns and always put the dignity and safety of the book's contributors above sensationalism and commercial concerns. My thanks also to Melissa Bond and Victoria Godden, who wrestled my jumbled references and errant semi-colons into place.

I count my blessings to have found a remarkable illustrator in Merieme Mesfioui, who treated the twenty-nine subjects I placed in her care with such warmth and attention to detail. You have truly brought this book to life.

I would also like to thank David Mildon and Anna Sutton, who extended enthusiasm and encouragement when my own reserves were running low and who provided invaluable feedback in the early stages of the drafting process. Academically, I was very fortunate to count on the co-operation and insight of Dr José Sánchez García, who has conducted some truly unique research in the region.

I am eternally indebted to those women from the Kingdom who reviewed my words and who answered endless, seemingly random questions about their homeland with patience and good humour. Especially the brilliant Alyah Shamsan and Muna Al Yusuf. Thanks also to Ms Al Mainman for answering legal queries.

Then there are the Saudi women who were, perhaps, not directly involved, but whose writing and other works for the women of their country informed and inspired my own efforts. To name but a few: Dr Thoraya Obaid; Dr Hala Aldosari; Dr Hatoon al-Fassi; and Manal al-Sharif.

I am also very grateful to those Saudi men who contributed by welcoming me in their cities, their homes and their families; teaching me local customs and history and putting me in touch with wonderful women I would never otherwise have found.

A thousand thank yous to my unsalaried interpreters, above all to Mirjam K., who gave up her evenings and weekends, and sometimes travelled with me to far-flung and decidedly non-touristy locations purely for the joy of the adventure.

To my long-suffering drivers, Abu Bakr and Siya, who waited for hours outside homes, palaces and airports, and not only greeted me with a smile, but even brought me dinners – thank you, you are family.

A special mention for friends and comrades including Suzanne, Tracy and Cynthia, who endured my obsession, lack of sociability and piles of paperwork for several years.

I do not think I would have passed the first page without the support of my own *mama* and *baba*. Thank you for your love and positivity; especially to *baba* for being my heroically long-standing sounding board and making me 'write it down'.

Thank you to my darling Olivier, who endured highs, lows and very late nights with never a word of complaint, who listened and cajoled and cooked an enormous amount of comfort food. And to Tallulah, the dog who provided cuddles and finished the leftovers.

The greatest thanks of all are reserved, of course, for the women who so generously shared the stories that filled these pages and, moreover, encouraged me in my venture. From those who have never spoken to an outsider before to those who openly share their experiences and opinions in the public domain, whatever the risks, you are my heroines.

Finally, and especially, to the girls of PNU; the girls of the lunch gang, the drama group, the green club. Although here unnamed out of respect of your privacy, it was in the light of your laughter, kindness, hospitality and friendship that any preconceived notions and stereotypes that I may have arrived to your country with fell away completely. This book is for you. You are the future, and the future is bright.

SOURCES

INTRODUCTION

Almana, A.; Al ash-Sheikh, H. (2013) 'The Sixth of November', Beirut: Jadawel

A WOMEN APART

'Saudi police "stopped" fire rescue', *BBC News*, 15 March 2002 http:// news.bbc.co.uk/2/hi/middle_east/1874471.stm
'Saudi female student dies after male ambulance crew denied access', *Gulf News*, 6 February 2014 https://gulfnews.com/news/gulf/ saudi-arabia/saudi-female-student-dies-after-male-ambulance-crew-denied-access-1.1287560

AFFAIRS OF THE HEART

Al Dosari, H. (2017) 'The Effect of Gender Norms on Women's Health in Saudi Arabia. The Arab Gulf States Institute in Washington'. Policy paper #1
'A rundown on reasons for rising divorce rate in Saudi Arabia', *Saudi Gazette*, 9 February 2018 http://saudigazette.com.sa/ article/527994/SAUDI-ARABIA/A-rundown-on-reasons-for-rising-divorce-rate-in-Saudi-Arabia
'Over half million Saudi men engaged in polygamy, report shows', *Alarabiya*, 25 October 2016 https://english.alarabiya.net/en/ variety/2016/10/25/Over-half-million-Saudi-men-engaged-in-polygamy-in-2016-report-shows.html
'Population In Saudi Arabia by Gender, Age, Nationality (Saudi / Non-Saudi) – Mid 2016 AD', General Authority for Statistics, Kingdom of Saudi Arabia https://www.stats.gov.sa/en/5305

HEALTH MATTERS

'Life expectancy at birth, female (years)', The World Bank https://data.worldbank.org/indicator/SP.DYN.LE00. FE.IN?locations=SA

'Mortality rate, infant (per 1,000 live births)', The World Bank
    https://data.worldbank.org/indicator/SP.DYN.IMRT.
    IN?end=2017&locations=SA&start=1960&view=chart
'Saudi police arrests man who shot doctor for helping wife deliver a
    baby', Alarabiya, 26 May 2016 https://english.alarabiya.net/en/
    variety/2016/05/26/Saudi-police-arrests-man-who-shot-doctor-
    for-helping-wife-deliver-a-baby-.html
Koenig, H. G., et al. (2014) 'Mental Health Care in Saudi Arabia:
    Past, Present and Future'. Open Journal of Psychiatry, Vol. 4, 113–
    30. http://dx.doi.org/10.4236/ojpsych.2014.42016
Alyusuf, M. (2011) In the Shadow of Her Voice: A Memoir of an Arab
    Woman. Fatema Sanctuary
Christianson, A., Howson, C. & Modell, B. (2006) 'Global Report
    on Birth Defects'. New York: March of Dimes Birth Defects
    Foundation
Al-Mogbel, E. S. (2012) 'Vitamin D status among Adult Saudi Females
    visiting Primary Health Care Clinics'. International Journal of
    Health Sciences, 6(2), 116–26
Al-Quaiz, AlJohara M., Gad Mohamed, Ashry & Khoja, Tawfik A.
    M., et al. (2013) 'Prevalence of Anemia and Associated Factors
    in Child Bearing Age Women in Riyadh, Saudi Arabia'. Journal
    of Nutrition and Metabolism, Vol. 2013, Article ID 636585, 7 pages
    http://dx.doi.org/10.1155/2013/636585
'IDF MENA Members', International Diabetes Federation
    https://www.idf.org/our-network/regions-members/
    middle-east-and-north-africa/members/46-saudi-
    arabia.html
'Diabetes country profiles, 2016: Saudi Arabia', World Health
    Organization http://www.who.int/diabetes/country-profiles/
    sau_en.pdf
'Noncommunicable Diseases (NCD) Country Profiles, 2018: Saudi
    Arabia', World Health Organization http://www.who.int/
    nmh/countries/sau_en.pdf?ua=1
Qureshi, N. A., Al-Habeeb, A. A. & Koenig, H. G. (2013) 'Mental
    health system in Saudi Arabia: an overview.' Neuropsychiatric
    Disease and Treatment, Vol. 9, 1121–35. http://doi.org/10.2147/
    NDT.S48782
Eldoseri, H. M., Tufts, K. A., Zhang, Q. & Fish, J. N. (2014)
    'Social Determinants of Domestic Violence Among Saudi
    Married Women in Riyadh, Kingdom of Saudi Arabia'. Eastern
    Mediterranean Health Journal, 20(11), 717–25

WOMEN'S WORK

'Budget Statement: Fiscal Year 2018', Saudi Arabia Ministry
of Finance https://www.mof.gov.sa/en/budget/
Documents/171228%20%20budget%20Statement%20eng%20
Single.pdf

'Education: The Key to Women's Empowerment in Saudi Arabia?',
Middle East Institute, 30 July 2015 http://www.mei.edu/
content/article/education-key-women%E2%80%99s-
empowerment-saudi-arabia

Saudi Arabia country profile, UNESCO Institute of Statistics http://
uis.unesco.org/country/SA

'Labor force, female (% of total labor force)', The World Bank
https://data.worldbank.org/indicator/SL.TLF.TOTL.
FE.ZS?locations=SA

'How Princess Reema Is Opening Doors For Women In Saudi
Arabia', *Fast Company*, 8 October 2015 https://www.
fastcompany.com/3048624/driven

VOICES UNSILENCED

Al Fassi, H. (2015) 'Sunday Women Group'. *Journal of Middle East
Women's Studies*, 11(2), 242–3

Al Nahedh, M. & Al Sheikh, H. (2018) *A Voice Unsilenced: Saudi Women
Advocating Their Rights, 1990–2017*. New Jersey: Center for
Women's Global Leadership

'Women voted in Saudi Arabia this week but they only won 1%
of available seats and still face systematic discrimination',
Business Insider (France), 12 December 2015 http://www.
businessinsider.fr/us/women-voted-in-saudi-arabia-this-week-
but-they-only-won-1-of-available-seats-and-still-face-systematic-
distrimination-2015-12

'Saudi Arabia: Landmark Elections for Women', Human Rights
Watch, 11 December 2015 https://www.hrw.org/
news/2015/12/11/saudi-arabia-landmark-elections-women

'Population In Saudi Arabia by Gender, Age, Nationality (Saudi /
Non-Saudi) – Mid 2016 AD', General Authority for Statistics,
Kingdom of Saudi Arabia https://www.stats.gov.sa/en/5305

Popular Culture 2.0

Sharif, M. (2018) *Daring to Drive: A Saudi Woman's Awakening*. New York: Simon & Schuster

'Kingdom of luxury shopping', *Arab Weekly*, 1 April 2016 https://thearabweekly.com/kingdom-luxury-shopping

'Saudi women spend over $3,000 on cosmetics yearly, experts say', *Alarabiya*, 31 May 2015 https://english.alarabiya.net/en/life-style/2015/05/21/Average-Saudi-woman-yearly-spends-over-3-000-on-cosmetics.html#

'Saudi Arabia Consumer Spending', *Trading Economics* https://tradingeconomics.com/saudi-arabia/consumer-spending

Life on the Edge

'Population In Saudi Arabia by Gender, Age, Nationality (Saudi / Non-Saudi) – Mid 2016 AD', General Authority for Statistics, Kingdom of Saudi Arabia https://www.stats.gov.sa/en/5305

'New conditions for Saudi marriages with foreigners', *Gulf News*, 18 March 2018 https://gulfnews.com/news/gulf/saudi-arabia/new-conditions-for-saudi-marriages-with-foreigners-1.2189750

Al-Seghayer, K. (2015) *Real Face of Saudi Arabia*. Riyadh: Hala Print Company

'5,000 maids run away in Saudi in 6 mths', *Arabian Business*, 3 June 2014 https://www.arabianbusiness.com/5-000-maids-run-away-in-saudi-in-6-mths-552603.html

'Saudi Arabia: Landmark Elections for Women', Human Rights Watch, 11 December 2015 https://www.hrw.org/news/2015/12/11/saudi-arabia-landmark-elections-women